TREASURING ALGONQUIN:
Sharing Scenes From 100 Years of Leaseholding

By Gaye I. Clemson

Order this book online at www.trafford.com
or email orders@trafford.com

Most Trafford titles are also available at major online book retailers.

Print information available on the last page.

ISBN: 978-1-4120-9227-2 (sc)
ISBN: 978-1-4251-9693-6 (e)

Cover background photo reprinted with permission of Theresa Bertolone and Cottage Life ©Cottage Life magazine. (www.cottagelife.com). Theresa, a Cache Lake resident, won first prize in the Landscape category of the 2004 Cottage Life Photo Contest. The original photo was published in the **Nov./Dec. '04** issue of ***Cottage Life Magazine***.

Lake maps and the related cartography provided by Chris Brackley, Canoe Lake resident and owner of As The Crow Flies cARTography 2006.

Cover design and layout by Kathleen & Troy Chasey/Capitola Design, Soquel, CA.

Trafford rev. 10/10/2019

www.trafford.com

North America & international
toll-free: 1 888 232 4444 (USA & Canada)
fax: 812 355 4082

Treasuring Algonquin: Sharing Scenes From 100 Years of Leaseholding

Table of Contents

Dedication and Acknowledgements

Among the many who treasure Algonquin Park are a small group of leasehold residents who have occupied small corners of the Park since the earliest days of the 20th century. I had originally wanted to call this book ***Guardians of the Jewel – Stories of 100 years of Leaseholding in Algonquin Park***. It was my attempt to point out our strong feeling of stewardship for what many in our community believe to be the crown jewel of Ontario's parks. Alas, though only a few mutterings in the beginning, it eventually became clear that a controversy was brewing. Being a leaseholder myself, the title at first seemed perfect for our stories and our contributions to the Park. It evoked all of the things that so many feel about being in Algonquin. But a concern was raised by members of the community whose credentials both as park residents and contributors to Algonquin are among the highest and whose stories form part of this book. Their concern was that such a title would ignore all those people other than leaseholders who have become guardians of Algonquin in their own way. To paraphrase their comments:

> *"We must not single ourselves out as stewards of Algonquin to the exclusion of those we share the park with. It would be an insult to them. Not one Algonquin leaseholder holds such intent certainly not the author of this book. Indeed we celebrate and treasure all of the accomplishments that have made the Algonquin "jewel" shine."*

So I bring to you here the fourth and final book in a series of narratives that makes an attempt to capture another aspect of the human history of Algonquin Park. It is a book about the Algonquin leasehold community. It is a book about their heritage, their families, their traditions, their passion for Algonquin, and their contributions both large and small. However, as with all histories of this sort, stories handed down from person to person or generation to generation can get distorted, perhaps embellished and the facts not quite right. I have tried, to the degree that is possible, to verify "facts" and guard against incorporating too many "tall tales". However, I expect that some have slipped through the cracks, so I apologise in advance for any errors or misinformation. I have tried to the best of my ability to provide a balanced and unbiased narrative.

My intent is to shine a small light and give some form and humanity to a small group of people who all call Algonquin Park home. To this end, I have dedicated this work to my twin 12-year-old sons, Taylor and Kristopher, who happily accompanied me on this journey of discovery into the depth and breadth of their summer home. It all began in 1996, when we first set out in our vintage green cedar strip canoe from the small cabin on a Canoe Lake ridge that my parents built in the early 1950s. Our objective was to meet and record the Algonquin Park experiences of some of our nearby neighbours. After that first venture I was hooked and my efforts took on a life of their own. Over the next decade, I spent many summer hours visiting residents from across the Park. As my collection of stories of their Algonquin Park experiences grew, I realized that the insights that I was gaining into Algonquin Park's human heritage might be also be of interest to a wider audience. So I hope that all will enjoy what I have created.

As with any work like this, there are many people who helped with its molding. Special thanks must first go to the many leaseholder families who shared with me their Algonquin Park heritage and experiences. Where it fits, I have footnoted the original text, and included an extensive bibliography. Secondly I thank those who willingly dedicated hours of time to the editing of the various versions of the manuscript including Valerie Young Argue, Rose Campbell, Lela Gamble, George Garland, Dan Gibson, Robin Rigby Howe, Don Lloyd, Martha Cochrane Newton, Roderick (Rory) MacKay John Ridpath, Helen Steinberg, Robert Taylor and Ron Tozer. An extra special thank you must go to Valerie Young Argue, Rory MacKay, George Garland and Ron Tozer whose invaluable advice and guidance in the later stages of this effort were invaluable. In addition, I must also extend many thanks to the Canoe Lake and District, Smoke Lake, Cache Lake and Rock and Whitefish Lake Leasehold Associations, and the Algonquin Park Residents Association, which provided both moral and early financial support to get this effort off of the ground. Other key financial supporters, to whom I am deeply indebted include Michael Budman, and Diane Bald, Peter and Camilla Dalglish, Mary and Keith Percival, Janie Roberts, Michael Davies, Fran and Bernie Goldman, Anne Chisholm, Dr. John W. Graham, Joyce Valliant Armour, Joanne Edwards, Charles Tator and Michael Tucker. Last but not least, I would also like to extend a very special thank you to both the Friends of Algonquin Park and the Algonquin Park Museum Archives staff for their help, support and guidance over the last decade.

Source Lake - View looking East from West End of Lake Dernoga Collection 2005

Aerial view of West End of Lake of Two Rivers MacKay Collection

Entrance to the Madawaska River 1916 APMA #76

Rock Lake View Looking South c1910 McCourt Collection

Introduction

Photos this page: Clemson Collection

Clemson Cottage Bunkees 1970s

Clemson Path to Cottage 1950s

View of Canoe Lake North from Clemson Dock 1980s

Clemson Cottage Spring 2004

Clemson Path to Cottage 1990s

Introduction

One of the crown jewels of Ontario's park system, it was originally called Algonquin National Park. This large tract of land (today over 7,700 square kilometers) that sits about 500 meters above sea level contains the headwaters of five major rivers. Created by statute in 1893, it was "reserved and set apart as a public park and forest reservation, fish and game preserve, health resort and pleasure grounds for the benefit, advantage and enjoyment of the people of the Province of Ontario."[1] Renamed Algonquin Provincial Park in 1913 after the addition of several neighbouring townships, it is today an important member of Ontario's 800-park system. Yearly, over one million visitors come to experience Algonquin in a wide variety of forms. For some it's a canoe trip to the interior, and for others it's a camping experience at one of the public campgrounds along Highway 60. The activities these visitors engage in vary widely, from bicycle trips up the old Minnesing Road or along the Rock/Whitefish Trail, to self-guided day hikes on any one of the 12 trails that lie adjacent to Highway 60. A visit to the Algonquin Logging Museum, the Algonquin Park Visitor Centre, or the new Algonquin Art Centre at Found Lake is always a memorable part of every Park itinerary. Some brave tourists rent canoes on Opeongo Lake or Canoe Lake and spend the day paddling around and exploring on their own.

Along the shores of Canoe, Smoke, Cache, Rock Whitefish, and a handful of other lakes, you will notice a few little cabins tucked away amid the darkness of the local forest. In these cabins live quiet, unobtrusive groups of leaseholders and their extended families whose forebears were invited by the Ontario Government to establish cottages in the Park. Until 1954 cottagers were welcomed with open arms, support and encouragement. For some families it's the fifth generation who now are learning to appreciate the Park and its beauty. Most of the time, you'd hardly know they were there—until you run into trouble while paddling on one of the lakes, lose your way, need medical attention, or get caught in a storm or a heavy north wind. Then they miraculously appear to provide help and guidance and occasionally save your life. Mostly in residence on weekends from ice-out to ice-in, and for a few weeks in the summer, members of

[1] Algonquin Provincial Park Note, Archives of Ontario, Rg1-47-3, File 27-1501-17-Box 45.

this small but vibrant community of 9,000+ extended family members across 304 leaseholds have been coming to Algonquin for well over 100 years.[2]

Most of these cabins are quite primitive with unlined walls and uncurtained windows. Most are modest in size and designed to blend in with the forest surroundings to ensure that their environmental impact is kept to a minimum.[3] *Leaseholders have resisted development, generally preferring to supplement rather than rebuild. These cabins are usually heated by wood stoves and lit by kerosene lamps. Water is usually pumped by hand, and refrigerators and stoves are often fueled by propane. Most leases in the south are on lakes adjacent to the route taken by the old Ottawa, Arnprior and Parry Sound railroad right of way.*[4] *The cottages in the northeast side of the Park follow the rail bed of what was once a CNR line that ran from North Bay to Ottawa.*[5] *One might wonder how and why leaseholders came in the first place and why they continue to stay.*

It seems that Alexander Kirkwood, one of Algonquin Park's original founding fathers, was the first to suggest that private individuals be allowed to 'lease locations in the Park for summer cottages or tents.'[6] *According to early Park Superintendent annual reports, though there was some interest in leasing as early as 1896, in the early years after the Park's founding, not much happened in this regard. Most of the Park was home only to logging and railroad operations and the occasional fishing party in the early spring and late fall. It wasn't until the arrival of Dr. Alexander Pirie in 1905 that there was much interest in camping or cottaging. Not only was the Park generally inaccessible, but also few in Canada had time or money for recreational tourism. Dr. Pirie, a Canadian who practiced medicine in Costa Rica, wanted a place where he could bring his far-flung family together in the summer. The old abandoned houses on Canoe Lake owned by the Gilmour brothers that were built in the late 1890s provided the perfect place.*

At about this same time, the then-Park Superintendent George Bartlett had begun to encourage the Ontario Department of Lands and Forests to develop Algonquin Park as a "tourist resort for an affluent middle class clientele."[7] *It began with the construction of the Hotel Algonquin at Joe Lake Station and the Highland Inn on Cache Lake, and the leasing of a few parcels to long-time campers also on the shores of Cache Lake near the Park Headquarters. Over the next few years, the community grew to include more hotels, fishing lodges, outfitting stores, youth camps, and private leases. According to Gerald Killan, who has written extensively about the history of Ontario's Provincial Park system, Bartlett took a utilitarian approach to park management. His intent was to balance recreational activity with revenue producing commercial interests while still protecting the Park watershed and preserving its essential wildness. He encouraged the trapping of surplus beaver (generating nearly $15,000 in revenue in 1920), and arranged a controlled hunt of deer to supply Toronto meat markets during WWI. He also allowed the select logging of mature trees along certain lake shorelines during a coal shortage. But one of his most*

---

2. This estimate is based on a spreadsheet analysis of the average size of various extended family groups multiplied by the estimated number of leaseholds in each group.

3. Cache Lake submission to the Algonquin Park Master Planning process, 1975.

4. Rain Lake, Brulé Lake, Canoe Lake, Tea Lake, Smoke Lake, Joe Lake, Cache Lake, Lake of Two Rivers, Source Lake, Whitefish Lake, and Rock Lake.

5. Kioshkokwi Lake, Couchon Lake, Cedar Lake, Radiant Lake, Grand Lake, and Lake Traverse.

6. Memorandum concerning Algonquin Park by Alexander Kirkwood 1893

7. Gerald Killan, ***Protected Places: A History of Ontario's Provincial Park System,*** 1993, pg. 49.

important contributions was to establish regulations that protected the interior by making cottage lease sites available only on lakes near the railway line.[8] This meant that over the next 30 years, leases were restricted to four key areas:

- *Canoe Lake and District, including Rain, McIntosh, Brulé, Joe, South Tea and Smoke Lakes*
- *The Park Headquarters area at Algonquin Park Station on Cache Lake, including Lake of Two Rivers and Source Lake along Highway 60*
- *The Rock Lake Station area, including Rock and Whitefish Lakes and part of Galeairy Lake*
- *The northern section, including those lakes running parallel to the CNR rail line from Lake Traverse to Kisohkokwi Lake and a few remote outposts on Manitou and North Tea Lakes*

Though the response to government and railway advertising was slow, the idea of leaseholders as important members of the Algonquin Park community of users was firmly in place and supported by Park Superintendent Frank MacDougall in the 1930s. By 1930, there were only 31 leases on Cache Lake and about half a dozen on both the north end of Canoe Lake and Rock Lake near Rock Lake Station.[9] Even as late as 1945 the total number of leaseholds had only grown to just over 200 (including 85 on Cache Lake, 85 in the Canoe Lake and District area, and 31 in the Rock/Whitefish area). There were also a few scattered in the north and a few on Source Lake and Lake of Two Rivers. As can be seen in the chart below, it wasn't until the post-war recreation boom, during the time of Park Superintendent George Phillips, that the number of leases issued doubled again.

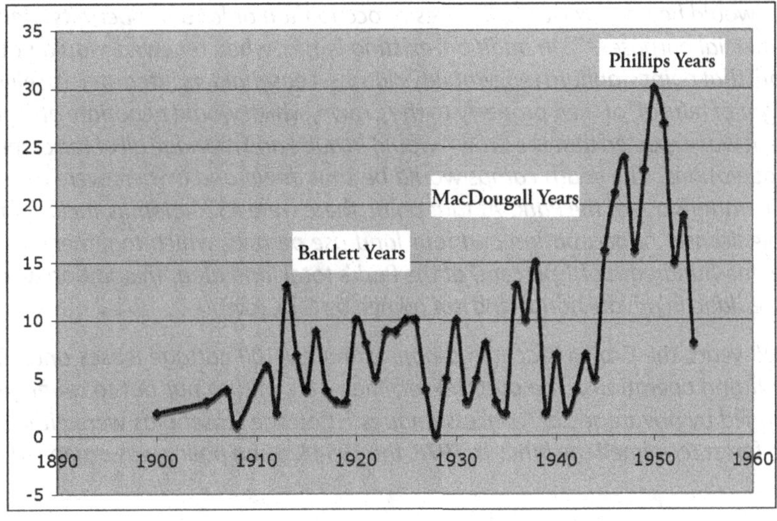

[8] Gerald Killan, ***Protected Places: A History of Ontario's Provincial Park System,*** 1993, pgs. 47-52.

[9] For details on the history of Rock Lake, see ***Rock Lake Station*** by Gaye. I. Clemson, 2005.

For the first half of its existence, leaseholders, summer youth camps, commercial lodges, and canoe trip outfitters were a welcome addition to Algonquin Park. A few leaseholders came in response to Ontario Government advertising campaigns in Ontario and the northeastern United States. One memorable Ontario Lands and Forest exhibit was featured at the Canadian National Exhibition in 1932. The exhibit advertising cottage lots to lease in Algonquin Park was a large reconstructed slice of the Park complete with a forest of evergreens, a log cabin, a canoe, a tent, camping supplies and uniformed Park Rangers all part of the scene.[10] *The Reverend Rasey on Tea Lake, for example, saw an advertisement in the Ford (Motor) Times magazine that he'd been reading while waiting at a local photography studio in Illinois in the late 1940s.*[11] *These ads encouraged ordinary Canadians and Americans from all walks of life, especially veterans from WWII, to apply for what at the time was advertised as being an "arrangement in perpetuity." Even as late as 1939, prospective leaseholders were being advised by the then Park Superintendent:*

> *"The expiry of the lease in 1944 does not mean much. All leases are for 21 years and are renewable for another 21 years and the renewal goes through as a matter of routine. The 21-year period gives the government the opportunity to raise or lower the general rental conditions or otherwise revise its statutes. Most of the Park leases are now in their second term of 21 years and some are in their third period.'"*[12]

As previously mentioned, these "arrangements" were not in perpetuity to the chagrin of the second and third generation, who on a cold winter night sometimes wish that their relatives, like our friend and colleague Roy MacGregor, had settled just a few miles outside of the Park's boundaries.

In the summer of 1954 the post WWII pressures for more public recreation alternatives in Ontario led to the adoption of a new park policy. The long-term plan was to restore the Park to a more natural state. "In the future, there would be no new leases, licenses of occupation or land use permits granted for public, private or commercial purposes."[13] *In addition, existing leases, when renewed, would not contain what had been up until that point standard renewability clauses. Leaseholders interested in selling would need to grant "first right of refusal" of their property to the Crown, which would negotiate an agreeable selling price. Over time, it was expected that the Crown would acquire and manage all of the commercial lodges, and outfitting operations. The youth camps would be shut down and owners were expecting to move their bases of operations out of the Park. At that point, there were 432 holdings, including 420 leases, 12 yearly renewable licenses of occupation and four land-use permits, which together accounted for less than .01% (one one-hundredth of 1 percent) of the Park's total land area. In addition were four areas of patented land, i.e., land in private hands and not owned by the Crown.*

Over the next 25 years, the Crown reacquired approximately 100 cottage leases and all leases of the commercial outfitting operations. The outfitter facilities were in turn put out to management bid and today are managed by private sector "concessionaires." Cottage leaseholds were either dismantled or burned and the forest reclaimed the land. In 1978, the 1954 leasing policy was amended to permit both

---

10. Recollections from Gordon Willson, 2003.
11. Recollections from the Rasey family, 2004.
12. Correspondence from the Park Superintendent, 1939, Algonquin Park Museum Archives.
13. Gerald Killan, ***Protected Places: A History of Ontario's Provincial Parks System,*** 1993, pg. 88.

commercial leases and children's camps to stay in private hands and their leases were extended to 2017. At the same time, as a result of extensive lobbying, leaseholders whose leases were to expire prior to 1996 were allowed to extend their leases to 1996 as long as they were willing to pay "market rents." In 1986, again after extensive lobbying, a new Liberal government agreed to look at the issue of why cottagers were now the only leaseholding group still subject to the 1954 policy. The Provincial Parks Council (a citizens advisory committee that reported directly to the Minister of Natural Resources), chaired by Fred Gray, was asked to conduct public hearings, review the Algonquin Park leasing policy, and make recommendations to the Ontario Cabinet. During the spring of 1986, over 900 people attended the various hearings and town meetings that were held across the province. The committee received over 250 briefs or pieces of correspondence. In April 1986, the Provincial Parks Council released its recommendation that, for those who joined the plan, leases would be extended to 2017.[14] *In return, the Ministry of Natural Resources acquired the ability to:*

- *Charge market value rents and adjust them periodically*
- *Charge additional rents for services such as garbage pickup on some lakes*
- *Charge leaseholders vehicle permit fees as it did other park users*
- *Have first right of refusal at the time of any lease transfer*
- *Approve in writing all building activities, based on a set of regulations designed to minimize evidence of leaseholder presence and impact on the lakes*
- *Eliminate all year-round residency*

The majority of leaseholders agreed to the new plan, such that today there are 304 leaseholds still in existence that have been home to nearly 600 families over the last 100 years. Nearly 40% are in the hands of the same original leaseholder families and 37% have changed hands only once. Across all of these sites, the overall average tenure has been just over 68 years.[15] *Over 30% have been summer residents for over 30 years. The author estimates that the commnity contributes over 150,000 person days to overall Algonquin visitorship. Many are friends and friends of friends who otherwise may never have experienced the beauty of Algonquin. Some 95% of them are still located within a few kilometers of the Highway 60 corridor. These seasonal residents live and breathe Algonquin, care about its health and its welfare, and know it better, longer, and more intimately than just about any other group of Park users. As indicated previously, my hope is that these stories will shine a small light on a valuable part of the Algonquin Park community, a community of people who prefer to know a small piece of land and lake intimately, as season leads to season and year leads to year. I hope that by reading their stories their contribution to the Park and its welfare will not be forgotten.*

---

14. Ontario Parks Council Report, 1986, Algonquin Park Museum Archives.
15. These figures are based on a detailed analysis of leaseholds by the author during the winter of 2005-2006

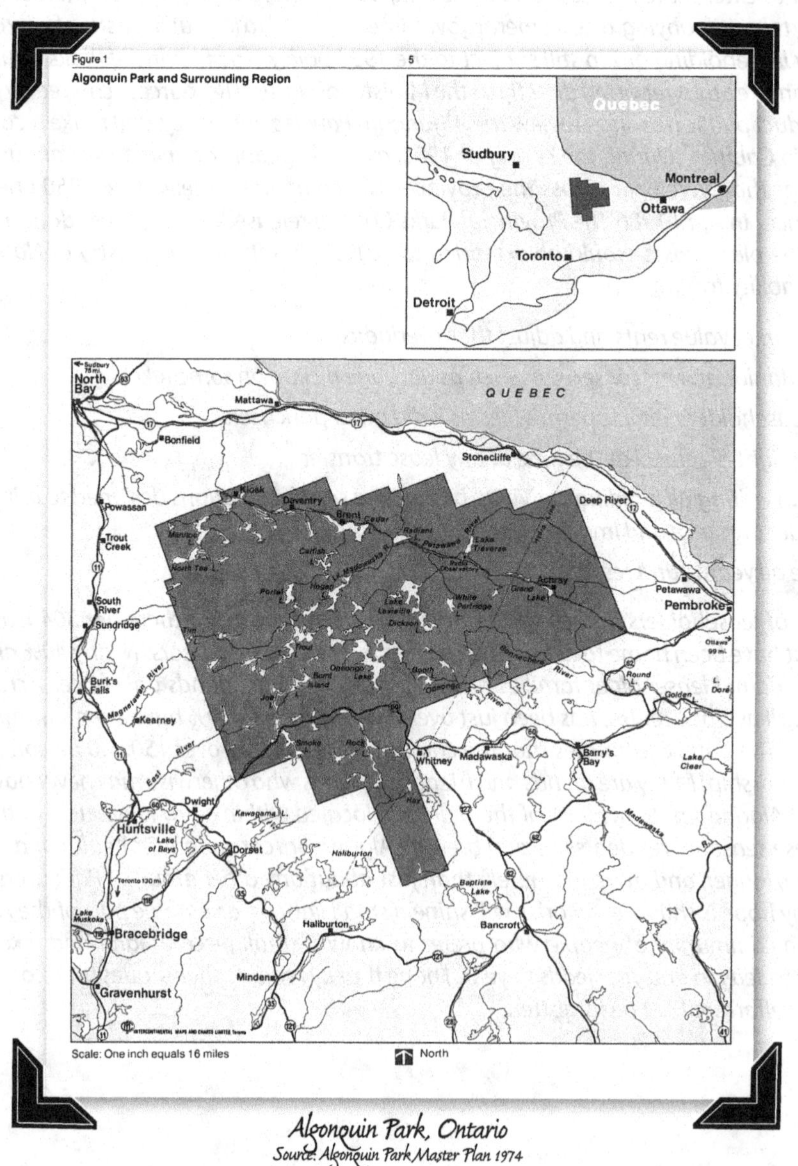

Algonquin Park, Ontario

Source: Algonquin Park Master Plan 1974

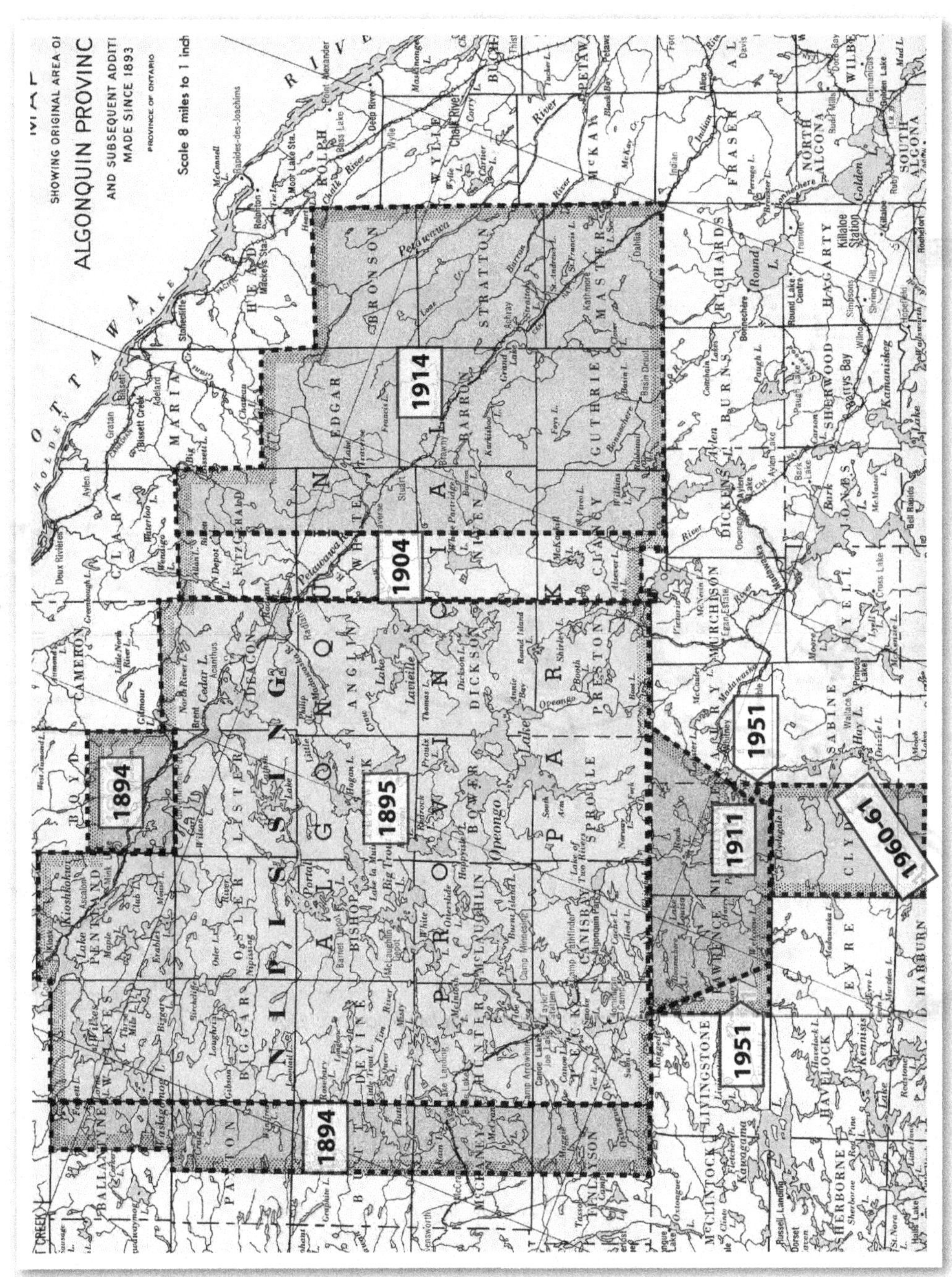

Algonquin Park and Subsequent Additions since 1893

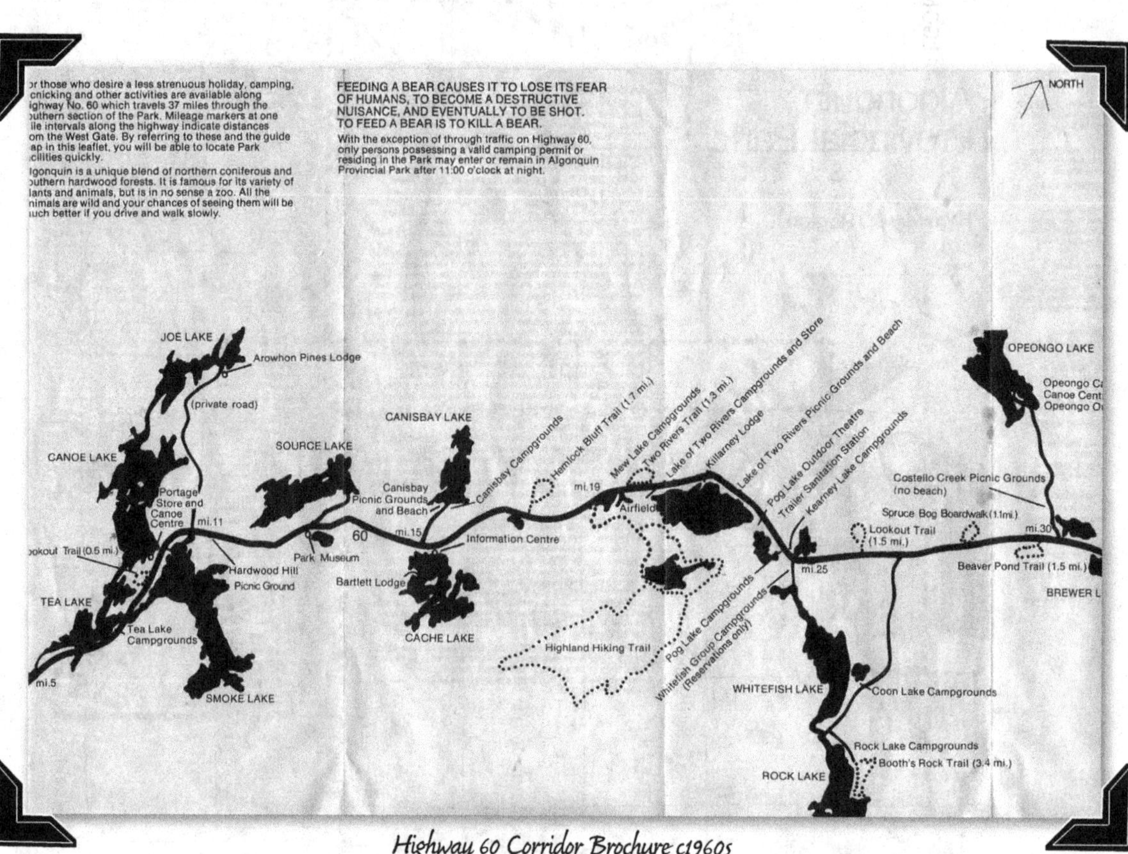

r those who desire a less strenuous holiday, camping, cnicking and other activities are available along ighway No. 60 which travels 37 miles through the uthern section of the Park. Mileage markers at one ile intervals along the highway indicate distances om the West Gate. By referring to these and the guide ap in this leaflet, you will be able to locate Park cilities quickly.

lgonquin is a unique blend of northern coniferous and uthern hardwood forests. It is famous for its variety of lants and animals, but is in no sense a zoo. All the nimals are wild and your chances of seeing them will be uch better if you drive and walk slowly.

FEEDING A BEAR CAUSES IT TO LOSE ITS FEAR OF HUMANS, TO BECOME A DESTRUCTIVE NUISANCE, AND EVENTUALLY TO BE SHOT. TO FEED A BEAR IS TO KILL A BEAR.

With the exception of through traffic on Highway 60, only persons possessing a valid camping permit or residing in the Park may enter or remain in Algonquin Provincial Park after 11:00 o'clock at night.

Highway 60 Corridor Brochure c1960s

Leasehold History Timeline since 1893 Park Creation

Park Superintendents

Peter Thompson – **1893-1895**
John Simpson – **1985-1898**
George Bartlett – **1898-1922**
J.W. Millar – **1922** (Acting)
Mark Robinson – **1922-1924**
J.W. Millar – **1924-1930**
J.H. McDonald – **1930-1931**
Frank MacDougall – **1931-1941**
James Taylor – **1941-1944**
George Phillips – **1944-1958**
R.C. Passmore – **1958-1962**
U.W. Fiskar – **1962-1966**
T.W Hueston – **1966-1972**
J.H. Lever – **1972–1975**
John Simpson – **1975-1980**
Tim Millard – **1980-1983**
George Whitney – **1983-1987**
Chris Goddard – **1987-1988**
Ernie Martelle – **1988–1997**
John Winters – **1997-Present**

Key Events

1895 - Park HQ established at Cache Lake
1896 - Ottawa, Arnprior & Parry Sound Railway opens
1900 - Dr. Bell builds on Cache Lake and Men-Wah-Tay completed on Rock Lake
1905 - Dr. Pirie buys Gilmour houses on Canoe Lake - Park's first leasehold
1908 - Highland Inn and Hotel Algonquin built. Northway Lodge Girls Camp established
1913 - Nominigan and Minnesing Camps open
1923 - Bartlett Lodge opens on Cache Lake
1927 - Kish Kaduk Lodge opens on Cedar Lake
1931 - Gar Northway acquires Nominigan lease
1933 - Cache Lake main trestle condemned, CNR closes the Highland Inn, Turtle Club built by Booth grandson on Lake Traverse
1936 - Highway 60, Portage Store & Killarney Lodge open
1938 - Whitefish Lodge opens
1940 - Highland Inn reopens under lease
1941 - Arowhon Pines Resort opens on Baby Joe Lake
1946 - J. R. Dymond establishes first Park Interpretive Program from a tent on Cache Lake
1947 - Manley Sessions acquires Minnesing lease
1949 - Glen Donald Lodge opens on Source Lake
1953 - Crown acquires and dismantles Minnesing and Glen Donald Lodge
1954 - New Park Policy bans all new leasing
1955 - Highland Inn and Men-Wah-Tay acquired by the crown and dismantled soon after
1965 - Whitefish Lodge acquired by Crown
1975 - First leases expire and Kish Kaduk Lodge closes
1977 - Nominigan Camp dismantled
1978 - Youth Camps and commercial lodges granted lease extensions to 2017 and cottage leases given common end dates of 1996
1986 - Leases extended to 2017
1993 - Park Centennial Year
2005 - Leasehold Centennial Year

1932 DLF Canadian National Exhibit Display.
The Availability of Cottage Sites was Actively Promoted to Increase Park Use.

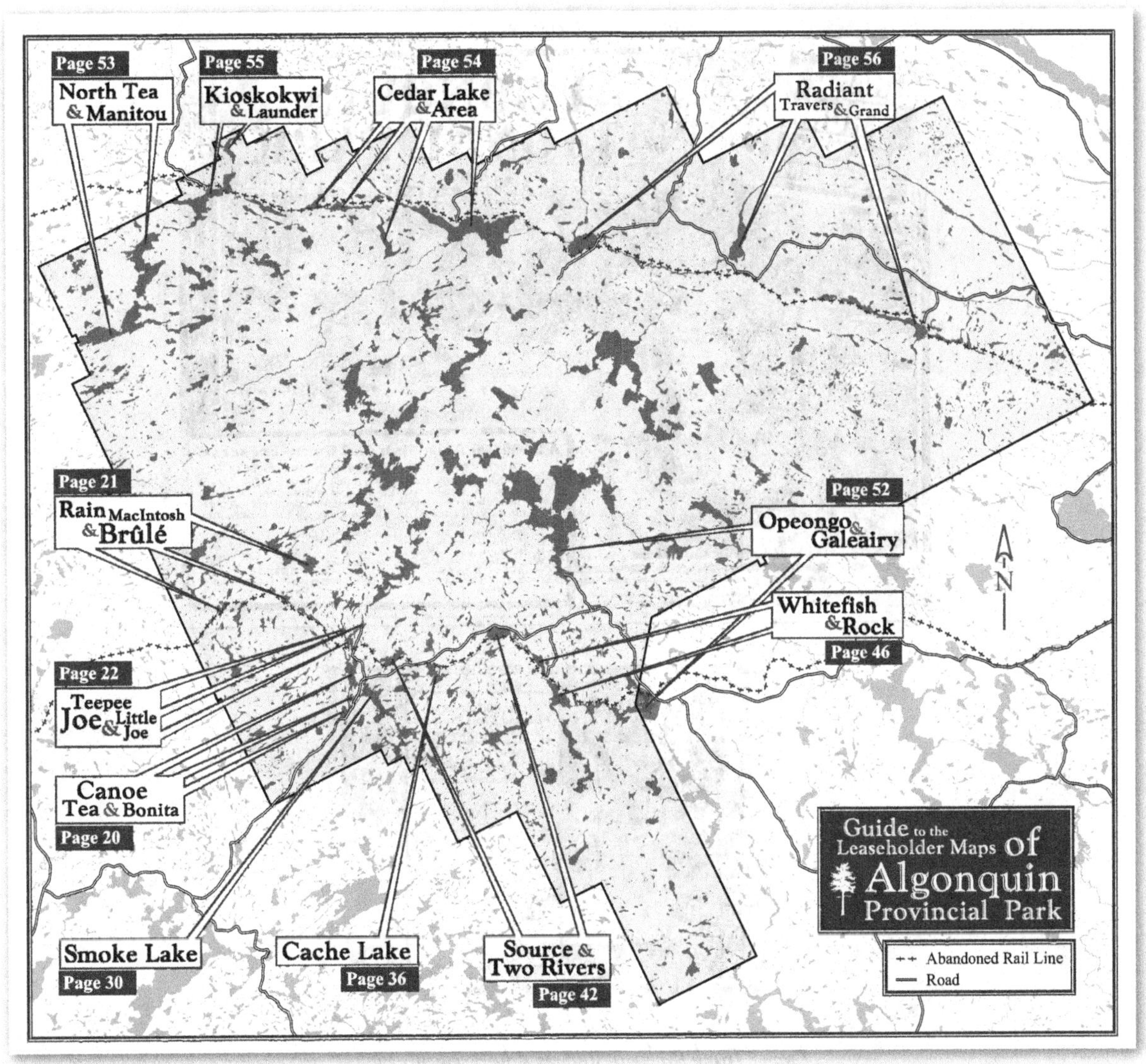

Leasehold Locations in Algonquin Park As The Crow Flys Cartography, Chris Brackley

Grand Trunk Railway Systems Advertisements 1909

Chapter 1

Depth and Breadth of Leasehold Roots

Where do I begin to write a story about Algonquin Park leaseholds? My first experience of the park was in the summer of 1954, when my parents built our little cabin. I was just nine months old and naturally don't remember those days, but old black-and-white photographs show me watching intently from the safe venue of a bushel basket beneath a giant foot pine tree as my parents worked. Two years previously they had built a small sleeping bunkee for shelter and did all of their cooking out of doors. As our family grew, additional bunkees and a bathhouse were added. Today a central cabin with kitchen and living space sits in a little clearing and is surrounded by four small bunkees tucked under the trees. The entire complex sits on the top of a relatively steep cliff, overlooking the lake. It provides a lovely view through the lower branches of trees that hide it from view from the lake, but hauling goods and supplies up the cliff gets harder and harder each summer. The composition of the forest has also changed significantly over the last 50 years. Except for two lone pine trees that luckily were too small to be taken in the late 1800s, when the original loggers went through, most of the surrounding bush is hardwood with a few cedar, hemlock and birch trees thrown in for good measure. As the forest has grown, the vegetation on the forest floor has gotten sparse such that today there is very little ground cover and we can easily see the cabin of our nearest neighbour. In areas to the back, where some of the larger trees have fallen down and been cleared away, small trees and shrubs that now have access to sunlight are now starting to grow. A new generation of forest is beginning.

For my entire life, I have spent some part of virtually every summer on the shores of Canoe Lake. Though I know the Canoe Lake and District area pretty well, I've had little or no contact with those who call other parts of Algonquin Park their summer refuge. So, an important part of this journey of discovery of the human heritage of my community has been to uncover the depth and breadth of leasehold roots in other parts of the Park. Here is what I discovered.

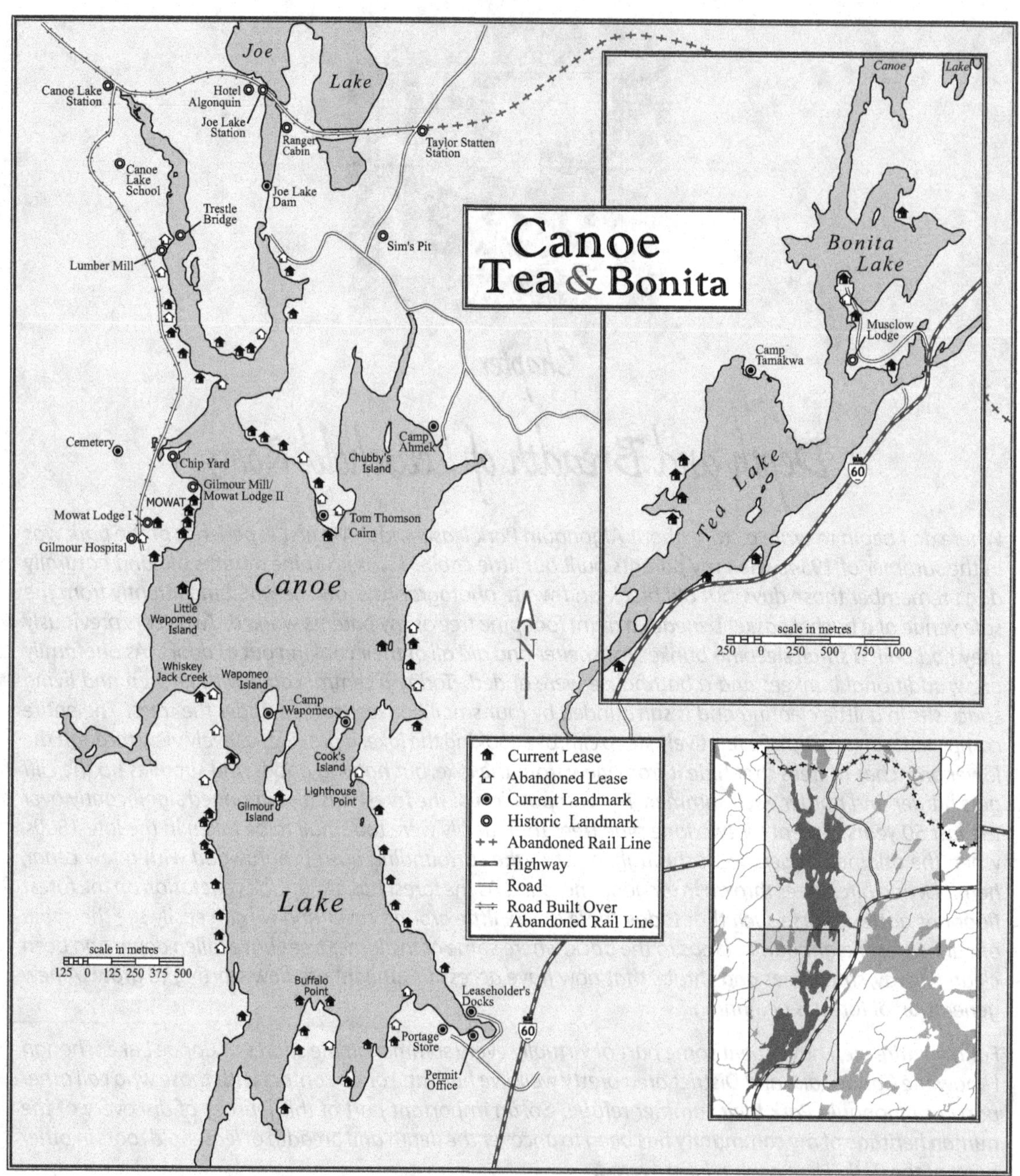
Canoe
Tea & Bonita
Joe
Lake
Canoe Lake Station
Hotel Algonquin
Joe Lake Station
Ranger Cabin
Taylor Statten Station
Canoe Lake School
Joe Lake Dam
Trestle Bridge
Sim's Pit
Lumber Mill
Cemetery
Chip Yard
MOWAT
Gilmour Mill/ Mowat Lodge II
Mowat Lodge I
Gilmour Hospital
Camp Ahmek
Chubby's Island
Tom Thomson Cairn
Canoe
Little Wapomeo Island
Whiskey Jack Creek
Wapomeo Island
Camp Wapomeo
Cook's Island
Lighthouse Point
Gilmour Island
Lake
scale in metres
125 0 125 250 375 500
Buffalo Point
Leaseholder's Docks
60
Portage Store
Permit Office
N
Canoe
Lake
Bonita
Lake
Musclow Lodge
Camp Tamakwa
Tea Lake
60
scale in metres
250 0 250 500 750 1000
Current Lease
Abandoned Lease
Current Landmark
Historic Landmark
Abandoned Rail Line
Highway
Road
Road Built Over Abandoned Rail Line

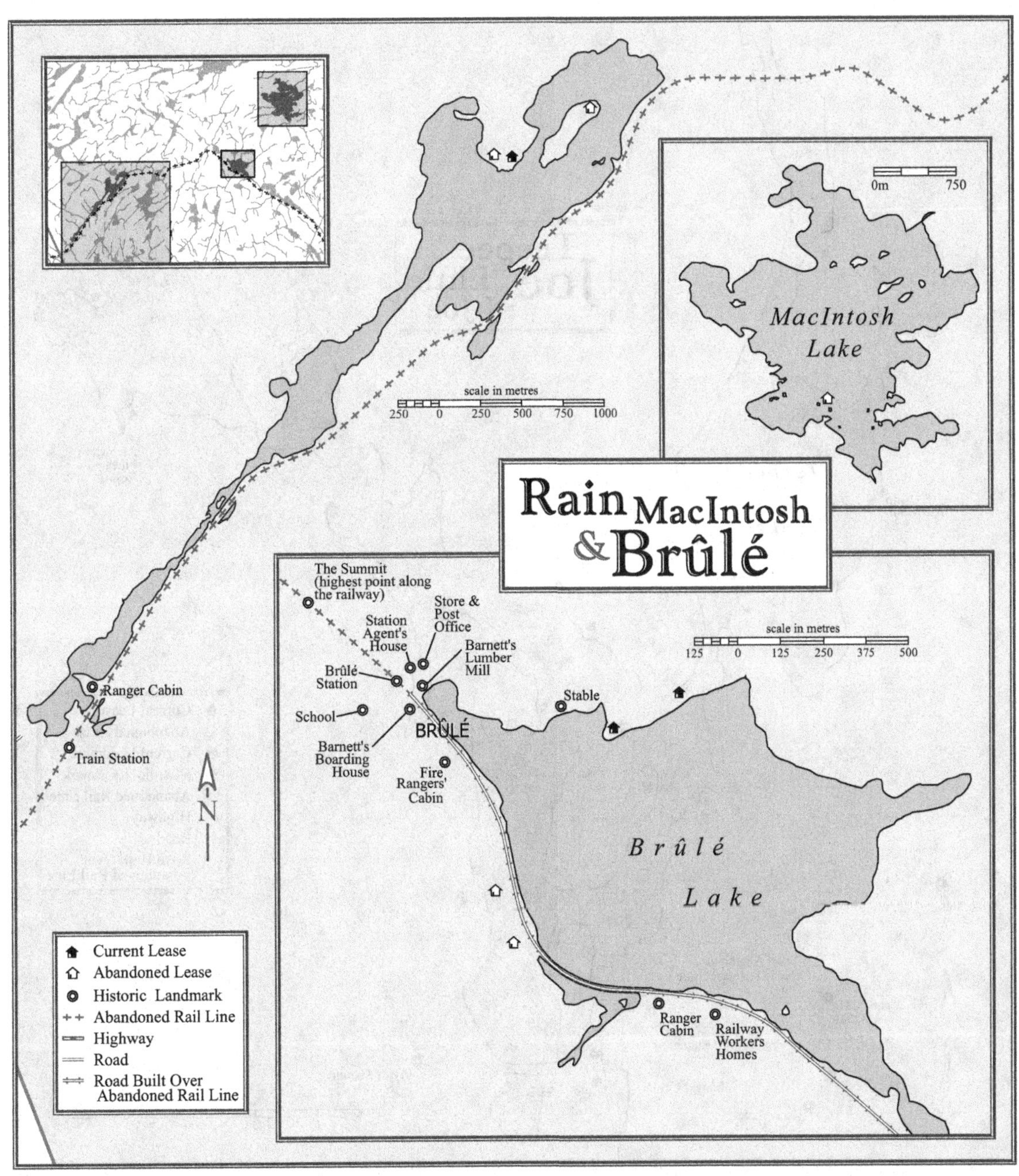

Rain MacIntosh & Brûlé
MacIntosh Lake
0m 750
scale in metres
250 0 250 500 750 1000
Ranger Cabin
Train Station
N
The Summit (highest point along the railway)
Station Agent's House
Store & Post Office
Barnett's Lumber Mill
Brûlé Station
School
BRÛLÉ
Barnett's Boarding House
Fire Rangers' Cabin
Stable
scale in metres
125 0 125 250 375 500
Brûlé Lake
Ranger Cabin
Railway Workers Homes
Current Lease
Abandoned Lease
Historic Landmark
Abandoned Rail Line
Highway
Road
Road Built Over Abandoned Rail Line

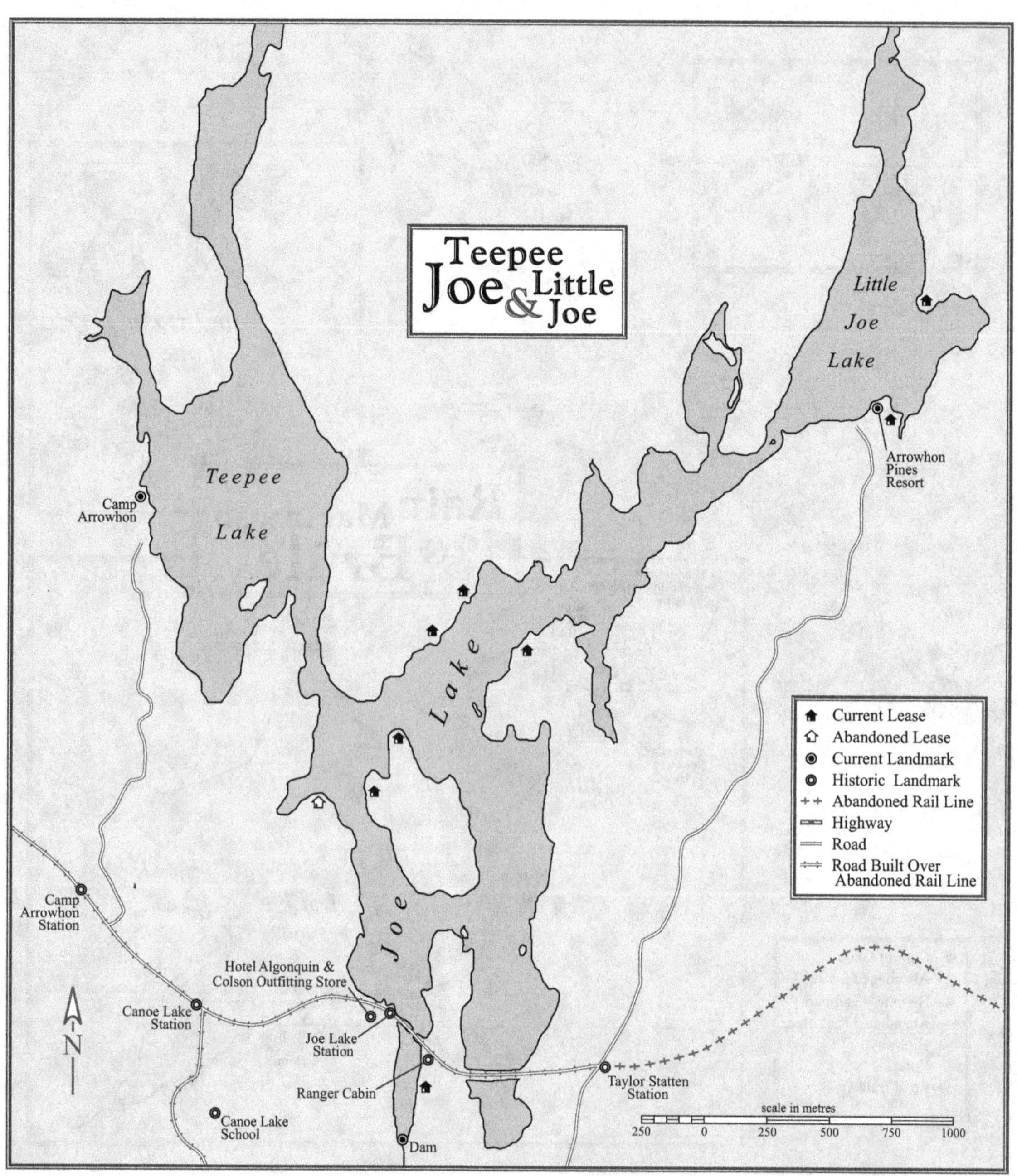

Teepee
Joe & Little Joe
Little Joe Lake
Teepee Lake
Joe Lake
Camp Arrowhon
Arrowhon Pines Resort
Current Lease
Abandoned Lease
Current Landmark
Historic Landmark
Abandoned Rail Line
Highway
Road
Road Built Over Abandoned Rail Line
Camp Arrowhon Station
Hotel Algonquin & Colson Outfitting Store
Canoe Lake Station
Joe Lake Station
Ranger Cabin
Canoe Lake School
Dam
Taylor Statten Station
scale in metres
250 0 250 500 750 1000
N

Canoe Lake and District 16

Much has been written about the early exploration and exploitation of Canoe Lake. In summary, in 1826 the first military explorer who came close by was Lieutenant Henry Briscoe, the first white person to paddle up the Oxtongue River to Tea Lake. He then turned east to Smoke Lake, headed south through Ragged and Big Porcupine and then traveled on to the Ottawa River via the Petawawa River. Next was Alexander Shirreff of Fitzroy Harbour, who in 1829 was the first to explore what is now colloquially called "The Trippers Highway" or "Main Street" from Big Trout Lake to Burnt Island Lake and on down through the Otterslides to Joe Lake and Canoe Lake. In 1837, David Thompson, a great Canadian explorer and mapmaker, passed through and was the first to make a detailed survey of Tea, Smoke, Canoe, and Ragged Lakes. Canoe Lake got its name from Alexander Murray, who in 1853 came to examine the geology of the region. His party spent a few days in what is now called Ahmek Bay (site of an old Indian camp) to build a new birch bark canoe. Later in 1886 another surveyor, James Dickson, passed through and camped on what is now Gilmour Island and spent a pleasant few days fishing and enjoying the wilderness scenery.[17]

The Canoe Lake and District includes a broad area on either side of what was once the Ottawa, Arnprior and Parry Sound railway line. At the turn of the 20th century, this railway, built by lumberman J. R. Booth, wound its way from Parry Sound on Depot Harbour at Georgian Bay, through Scotia Junction on the west side of the Park to Whitney on the east side and eventually made its way to Ottawa. The area included Smoke, Tea and Bonita Lakes to the south and Joe, Rain, and Brulé Lakes to the north. Brulé Lake is a significant landmark because approximately 2 miles west of the lake, at 1,607 feet above sea level, is marked the highest point of land on the rail line. Apparently, the grade of the rail line was so steep that it took two engines to pull the train up and over down to what was then called "Algonquin Park Station" on Cache Lake.[18] For most of its existence, Brulé Station was a lumber town anchored by the Barnet Lumber Company. Barnet had a mill and a boarding house that was home to 50 or 60 men as well as about 30 families. Brulé Station had a waiting room, a ticket office where a station agent worked during the day, and a baggage section where they stored baggage and freight. The train would stop at Brulé Lake to pick up lumber, and the train crews would have their dinner at the lumber camp. In the early 1930s, the Barnet Lumber Company closed the mill, and most of the families moved away and the town soon disappeared. In 1937 there was a big fire at Potter Lake between Canoe and Brulé Lakes that took six weeks to put out. Later that year, the P. A. Duff Lumber Company built another mill on Brulé and did a second cutting on the old J. R. Booth limits until the early 1950s.[19] Only two leaseholds ventured into Brulé Lake, both of which are still there today.

After the demise of the railway, getting to Brulé Lake was not (and still is not) easy. An old lumber road still exists to the lake, but over the years sections of it have periodically washed out in heavy rains, isolating residents for varying periods of time.

---

16. Excerpted from the ***Canoe Lake Chronicles*** by Gaye. I. Clemson, 2001.
17. S. Bernard Shaw, ***Canoe Lake, Algonquin Park: Tom Thomson and Other Mysteries.***
18. Richard Eldridge and Orville Osborne, ***Cache Lake Reflections,*** 1995, pg.13.
19. Mary McCormick Pigeon, ***Life on Brulé Lake,*** 1995.

Before 1896 and the completion of J. R. Booth's railway through the Park, Canoe Lake was the centre of the region. A small lumber camp had existed on its north shore since the time of Algonquin Park's creation as a result of the purchasing at auction in 1892 of timber rights in the area by the Gilmour Lumber Company, which was owned by David Gilmour and his brother, Alan, of Trenton, Ontario. In the fall of 1893, the first official Algonquin Park Rangers established a Park Headquarters—a small log shanty with a hewn timber floor, a scoop roof, bunks, chairs, a table for six, a sheet iron wood stove for heat and kerosene lanterns for light—at the northwest corner of the Canoe Lake, just south of Potter Creek. Being only a short journey by water from the Gilmour Depot on Tea Lake and near the projected location of the Ottawa Arnprior and Parry Sound Railway, this site was chosen:

> *"On account of its position commanding the route to the chains of water which lie to the north and east and convenience for getting supplies and mail."*[20]

Within weeks of the Park Rangers' arrival and to the dismay of Peter Thomson, the Park's first superintendent, the logging company built a logging shanty less than a dozen feet from the new headquarters. In the process they cut down many of the beautiful trees that surrounded the site.[21] Later, after several complaints, the Gilmour Lumber Company erected a fence between the two buildings to give the headquarters staff a bit of privacy. During its peak in 1895, according to the "Bobcaygeon Independent" newspaper, the Gilmour Lumber Company had 11 lumber camps, 10 of which were located along the Oxtongue River. With pay of about $1.50 a day, each camp had 55 men and 150 pairs of horses. Sixty-five "cadge" or "tote" teams hauled supplies all winter up and down the "tote" road north (which ran from Dorset to the outskirts of the Park), and then on to where Tea Lake met the Oxtongue River, inside the Gilmour timber limits. Here they established a supply depot and administrative headquarters. As has been well documented in other Algonquin Park histories, the Gilmour Lumber Company plan was to float millions of cubic feet of timber 200 miles from Canoe Lake to Trenton, over a height of land between the Trent System and Lake of Bays.[22] The endeavour cost millions and was said to have employed over 1,000 men. Unfortunately, by the time the logs had made their way to the Gilmour Trenton sawmill, nearly two years had passed, and much of the lumber was severely water damaged and riddled with ring-rot.

To make some of the smaller waterways more navigable and to store the water needed to help flush logs down the Oxtongue River, Gilmour constructed dams in 1894 at Joe and Tea Lakes. The water level was raised a good two feet, devastating the shoreline. Gilmour Island became separated from what is now called Big Wapomeo Island. The Little Wapomeo, Chubby's, and Popcorn peninsulas became islands. Smoke, Canoe and Tea Lakes became connected together into one continuous waterway. Over the years, thousands of trees died and the landscape became desolate and gray. All of the little bays became wastelands of stumps and sunken logs. Canoe Lake became, as A. Y. Jackson, one of the renowned "Group of Seven" Canadian painters, would say a few decades later:

---

20. George Garland, ***Glimpses of Algonquin Park***, 1993, pg. 47.
21. Audrey Saunders, ***The Algonquin Story***, 1946, pg. 101.
22. For details of the adventures of the lumbering Gilmours, see ***When Giants Fall*** by Gary Long, 1998.

"A ragged piece of nature hacked up many years ago by a lumber company that went broke, fire-swept, damned by both man and beaver and overrun with wolves."[23]

Later when the sawmill was established at Mowat, the north end would become a complete mass of floating logs. Flat-bottomed scows with side-mounted paddle wheels and a powerful winch to haul logs on water or on land (called alligators), and long shallow-draught row boats with points at both ends to transport men and suppliers (called pointers) were brought in from Lake of Bays to ply the three-lake water system.

After the disastrous attempt to drive logs from Canoe Lake to Trenton, David Gilmour decided in 1896 to build a saw and planing mill on the northwest shore of Canoe Lake.[24] He was granted a 10-year "license of occupation" for 326 acres south of the new railway line and west of Potter Creek for $40 per year. The "tote" road was extended up the west side of Canoe Lake to the new town site. Since the railway wasn't yet operational, the huge boiler for the mill had to be hauled along the tote road from the Dorset pump house. Nine teams of horses were used to pull the boiler on birch rollers that allegedly wore out almost as fast as the men could replace them. The construction workers worked three shifts per day to get Canoe Lake Mills in operation in time for the spring log drive of 1897. The function of the mill was to prepare four-inch thick boards called "deals" that were then shipped out to Ottawa finishing mills. A 2.4-kilometer rail spur called the "Gilmour Spur" was built from the mill site to the main line at Canoe Lake Station to the new mill with its water tank, pump house, and numerous sidings.

Over the course of the next few years, over 700 people came to reside in the town that sprang up around the Gilmour mill and the railway line. Named after Oliver Mowat, who was the Ontario Premier at the time, the town had a hospital, a boarding house, stables for 50 teams of horses, a large warehouse, cookhouse, various storehouses, farm buildings, shacks, and a small cemetery up on a knoll northwest of town. A post office was established in 1897 with E. T. Marsh as the first postmaster. In 1898, prices for white pine dropped so much that the Gilmours decided to stockpile most of the top grade lumber. In order to create a large enough storage area, sawdust, slabs (outside pieces) and inferior logs were dumped into the lake alongside of the mill until it made a solid surface, which became known as the chip yard. By 1900 the whole logging scheme went bankrupt, and the Gilmours abandoned the area. Little effort was made to clean up the mess or return the area to its original condition as required in their license of occupation. By 1901, there were only 205 inhabitants. Some worked for the railway, some for the Park, and others for the Gilmour bankruptcy receiver.

During the summer of 1905, Dr. Alexander Pirie and his close friend, Dr. Thomas Bertram, decided to take a trip through Algonquin Park.[25] While paddling north up Canoe Lake they discovered two houses, owned and built by the Gilmour Brothers, on the south end of the island in the middle of the lake. Each of the frame houses, at more than 1,700 square feet in size, was sturdily built with brick and stone fireplaces, plastered walls, and double-planked floors that enabled year-round occupancy. They had been used by the Gilmours when inspecting their timber operations in the area, but had been unoccupied for at least half a dozen years due to

---

23. Meehan, B., (curator), Millard, L. (text), ***Algonquin Memories: Tom Thomson in Algonquin Park***, exhibit for the Algonquin Gallery, Algonquin Park 1998, opposite Plate #3.

24. For additional details on the Trenton logging experiment, see ***When Giants Fall***, by Gary Long, 1998

25. For additional details see Chapter 1, ***Algonquin Voices: Selected Stories of Canoe Lake Women*** by Gaye I. Clemson, 2002.

the bankruptcy of the firm in 1900. Though the shoreline was desolate and uninviting, Dr. Pirie, a native of Hamilton who lived and practiced medicine in Costa Rica since 1897, was enamoured with Canoe Lake and decided to see if the buildings were for sale. He purchased them both from the Gilmour receivers and became the first leaseholder in Algonquin Park, though an official lease wasn't issued until 1926.

Over the next decade, a few leaseholds were established around the old Mowat town site and across the lake at the north end. In 1913, Taylor Statten arrived and leased what is now called Little Wapomeo Island. Later, in 1921, he went on to establish Camp Ahmek on the northeast shore, and in 1924 his wife Ethel established Camp Wapomeo on another island in the middle of the lake just north of what by then was called Pirie's Island. By the early 1940s most of the available sites at the north end had been taken, and a number of alumni from Taylor Statten Camps began to populate the south end. Easy access via Highway 60, which had opened in 1935, and the supplies at the Portage Store that opened in 1936 made Canoe Lake a popular choice. By 1953 it was fully leased with 72 leaseholders, a few of whom lived year-round on Potter Creek near the old rail line.

In 1952, Ontario Hydro had enough customers in the area that the construction of a feeder line into Canoe Lake and some of the other developed lakes along Highway 60 became feasible. It was, however, not inexpensive and only those close to Highway 60 accepted the available services. Leaseholders had to obtain a right of way from the existing hydro line on Highway 60 to their individual parcel. They also had to promise that they would ensure that brush and debris was disposed of to the satisfaction of the Department and not cut down any merchantable timber.[26]

The Thompsons were the first leaseholders on the lake to get hydro because the first power line went to Camp Wapomeo right next door. Tess Thompson just happened to be making pies on the day that the installation was taking place. She took a pie fresh from the oven over to the boys who were cutting the line. Then she suggested that there was "more where this one had come from that would be just about ready, had their names on them, if and when they should feel like running the hydro line over to her cottage."[27] In a heartbeat it was done, with the cost being $10 per pole and about a half a dozen blueberry pies. Tess was one of the earliest pioneers in the Park and in addition to great pie-making skills: she also had a unique way of fishing, one of her favourite pastimes. She would sit on the shoreline with her line out until some hapless fish would happen upon her hook. She would then stand up, pick up the rod and march up the hill, the line dragging behind, until the fish hit shore. Locals were astounded at her regular success with this method.[28]

Most of the Park ranger cabins were connected by bush telephone and upon occasion were available for use by local leaseholders. For a long time the only exception was Camp Nominigan. Built over the winter of 1912-13 by the Grand Trunk Railway on a protected peninsula mid-way down the east side of Smoke Lake, Camp Nominigan was until the late 1920s a popular tourist resort. In 1928, a fire destroyed all of the sleeping cabins and the hotel was shut down. In 1931, Garfield Northway, a department store retailer from

---

26. Thompson lease records correspondence, 1955.
27. Thompson cottage log, 1973.
28. ***Algonquin Voices: Selected Stories of Canoe Lake Women*** by Gaye I. Clemson, pg. 140.

Toronto, purchased the buildings and assumed the lease for 10 acres from what was the Canadian National Railway, which had purchased the Grand Trunk Railway in 1923. In 1933, the Ontario Department of Lands and Forests (DLF) agreed to install a direct telephone line from Nominigan to the Smoke Lake Hangar to Algonquin Park Station at Cache Lake.[29] Gar Northway agreed to pay for the materials, and the DLF did the installation and maintenance. The ongoing cost was expected to be $15 a year for the duration of his lease. Since this was the only phone on the lake, Jack Hamilton, Northway's caretaker, became the lake messenger. Callers had no idea what Jack had to go through to deliver their messages to the appropriate recipient. Many residents were fearful when he appeared, afraid that he had a dour message for them.

At its peak, when it was easily accessible by rail, Rain Lake had a small community of four families, which included well known writer and fishing camp owner Ralph Bice and Leopold MacCaulay, a barrister and member of the Ontario Legislature in the late 1930s. Access to a telephone was a major concern as the few summer residents were mostly women with young children. Though Park officials tried, they were unable to obtain permission from the CNR to connect a telephone at the railway station in the vicinity. Eventually they resolved the situation by removing the bush telephone from inside the Park Ranger cabin and placing it in a box outside for use by residents. The only proviso was that residents had to agree to make collect telephone calls, as there were no provisions in the Park regulations for collecting revenue from such a source. Today only the Bice family lease remains.

North and a little west of Canoe Lake is Brulé Lake and directly north is the Joe Lakes chain, composed of Big Joe, Little Joe, and Baby Joe Lakes. On Brulé Lake, a license of occupation was issued to Jane Barnet widow of Alex Barnet of lumbering fame in 1922. In 1930 the Barnets transferred their interest to their daughter Grace who was married to a Lt. Col. Irving. They called the cottage Pringrove. In 1935 the lease was sold to Dr. Edmund H. Kase Jr. from Princton, New Jersey. Dr. Kase was an amazing Algonquin legend, known for his significant contributions towards the appreciation of Algonquin Park. He first came to the Park to canoe trip in 1932 and through his many academic affiliations organized scores of challenging summer and winter trips into the interior of the Park for his students. As Smoke Lake resident George Garland so eloquently stated when Dr. Kase was appointed a Director of the Friends of Algonquin Park in 1987:

> *"Dr. Kase made full use of these experiences to instill in his companions the highest standards of character and sportsmanship" Through his books,* **"Pringrove Through the Years"** *and* **"Jack Gervais: Ranger and Friend"**, *and Jan and Bob Bignell's follow on book called* **"Pringrove – The Later Years"**, *Dr. Kase has given us a permanent record of his activities and a feeling for the love of Algonquin that was developed in his former students and companions."*

A single cottage lease exists near the Joe Lake station railway bridge at the south end of Big Joe Lake, a second lease is the home of Arowhon Pines Resort at the north end of Baby Joe Lake, and about a half dozen are leases scattered along waterways between the two lakes. North of Little Joe Lake, on Burnt Island Lake lie the forgotten remains of what once was the home of the majestic Minnesing Lodge.[30] South of Canoe Lake and

---

29. See Chapter VI for more details on Nominigan and the Northways of Smoke Lake.
30. See Chapter VI for details on the history of Minnesing Lodge.

also part of the Canoe Lake District is Tea Lake. Though close to the highway, Tea Lake is not well populated. Its main occupant is Camp Tamakwa, located on a height of land on the north shore started by Detroit native Lou Handler in 1936. In addition to the camp, there are only six other leases spread on the west and south shores, with several accessible by car from Highway 60. On the far east side of the lake, near the Smoke Creek Bridge and up Bonita Narrows, are a few other remote outposts. One is where Gertrude Baskerville spent her 35 years alone in the wilderness.[31] On Bonita Lake are two leases, both established in the 1950s.

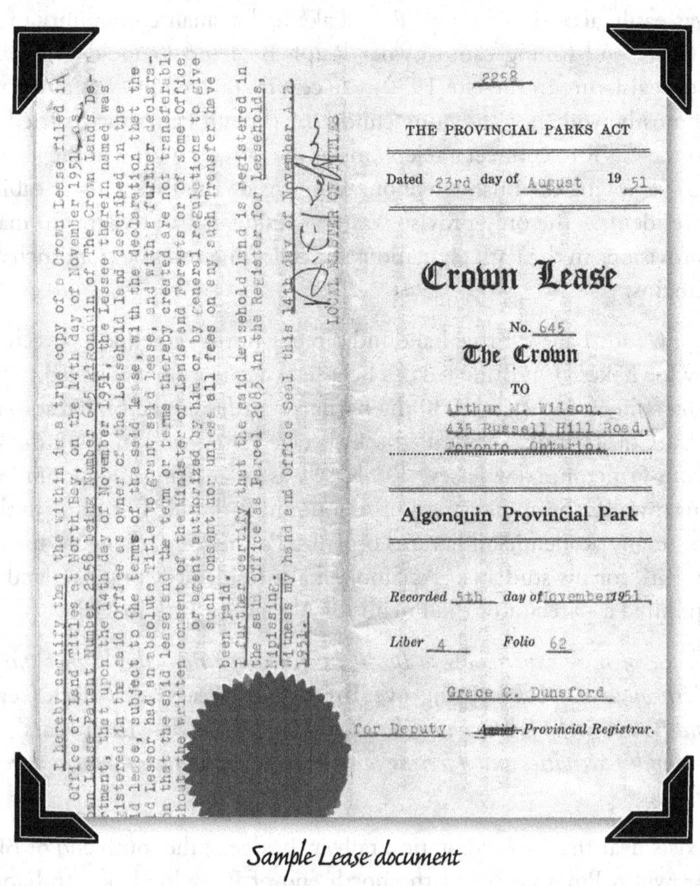

I hereby certify that the within is a true copy of a Crown Lease filed in Office of Land Titles at North Bay, on the 14th day of November 1951, as Crown Lease Patent Number 2258 being Number 645 Algonquin of The Crown Lands Department, that upon the 14th day of November 1951, the Lessee therein named was registered in the said Office as owner of the Leasehold land described in the said lease, subject to the terms of the said lease, with the declaration that the said Lessor had an absolute title to grant said lease, and with a further declaration that the said lease and the term or terms thereby created are not transferable without the written consent of the Minister of Lands and Forests or of some Officer or agent authorized by him or by General regulations to give such consent nor unless all fees on any such Transfer have been paid.

I further certify that the said leasehold land is registered in the said Office as Parcel 2083 in the Register for Leaseholds, Nipissing.

Witness my hand and Office Seal this 14th day of November A.D. 1951.

LOCAL MASTER OF TITLES

2258

THE PROVINCIAL PARKS ACT

Dated 23rd day of August 1951

Crown Lease

No. 645

The Crown

TO

Arthur M. Wilson,
435 Russell Hill Road,
Toronto, Ontario.

Algonquin Provincial Park

Recorded 5th day of November 1951

Liber 4 Folio 62

Grace C. Dunsford

for Deputy ~~Assist.~~ Provincial Registrar.

Sample Lease document

31. For more details see ***Gertrude Baskerville: The Lady of Algonquin*** Park by Gaye I. Clemson

Smoke Lake

Although Smoke Lake is the largest and deepest of all of the leaseable lakes in Algonquin Park, the establishment of a leasehold community didn't really begin after Highway 60 was opened in the mid-1930s. Initially a few leases were taken during the highway construction in the area around what began as No. 2 Camp and is now the Smoke Lake Hangar, and at the south end near what was then the park's southern boundary. The lake's original draw was Camp Nominigan, a sister lodge to Minnesing Lodge and outpost to the Highland Inn that was built by the Grand Trunk Railway in 1912 on Loon Point and as previously mentioned, acquired by A. Garfield and Jessie Northway in 1931.

Loon Point, now known as Nominigan Point, was and is today a strategic feature of the lake. Its flat, rocky, low shoreline to the west and rocky ridge protecting a sandy bay to the east offers shelter from the prevailing northwest wind, and its unusual flat terrain made an ideal place for camping. The site was also a vantage point from which the vistas of Smoke Lake could be viewed in all directions, and enemies, intruders, or friends spotted while they were still far off.[32] In the early years of the Highland Inn, before Nomingan was built, a visit to Loon Point was called the "Grand Outing." As longtime Smoke Lake resident George Garland recalls his aunt telling him:

> *"This day trip generally involved taking a train to Canoe Lake Station then a boat, in summer, and a sleigh, in winter, to Nominigan Point for lunch with the return by paddle, and portage or stage or sleigh back to the Highland Inn."*

According to the diary of Park Ranger Bud Culligan, who lived in a shelter hut across the lake, the site was cleared over the summer of 1912. The following winter a main lodge and six cabins were built and Nominigan Camp, which meant "Among the Balsams," opened for guests after the ice went out in spring of 1913.

By the mid-1920s, Nominigan had become the favourite lodging spot for families who would come and stay, often for two months, year after year. Accommodations were $2.50 per day or $16-$18 per week.[33] To get there, guests would disembark the train at Algonquin Park Station at Cache Lake. From there, they would be driven by a horse-drawn taxi called a "democrat," over a seven-mile rough corduroy road—built partially with logs arranged in a corduroy fashion—that ran along the Source Lake Road for part of the journey. According to a 1977 interview with Tom Murdock, a stagecoach driver at Highland Inn in early 1920s:

> *"There were three stagecoaches at the Highland Inn; a company team and two hired teams. The company team usually stayed at the Highland Inn and the other two teams went to Nominigan and Minnesing every day loaded with supplies going in and returning the next day, usually with three or four guests. The stagecoach had three seats and could hold six passengers with a driver. On busy days the company team would also be put into service to help ferry guests [for $1.00 each way]. They'd leave the Highland Inn around 2:30 p.m. after the train had arrived and it would take four hours to get there so they would arrive around 6 p.m. in*

---

32. Mary Northway, ***Nominigan: The Early Years,*** pg. 1.
33. Barney Moorhouse, ***Centennial Series 1993,*** pg. 31.

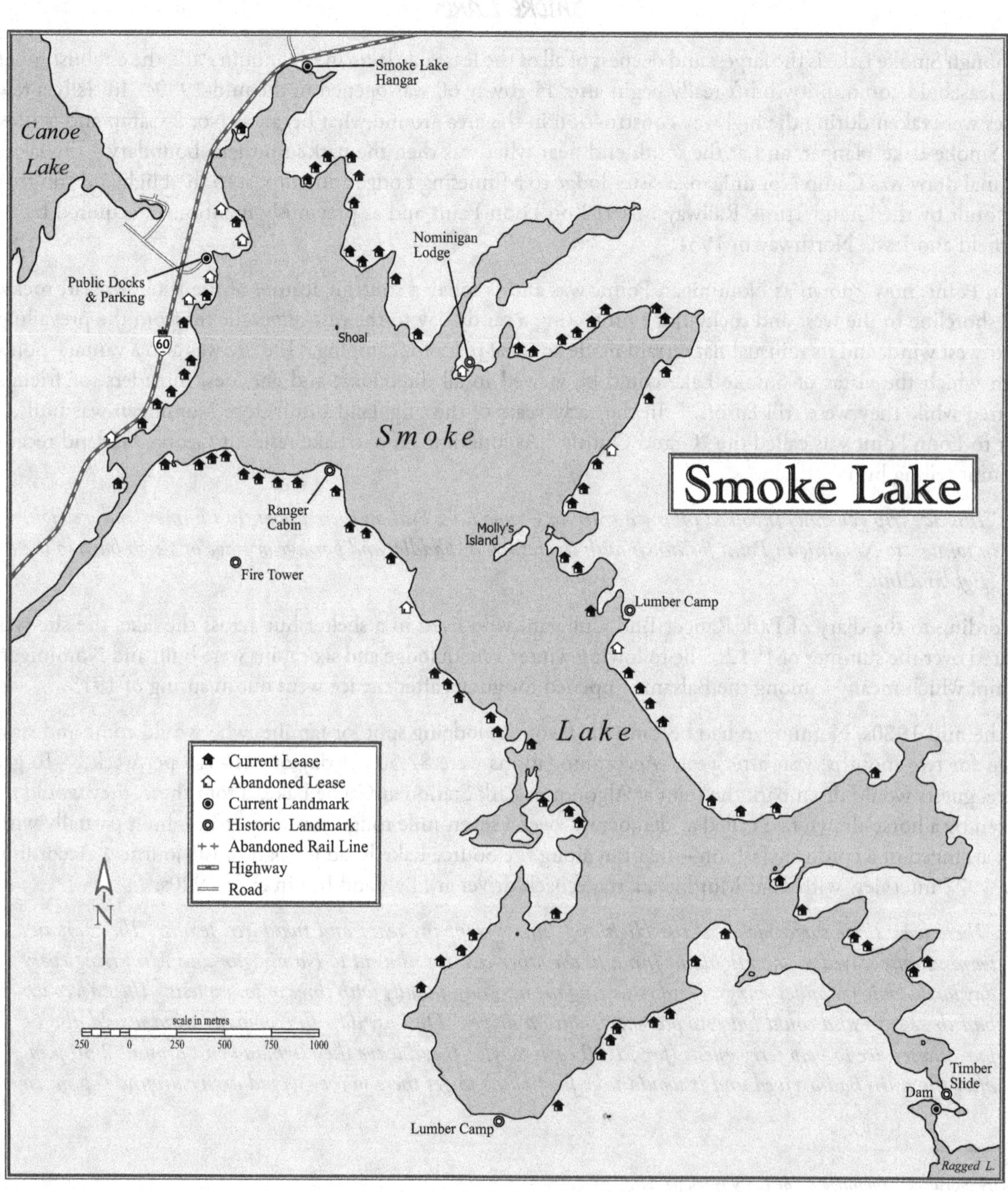
Smoke Lake
Smoke Lake Hangar
Canoe Lake
Nominigan Lodge
Public Docks & Parking
60
Shoal
Smoke
Ranger Cabin
Molly's Island
Fire Tower
Lumber Camp
Lake
Current Lease
Abandoned Lease
Current Landmark
Historic Landmark
Abandoned Rail Line
Highway
Road
N
scale in metres
250 0 250 500 750 1000
Timber Slide
Dam
Lumber Camp
Ragged L.

the evening, stay overnight and leave the next morning right after breakfast around 8 or 8:30 a.m. The road was about 12 feet wide with the damp spots filled in with hollow logs and very rough. You couldn't go as fast to Nominigan Camp as you could to Minnesing, due to twin hills about two miles from Smoke Lake. In the spring it was quite busy getting all of the summer supplies in. At that time it was up to the stagecoach driver to inspect the telephone lines that were fastened onto the trees, running parallel to the road. With them [was the appropriate] equipment so that they could fix the lines."

The main activity for the men was fishing expeditions, according a lovely little history of Nominigan written in the 1960s by Mary Northway, the daughter of Garfield and Jessie Northway.[34] Sometimes as many as thirty people in 10 canoes (10 guides and 20 guests) would head out to prime fishing spots on Ragged, Hellingone, or Porcupine Lakes. The guides portaged the canoes and carried the food packs. Another common fishing expedition was a two-week trip from Nominigan through Canoe Lake, and on the Petawawa River to the town of Pembroke. From Pembroke the group would load the canoes on the train and return to the Highland Inn.[35] When in residence, guests would play cards, talk, or go out for a walk in the woods or a canoe ride. In the mid-1920s, Nominigan also became summer lodging for parents of campers attending local children's camps, and a meeting place for camp counselors on their days off.

In the spring of 1928, a fire destroyed the six cabins due to a suspected blockage in the acetylene system. The cabins were not rebuilt and the hotel was shut down. It remained empty until 1931, when Garfield Northway from Toronto bought the buildings and assumed the lease for the 10-acre parcel from the CNR, which had taken over operation of the railway and its hotel operations from the Grand Trunk Railway in 1923.[36]

According to Mary Northway, the Northway family first visited Algonquin Park in 1913, when John and Kate Northway came to spend their summer holidays at the Highland Inn. John Northway came to Canada in 1868, and went to work for a tailor in Embro, Ontario. From this inauspicious beginning, Northway, using his sound business judgment, became by 1901 a merchant, manufacturer, and financier with partnerships throughout the province and investments throughout the continent. Upon his death in 1926, leadership of his manufacturing concern, The Northway Company Limited, and the retailer John Northway and Son Limited fell to his sons, A. Garfield and John A. Northway. John Northway and Sons Limited grew to include three stores in Toronto, and one each in Hamilton and Stratford.[37] Garfield Northway, known as "Gar," went on to become a major presence in Canadian retailing from the 1930s until his death in 1960.

Gar and wife Jessie loved to entertain, and their new summer home became the social centre for Smoke Lake and its environs. For decades they "were considered the King and Queen of the territory."[38] First they hired Jack Hamilton, who came as cook and caretaker and ended up staying for 29 years. He'd been a cook in a lumber camp and was an expert at making pies, cakes breads, rolls, muffins, homemade pickles, and jams. He became famous in the area for his pies with whipped cream, as apparently the Northway cow, Medusa,

---

34. Mary Northway, ***Nominigan: The Early Years,*** pgs. 20-26.
35. Interview with Tom Murdock by Ron Pittaway, 1977.
36. Mary Northway, ***Nominigan: The Early Years,*** pgs. 20-26. For more details on the early years of Nominigan see Chapter VI.
37. Biography of the Northway family found in the Trent University Archives.
38. Mary Northway, ***Nominigan: A Casual History,*** pg. 16.

tended to produce more cream than milk. A houseboy who donned a white jacket always served meals and was a stickler that guests appear on time. All of the laundry went to Huntsville and took 10 days to return. Northway put in a Delco electric generating system with a total output of 600 watts, with no bulb being more than 25 watts. According to his daughter Mary, this lighting was the most talked about feature of Nominigan, except for the coloured, scented toilet paper in the bathrooms.

The front of Nominigan was originally very swampy, so Northway decided to turn it into a lawn. This necessitated a breakwater. For several summers, all guests physically capable were expected to bring in two rocks a day as their ticket for a meal. The area eventually became a large lawn with a vegetable garden, flowering shrubs, lilacs, cultivated bushes, blueberries, and a strawberry bed. Store assistants laid out the gardens from Newton-and-Lawson, a famous garden shop at the time. Every May 24th holiday, dozens of flats of flowers were brought in and each guest was commandeered to assist with the planting. This was a challenge since the black flies were usually out in full force that time of year. The gardens were expanded for 20 years and according to Mary Northway, became rather celebrated in the park.[39]

Guests would usually come for a week or more and were generally of two types. The first was what Mary called the "White Flannel Crowd." These people were generally successful in the business world, and several had children at the Taylor Statten Camps. The second group was the "Store Crowd," which included store managers and assistants in the family business. The main activities were fishing during the day followed by bridge in the evenings. There was no radio, record player, or TV but for a while there was a player piano, until a mouse ate the mechanism one winter.[40]

Nominigan continued to be a popular a midway stopping point on the lake for canoe trippers, previous guests, and Park Rangers. As Mary Northway wrote:

> *"Because at one time the CNR had a snack bar, canoe trippers would often stop to see if they could get a chocolate bar. Private travelers who had stayed in the old days called, as did rangers, wanderers and guides. It was a port in the storm, with the only shelter for miles. Sometimes the Park Rangers would use it as an emergency headquarters. Once for a fire down the lake, Nominigan was the operations headquarters from dusk until dawn. Gar was good friends with Park Superintendent Frank MacDougall. He and his family would stay at my parents' home when visiting Toronto."*

For years the Northways were also the only leaseholders on the lake with a large boat. Their first one was an old one of Taylor Statten's, from Canoe Lake, that was later replaced by one from Brevettes with a Buchanan engine.[41] They often made it available to Park staff for both inspections of the lake and support of firefighting efforts. Gar Northway was also a major force behind the Canoe Lake and District Leaseholders Association that was formed in 1936. Over the years he hosted many discussions concerning the Park, its policies and future, including such topics as the advisability of building Highway 60, the new west gate, the nature museum, nature trails, mail delivery, the new parking lot, and the services provided at the Portage Store on Canoe Lake.

---

39. Mary Northway, ***Nominigan: A Casual History,*** pgs. 11-12.
40. Mary Northway, ***Nominigan: A Casual History,*** pg. 8.
41. Mary Northway, ***Nominigan: A Casual History,*** pg. 7.

In the early 1950s, Gar and Jessie Northway, became concerned as to what to do with Nominigan after their death. Their daughter Mary had already settled in the Haliburton area. At one time they thought they'd bequeath it to the Royal Ontario Museum for use as a headquarters for the interpretive programs that J. R. Dymond was developing. They also considered leaving it to the Sick Children's Hospital for use as a convalescent camp. Ultimately, they decided "it was too remote to be practical and would require too much expansion and renovation." The lease was renewed without incident in 1954 but Jessie died in 1957, and Gar in 1961. The Northway Company Limited was put into voluntary liquidation and Nominigan was bequeathed to the Northways' old and dear friends, Dr. Harry and Adele Ebbs, directors of Camp Wapomeo on Canoe Lake.[42] In 1968, a historical plaque recognizing Nominigan's 57 years as a Park landmark was unveiled. It read: "May Nominigan have a future worthy of its past; let that past be truly prologue."[43]

In 1976, the Nominigan lease expired. Extensive discussion and lobbying occurred at very high levels of government to get it renewed, but to no avail. At one point the Ontario Heritage Foundation got involved, but in the end its Architectural Conservation Committee "expressed great regret that the historical and architectural significance of Nominigan could not be adequately recognized within the terms of [the Ontario Ministry of Natural Resources'] policy with respect to buildings in the Park." However, the Committee could not justify the removal of the building from the Park.[44] In addition there was much dissent from Park residents anxious to protect and preserve a local landmark. As one wrote in great distress:

> *"Nominigan is a landmark of the Park and part of its heritage. To destroy such a unique building is as wanton an act as to burn an early sketch of Tom Thomson's simply because it is no longer the style of the times."*[45]

None of the appeals was successful, and in 1977 Dr. Ebbs was authorized to salvage whatever he wanted before the Crown began demolition.[46] Robert Bowes, then a Director in the Historical Planning and Research Branch of the Ministry of Culture and Recreation, documented complete information on the architecture, condition location, and construction techniques concerning the site and its building.[47] Knowing that it was a building of some historical significance, Park officials took pains to photograph the building for posterity and those photographs may be found in the Algonquin Park Museum Archives photo collection. According to local legend, Dr. Ebbs couldn't bear to see the main lodge demolished so he sold the logs to the director of nearby Camp Kandalore with the plan to reassemble at the Camp Kandalore site. It was dismantled piece-by-piece, with each log numbered and then moved it to the landing in the fall of 1977. The logs were taken to Camp Kandalore, but never rebuilt and those magnificent pine logs eventually rotted away.[48] A landmark

---

42. Biography of the Northway family found in the Trent University Archives.

43. Mary Northway, Nominigan: A Casual History, pg. 29. During her time at Nominigan, Mary graduated from the University of Toronto with a B.A. in 1933, a M.A. in 1934 and a Ph.D. in 1938. She taught psychology at the University of Toronto from 1934 to 1968 and spent 15 years as Supervisor of Research at the Institute of Child Study. She also earned international recognition as a pioneer in the field of Sociometry and was named an Honorary Life Member of the Ontario Camping Association.

44. Report from the Architectural Conservation Committee of The Ontario Heritage Foundation, 1977, found in Northway lease correspondence, Algonquin Park Museum Archives.

45. Minutes of the Smoke Lake Leaseholders meeting, 1976.

46. Mary Northway, ***Nominigan: A Casual History,*** pg. 29.

47. Letter from Robert Bowes, Director of the Historical Planning and Research Branch of the Ministry of Culture and Recreation, found in 1977 Northway lease correspondence, Algonquin Park Museum Archives.

48. Interview with Sue Ebbs, 2005.

of Algonquin Park history and development was now an empty field. Today, the point is still often used as a mid-lake stopping point by passing canoe trippers. Traces of the lovely gardens and natural rock steps can still be seen.

Other early Smoke Lake residents were Manley Sessions and his sister Esther Sessions (later Keyser). Manley, 10 years Esther's senior, had first come to Algonquin Park in the mid-1920s to visit Dr. Wilson Dods, a friend of their father who owned a cottage on Cache Lake called Loon's Ledge. Manley had asthma and severe seasonal allergies. At the time, conventional medical opinion was that summers in the fresh air of the Park would help his condition. He fell in love with the Park and strongly encouraged Esther to attend Northway Lodge, which she did in 1927. In 1936 and 1937, he and Esther took out leases next door to each other on the extreme south end of the lake, well off the beaten path. Over the years, other friends and relatives would visit, and a few took up leases. Getting there, though, was not so easy. As Esther Keyser wrote in her memoirs called ***Paddling My Own Canoe*** in 2004:

> *"That first summer it was a 12-hour drive from home. Our little bay was jammed with logs. The shore was crowded with flotsam and we could scarcely find a place for even one canoe to land. Manley and I lashed our two canoes together to bring lumber, supplies and bulky items that 6.4 kilometers down the lake. The water level was lower in the lake than it is now and there were small sandy beaches along the shore. Most groceries were brought in and we consumed a lot of canned goods, cases of dried fruit and lots of potatoes. Of course we ate fish nearly every day. On rare occasions we would purchase groceries and supplies at the Hotel Algonquin store operated by Annie Colson. Mail was addressed to Canoe Lake and could be picked up at the train depot in Mowat. Usually I would purchase food for the whole summer on my first trip to the Park."*

Also in the 1930s, Keyser started a canoe-trip guiding business, whereby she introduced friends, and friends of friends, to the joys of canoe tripping in the Park. As she wrote in her book, ***Paddling My Own Canoe***:

> *"The opportunities for outdoor adventure for women were extremely limited at that time so my trips helped fill that gap. I relied on word-of-mouth advertising. To answer the increasing number of questions asked by potential clients, I prepared a marketing notebook called "A Wilderness Canoe Trip" featuring black-and-white photos taken on these early trips with brief explanations about the daily routine. I supplied long thin Ojibwa style paddles. Equipment and food was packed in Woods canoe packs. Customers brought their own bedrolls, which usually consisted of a Hudson Bay blanket and several blanket pins. Sleeping bags weren't conveniently available until after WWII. One of the practices I adopted was the use of a kitchen canvas tarp with grommets for multiple tie downs in about a four-metre by five-metre size and made possible to comfortably weather Algonquin rainstorms. I encouraged people to sleep out under the stars and almost always did so myself. If the bugs were biting we used a shirt or towel over our faces and wrapped ourselves tightly in our Hudson Bay blankets. If bad weather moved in, we'd sleep under one of the canoes or under a tarp."*[49]

By the end of the 1930s, Smoke Lake had nearly 40 residents with an additional 58 being added in the post-WWII decade. Today, 87 leases remain, and the lake is still the main site for lake trout anglers in the spring and fall.

---

49. Esther Keyser, ***Paddling My Own Canoe,*** 2004, pg. 59.

Cache Lake

Algonquin Morning

All calm and still Cache Lake it lies
No cloudlets blur deep azure skies,
Scarce through the trees a breath of breeze,
Tall fir trees stand a stately frieze
Against the hills so misty green,
Reflecting summer sunshine sheen,
Algonquin day again begun,
All bright and warm with August Sun

Poem by Charles Hewitt, Cache Lake Resident

Cache is truly a beautiful lake. It was once known as "Lake of the Isles" because of the two big islands, Delano and Waubuno, which separate the lake into two sections. James Dickson, who cached some of his goods here while surveying the area in 1886, allegedly gave it its name. Other key landmarks got their names as a result of the railway. Laurier Point was so named when the first Ottawa, Arnprior and Parry Sound Railway train came through in 1896. According to local legend, amongst the 100 passengers that J. R. Booth invited on the inaugural train ride was Sir Wilfred Laurier, then the Prime Minister of Canada. When the train stopped at Cache Lake, Laurier was so taken with the area that he decided he wanted a tour. A small group piled into canoes and when they came to a spot he liked, they had a picnic beneath a huge pine tree. Minto Point got its name in 1903 when Lord Minto, then the Governor General of Canada, took a train ride across the Park and at Cache Lake decided he wanted to go on a canoe trip. Quickly a canoe was arranged, and he and his party camped overnight on this scenic point.[50]

Not only is it beautiful, but Cache Lake also holds in its clutches the history of much of Algonquin Park. This is most notably because, after a short stint on Canoe Lake, the Algonquin Park Headquarters relocated in 1898 to the north shore of Cache Lake, near the railway line. Cache Lake's first known resident was Dr. William Bell, who built a summer home kitty-corner across the lake from Park Headquarters on a parcel that is now the home of Bartlett Lodge. According to local historians, Dr. Bell's original idea was to build a health spa for his Ottowa patients where they could recover from tuberculosis or asthma. As mentioned in other Algonquin Park narratives, it was commonly believed by medical professionals in those days that the smell of evergreens was good for healing the lungs. There is no record that Dr. Bell ever acted on his ideas, but he did attain some fame in Algonquin lore by drafting Algonquin Park's first canoe route map. He also became known in some circles as the man who introduced Molly Cox Colson to Algonquin Park in 1900. A nurse from Ottawa,

50. Richard Eldridge and Orville Osborne, ***Cache Lake Reflections,*** pg. 55.

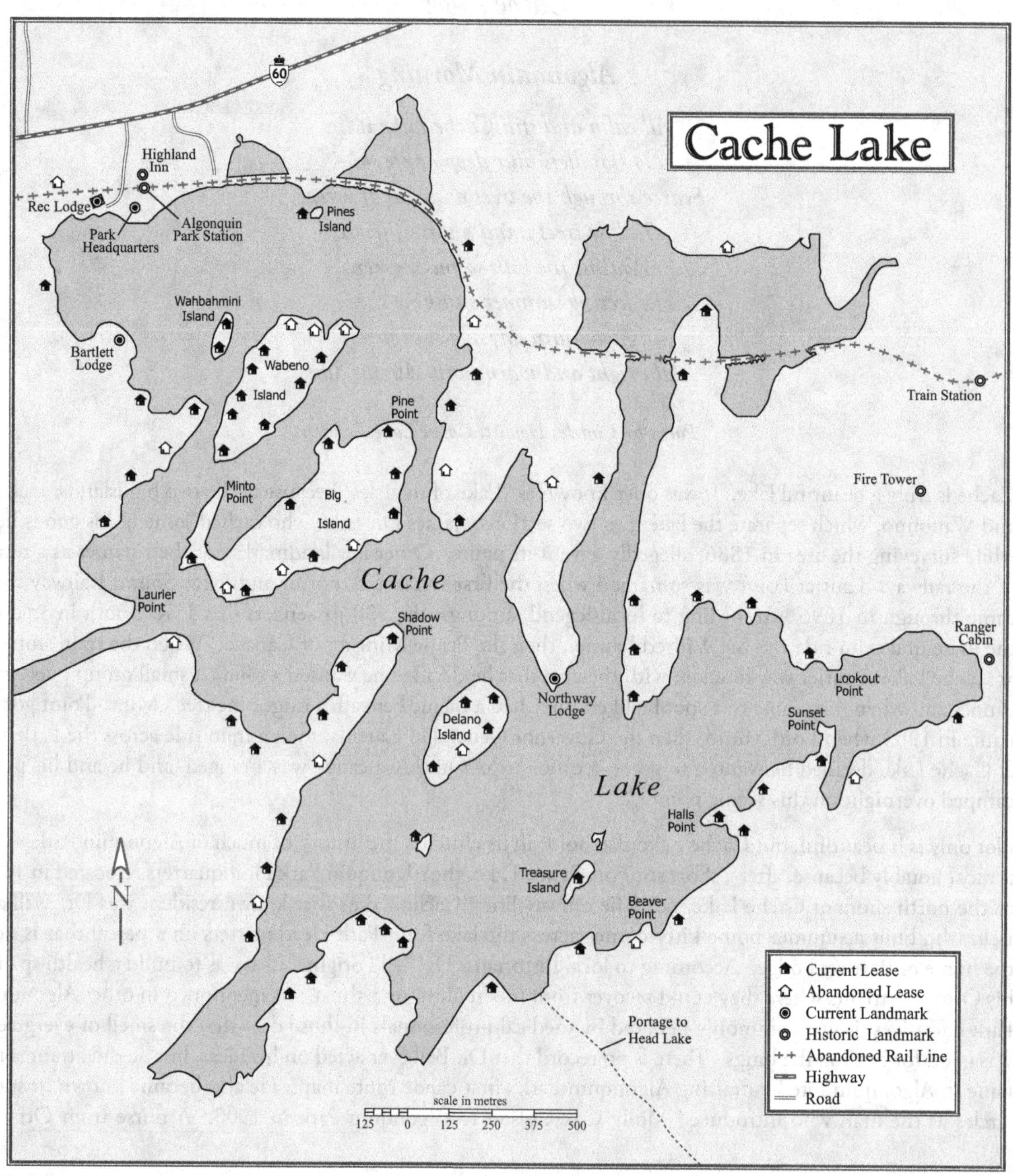
Cache Lake
60
Highland Inn
Rec Lodge
Algonquin Park Station
Park Headquarters
Pines Island
Wahbahmini Island
Bartlett Lodge
Wabeno Island
Pine Point
Minto Point
Big Island
Laurier Point
Cache
Shadow Point
Northway Lodge
Delano Island
Train Station
Fire Tower
Ranger Cabin
Lookout Point
Sunset Point
Lake
Halls Point
Treasure Island
Beaver Point
Portage to Head Lake
N
scale in metres
125 0 125 250 375 500
Current Lease
Abandoned Lease
Current Landmark
Historic Landmark
Abandoned Rail Line
Highway
Road

Molly became the housekeeper at the Park Rangers' boarding house to great acclaim. Later, she married Ed Colson and with him managed the Highland Inn from 1908 to 1917. In 1917 they acquired the Hotel Algonquin near Joe Lake Station and also established there an outfitting store, known locally as the Colson Store and run by Ed's sister Annie. Molly's influence as innkeeper, storekeeper, and healer was legendary. She also was apparently one of the last people to see Tom Thomson alive, on the fateful day of his disappearance in 1917. In 1935, she took out a "License of Occupation" and established the Portage Store at the south end of the lake. After her death, in 1945, Molly's Island on Smoke Lake, one of her favourite picnicking spots, was named after her.[51]

Other than the Park Headquarters, not much else happened on Cache Lake until 1908 when the Grand Trunk Railway decided to build the Highland Inn. It had become the central locomotive depot and the area around it was the most complicated section for the Ottawa, Arnprior and Parry Sound Railway to build. Within two miles it crossed the Madawaska River three times, each bridged by a huge wooden trestle structure. In 1899 the "Third Trestle" was replaced with a steel one. According to Cache Lake residents, it was a breathtaking experience to sit in a canoe under one of the trestles, as the train roared overhead.[52] One critical employee was the bridge keeper whose job it was to check to see that sparks from the passing train didn't catch the trestles on fire. Growing up on Cache Lake in the 1920s, Margaret Bennett remembers watching the trains rumble by. She'd wave, and the engineer would throw off the ice her family had ordered or drop off their mail. Sometimes they'd even stop and pick her up, and she'd ride with the engineer or on top of the coal car to the third trestle and walk back. Once a grain car overturned and dumped its load of grain between the track and the water and was burned in a giant bonfire.[53]

Along with the new Park Headquarters, built in 1898, there was a large collection of outbuildings, including a staff house called "Mahogany" that was used by the maintenance staff at the Highland Inn; quarters built in 1907 for married Park Rangers; a storage facility (later called the Recreation Hall) constructed in 1932; the "Stone House" for the airplane pilots in the MacDougall years; the "White House" residence for Highland Inn managers; and a barn for the DLF's horses. A little way down the CNR tracks was "Chester's Shack," the dilapidated cabin of train employee and famous local character Chester Nichols.

For most if its existence, the Highland Inn was a major centre of activity for Cache Lake residents. Allegedly designed by the architect who designed the Wawa Hotel on Lake of Bays, construction began by the Grand Trunk Railway in 1906 and Highland Inn opened in 1908. At first it was a small inn with eight rooms and a dining room with a verandah. Over the years it grew to have two wings that could accommodate 200 people. In its heyday, every weekend, all summer long, dances were held first on the open-air dance pavilion above the lakeside boathouse and later in the nearby Recreation Hall. Musicians would come from the Chateau Laurier Hotel in Ottawa. A gasoline-run generator would light a set of lights that ran right out to the end of the dock.

---

51. For additional details of Molly Cox Colson see *Algonquin Voices* by Gaye I. Clemson, pgs. 46-64.

52. Richard Eldridge and Orville Osborne, *Cache Lake Reflections*, 1995, pg. 14.

53. According to the *Cache Lake Reflections*, pg. 15, in the mid-1930s a flash flood disturbed the old foundation, so the trestles were condemned. Trains continued from Whitney to Two Rivers until 1944 and came from the west as far as Cache Lake until 1959. Bill Yaskovitch and his brother John dynamited one of the trestles in the late 1950s and sold the steel for scrap.

In 1908, Fannie Case, a high school teacher from Rochester, New York, came to Algonquin Park and decided to start a children's camp for girls. Called Northway Lodge, the camp is located on a peninsula across from Delano Island.[54] It was the first children's camp to open in the park and today is one of the oldest girls' camps in Canada. Case's philosophy of camping and canoeing had then, and still has today, a formative impact on a whole generation of women. According to Esther Keyser, who attended Northway Lodge in her youth, and went on to become Algonquin Park's first female licensed canoe-tripping guide:

> *"Fanny Case believed that women could do most things that men could do. She endeavoured to teach women survival skills in an environment that had been the domain of the opposite sex. Her connection to Mother Nature, displayed in her daily actions and expressions, provided much of the spiritual framework for the camp."*

Like Canoe Lake with its strong connections to Taylor Statten Camps, many Cache Lake residents can claim a connection in one form or another to Northway Lodge and Windigo, the nearby training facility for the male guides who took Northway campers out on canoe trips in the Park.

Like other social organizations, every lake has its own culture. Within a decade of Northway Lodge's opening, Cache Lake contained over 35 leases. When Frank MacDougall arrived in 1931 to take over leadership of the Park, there were over 70 leases on Cache Lake, most well separated with bumper parcels between them to maintain the natural tranquility everyone sought in coming to the Park. By 1936, the lake was fully leased. Whether it was due to the impact of the Highland Inn or just coincidence, Cache Lake was in its early years a place with class. A flag up the pole meant that you were in residence and that visitors were welcome. In the 1940s and 1950s the women would host afternoon teas, white gloves and all, with different tablecloths and salt and pepper shakers used for each meal.[55] The Pendletons, who apparently loved to entertain, had a cabin with a main hall, and a huge walk-in "cold box" set into the side of the hill. They would regularly seat and feed 20 people and often, without a thought, they would host parties to which over 40 people would be invited. Each lease had a specific colour scheme for their canoes that was recognizable by all. The Kings' colour scheme was red canoes with yellow gunnels. The Turners' was grey with a red and white band angled across one end. The Masons' was a royal blue and the Farmer-Waughs' was deep red. The Browns' was orange and the Rigbys' was green. Alas, when cedar strip canoes became too expensive to maintain and fiberglass canoes became common, the colour schemes pretty much disappeared.

To keep everyone on the lake informed, a group of leaseholders established a newsletter. The first one, a summer weekly newspaper called "The Algonquin Weekly," was published by full-time resident Mary Pigeon and cost 2 cents a copy. Kathleen Mitchell later started "The Bugle," which was one page filled with summer news. In 1970 it was renamed the "Cache Flash" by Marjorie Jackson and was produced by Hal King. The "Cache Flash" is still published several times a year to this day.

The roots of leasehold championing of Algonquin Park can also be found within the Cache Lake community.

---

54. To be completely correct, the camp was originally established outside of the Park in 1906. In 2005 it celebrated 100 years of operation.
55. Recollections from Susan Riddick, 2004.

It started with the formation of the Cache Lake Leaseholders Association (CLLA) in 1927. With 33 founding members, the group was "formed with a view to cooperative action in all matters affecting the common interests of its members," and by extension, the common interests of the Park.[56] With Dr. C. H. Juvet as the first President and a membership fee of $1 per year, one of the group's first and most visible efforts was in 1929 to lobby against the granting of timber rights to the McRae Logging Company to log in Canisbay Township, which included Cache Lake, Lake of Two Rivers, and Source Lake. Leaseholders were concerned that lumbermen would be at "liberty to cut down any tree of any substantial size on the lake. This spectre of woodsmen laying waste to the scenery near their cottages" drove the CLLA to orchestrate what became a very effective public protest in the Toronto press.[57] Their efforts were successful and resulted in a logging ban on all land within 30.5 meters of any lake, stream, or portage. The CLLA protested again when in 1930 the government announced the proposed construction of Highway 60 from Huntsville to Whitney without any sort of public consultation. Fearful that "an army of motorists would destroy the beauty and tranquility of the park and have a detrimental impact on fish and game stocks," the group launched another protest. They subsequently changed their minds, in 1935, when the railway announced that it planned to stop rail service into the Park and the road would be needed to gain access to their leases.[58]

Generally Cache Lake was not a lake that welcomed motorboats. Until the 1930s, motorboats weren't an issue as the only ones on the lake belonged to Bartlett Lodge and nearby Camp Tanamakoon. Northway Lodge would transport campers' trunks on top of a few planks laid across two canoes. But as usage of the Park increased, so did the number and size of resident and visitor motorboats. By the mid-1960s, residents had had enough and began a series of efforts to encourage Park Officials to introduce boat motor size restrictions. In 1975, a survey of Cache Lake Leaseholders showed that 91% were in favour of motorboat engine size restrictions and a ban on waterskiing. The Ministry eventually adopted these suggestions in the mid-1980s. Today it is hard to imagine that there ever was a time when the tranquility of Algonquin Park lakes was disrupted by waterskiing and high-powered motorboats.

Aerial of Cache Lake 1956 APMA #3344

56. Cache Lake Leaseholders Association Constitution, 1927.
57. Gerald Killan, *Protected Places: A History of Ontario's Provincial Parks System*, pg. 60.
58. Ibid, pg. 60.

Where Madawaska Flows

The day was still
As sun then starts to draw and paint with light
On every hill with lights and shadows
Its infinite skill
To produce the magnificent sight.

The early snow – which covers deeply all the open ground
The treasure trove – of Wintry Story passing
Time then wove
As every crevice shadowed then outlined every mound

The golden cloud, that slowly came in view and then just go
Dark evergreens that stand so tall and straight and proud
Bare Birch that seem to serve as Peace Look Out
There
Where Madawaska flow

Poem by Rudy Humber, Lake of Two Rivers Resident

Other Highway 60 Leasehold Lakes

Source Lake

A little over halfway between Canoe and Cache Lakes, along Highway 60, is Source Lake. It's a small community, and today contains only 13 leases, most of them established in the late 1940s and early 1950s. For a short time, there was also a commercial lodge called Glen Donald Lodge in existence on the north east shore.[59] It is not easily accessible via canoe routes, so it gets very little canoeing traffic. For most of its history, Source Lake's main claim to fame has been Camp Pathfinder. One of Canada's renowned canoe-tripping camps, located on an island on the east side of the lake, Camp Pathfinder was founded in 1914 by Rochester educators Franklin Gray and William Bennett. Over its nearly 100-year history, ownership of the camp has transferred from a number of people, including William Swift, whose son Bill Swift Jr. owns and operates Swift Canoe, and Kayak, a well known Canadian canoe and kayak builder and distributor. Today it is owned by Glenn and Heidi Arthurs and Mike and Leslie Sladden, who took over in 1999. The first leaseholder, Benedict Steimer, was a friend of a Camp Pathfinder Camp Director in the 1930s. Fred Maltman, an insurance adjuster from Toronto, followed him in 1947. Over the next two years, a dozen other leaseholders arrived, most of whom had a connection of one sort or another with Camp Pathfinder, Taylor Statten Camps on Canoe Lake, or other Source Lakers.

Lake of Two Rivers

Surveyor John Snow named Lake of Two Rivers in 1854, because two branches of the Madawaska River flow into the western side of the lake, just 100 or so meters apart. The north branch flows out of Lake Sasajewun, near the Wildlife Research Station, and the southern branch flows from Cache Lake out through the east end to Pog Lake and Whitefish Lake. During the last 50 years, three economic engines have driven the history of the area. Its first economic engine was a sawmill owned and operated by the McRae Lumber Company on the southwest shore, built in the early 1930s and closed in 1944. Aerial photographs in the 1930s show huge log booms hugging the north shore waiting to disgorge their contents at the mill. According to the locals, there were remnants of the mill building and burner still standing in the early 1950s, although these quickly disappeared into the forest landscape. The second economic engine was a Relief Camp that was built on a sandy plain between the two branches of the Madawaska River during the Great Depression in the 1930s. Run by the Department of National Defense, the camp for young unemployed men built the Lake of Two Rivers airfield and likely helped with the construction of Highway 60. The third economic engine was, and is today, the Lake of Two Rivers Campground, its location having been picked, no doubt, because of the fine beach. Built on 14 hectares of land, it opened for business in 1938 and was the first roadside campground in the Park. In the 1960s, after the airfield was closed, the space was used for overflow camping on busy weekends. In the summer, an outdoor theatre provides daily interpretive programs run by Park staff and Sunday church services.

The first leaseholder on the lake was Burt Moore, a traveling salesman from Toronto, who leased a parcel on a

---

59. For more details on Glen Donald Lodge see Chapter VI.

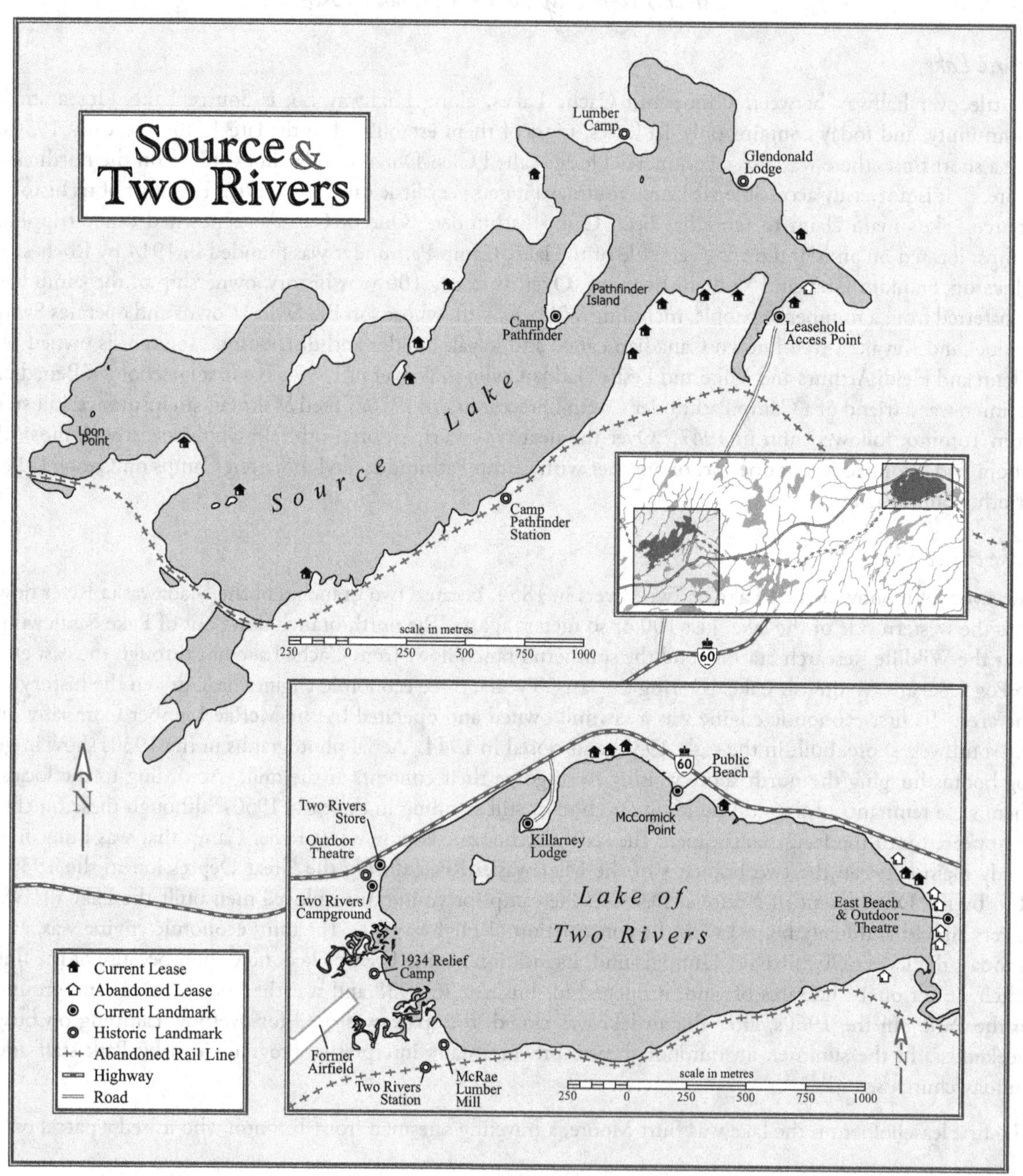

Source & Two Rivers
Lumber Camp
Glendonald Lodge
Pathfinder Island
Camp Pathfinder
Leasehold Access Point
Loon Point
Source Lake
Camp Pathfinder Station
scale in metres
250 0 250 500 750 1000
60
N
Public Beach
McCormick Point
Killarney Lodge
Two Rivers Store
Outdoor Theatre
Two Rivers Campground
Lake of Two Rivers
East Beach & Outdoor Theatre
1934 Relief Camp
Former Airfield
Two Rivers Station
McRae Lumber Mill
Current Lease
Abandoned Lease
Current Landmark
Historic Landmark
Abandoned Rail Line
Highway
Road

point on the north shore in 1935 and built Killarney Lodge on the site. According to historian Rory MacKay, Park Superintendent reports at the time indicate that a William Wise from the Bordentown Military Institute in New Jersey established a boys' camp (known as Camp Minnewawa) near Killarney Lodge, which was in operation until about 1930. A few years later in 1939, Tom McCormick, the Parks' Chief Ranger at the time, took out a lease on another nearby point. McCormick had joined the DLF as a summer Park Ranger in 1917. In 1922, he became Algonquin Park's Deputy Fire Ranger, Chief Fire Ranger in 1926, and Chief Ranger of the merged Fire and Park Ranger Departments in 1931 under Park Superintendent Frank MacDougall. He was deeply respected for his dedication to his work and his pride in and knowledge of Algonquin Park. According to his daughter, Mary McCormick Pigeon, McCormick was a tall, quiet-spoken man, who had a twinkle in his eye, a terrific sense of humour, and a calm bearing of authority.[60] He was an expert woodsman, scaler, fisherman, hiker, and canoeist and was never seen without a hat. It was he who blazed many of the hiking trails through the Park, staked out several of the campgrounds, and was the key contact person for people interested in leasing in the Park in the 1930s and 1940s During the post-war years about a dozen other parcels were taken up spread out across the north shore, running parallel to Highway 60.

In the mid-1960s, Park officials wanted to expand the picnic facilities in the area near the Lake of Two Rivers east beach and nearly a dozen of the leaseholders in the area were encouraged to abandon their leases. As will also be seen later in this narrative, and as was also true on Rock Lake, living right next to a public campground in the 1960s and early 1970s was not a pleasant experience. The noise and rowdiness was a major disturbance to the tranquility of the Park, and since resettlement in another part of the Park was not an option, these leaseholders were regretfully forced to leave. Their cabins were demolished or burned and as one former leaseholder commented:

> *"Only the hemlocks and the terraces on the hillside provided evidence that we were ever even there."*[61]

Today, Killarney Lodge still exists and operates under a commercial lease. The McCormick lease was acquired by the Crown in 1979 and about a half dozen residents are still there tucked away on the north shore of the lake.

Lake of Two Rivers Air Field c1940s
APMA #5377

---

60. His daughter Mary went on to write two narratives in 1995 of her time in Algonquin Park as a child, namely ***Born on Brulé Lake*** and ***Living at Cache Lake.*** The Pigeon family continues to maintain a lease on Cache Lake and grandson Jake Pigeon runs the Brent operation for Algonquin Outfitters. Another grandson, Roy MacGregor, is a well known Canadian writer and though he cottages now outside of the Park, he has many memories and has written extensively of his summers as a child visiting his grandfather.

61. For more details on Glen Donald Lodge see Chapter VI.

North End of Canoe Lake Looking Eest at Mowat Town Site c1920s APMA #625

Tom Thompson Totem Pole and Cairn c1930s
Gray Collection

Ranger Cabin on Eagle Lake APMA #3009

A Misty Source Lake 1896 APMA #166

View of Cache Lake from Skymount Tower 1917
APMA #6120

Madawaska River Near Rock Lake Taylor Collection

Rock Lake/Whitefish Lake and Galeairy Lake Area[62]

It all began for the little community at Rock Lake in 1896 when John Rudolphus Booth, a well known lumberman from Ottawa who at one time had some of the largest timber and sawmill interests in Canada, decided to build a railway from Parry Sound to Ottawa.[63] He wanted access to the shipping of wheat and other products from western Canada and the midwestern United States to Ottawa, Montreal, and points south into the United States. Though primarily a lumberman, Booth's interest in railroads had started in the early 1880s when he had financed the building of a rail line, which ran from Ottawa to Boston.[64] According to Rory MacKay, an Algonquin Park historian and resident of nearby Lake of Two Rivers:

> *"Ottawa provided too small a market for the [Canadian Atlantic Railway], so in 1892 Booth began the Ottawa, Arnprior and Parry Sound line, which crossed the Ottawa-Huron Tract through Booth's timber limits. The line followed the Bonnechère Valley to Golden Lake, crossed to the Madawaska Valley and [passed through the southern end of Algonquin Park]. From there it went on to Georgian Bay at Depot Harbour, just south of Parry Sound. The total distance was [just under 400 miles]."*

By early 1896, 30 camps had been built along the newly surveyed right of way that could accommodate up to 2,000 workers. Six hundred men with 150 teams were busy on construction with 50 new men being hired every day. Special trains delivered 150 tons of dynamite from the Ottawa Powder Works of Buckingham, Quebec, which was needed to blast the line through the Precambrian rock along the route. The dynamite was stored in magazines built on islands on nearby lakes.[65] In the process of laying out the right of way, the surveyors came upon a natural glacial sand and gravel deposit that lay between Whitefish and Rock Lakes. At the time, Rock Lake lay south of the Algonquin Park boundary. This sand and gravel was perfect as ballast for the railway bed so the first Rock Lake "day station," with the Morse code call letters "UF," was built just south of the Rock Creek Bridge.

In mid-November 1896, railway Secretary-Treasurer Andrew W. Fleck, who later married Booth's daughter Helen Gertrude Booth, officially opened the line for freight business. To celebrate, Booth hosted a special run from Ottawa to Potter's Lake, 80 miles east of Parry Sound. He invited 100 passengers, including members of Parliament, Senators, and newspapermen, feeding them lunch on the way up and dinner on the way back. Attached to the rear of the train was Booth's recently completed official business railcar No. 99, which he called "Opeongo."[66] It was on this trip that he earned the moniker "King of Canadian Lumbermen and Railway" from W. C. Edwards, a member of Parliament at the time.[67] On December 5, 1896, then-Prime Minister Wilfrid Laurier and Booth went on an inspection tour of the line that soon after opened for passenger traffic. At the time, return fare from Ottawa to Parry Sound was $14.85, with a special Christmas excursion fare that

---

62. Excerpted from ***Rock Lake Station*** by Gaye I. Clemson, 2005.
63. Rory MacKay and William Reynolds, ***Algonquin,*** 1993, pg. 43.
64. John Ross Trinnell, ***J. R. Booth: Life and Times of an Ottawa Lumber King,*** pg. 109.
65. John Ross Trinnell, ***J. R. Booth: Life and Times of an Ottawa Lumber King,*** pgs. 31-32.
66. Likely named after nearby Lake Opeongo, which means "Sandy at the Narrows," where it is believed there was at one time an Indian settlement. According to Algonquin Park Bulletin No. 10, ***Names of Algonquin,*** there was also a colonization road projected from near Renfrew towards Opeongo Lake that in 1850 was called the Opeongo Road and the name was given to a community near the beginning of this road.
67. John Ross Trinnell, ***J. R. Booth: Life and Times of an Ottawa Lumber King,*** pgs. 51-53.

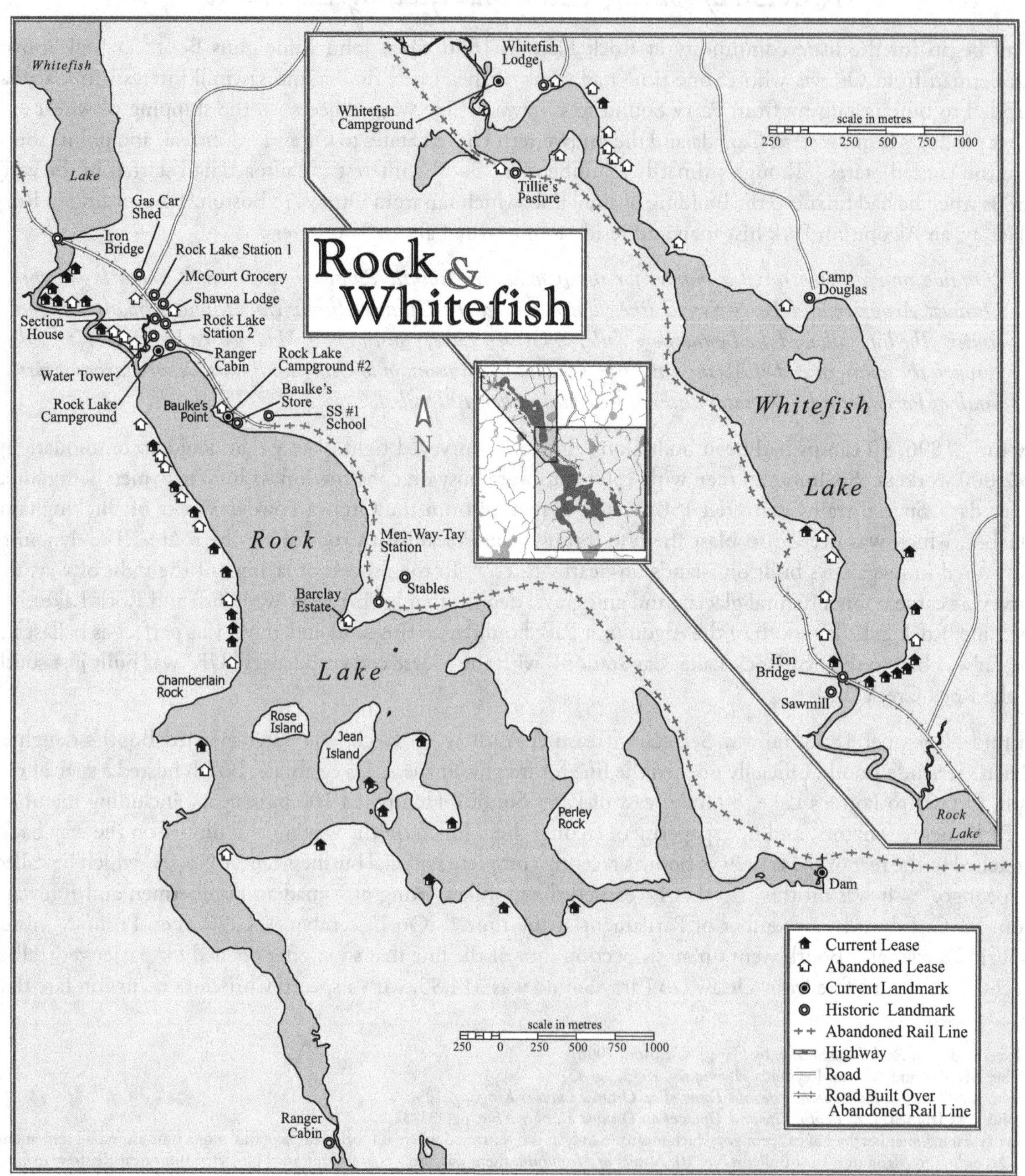
Rock & Whitefish
Whitefish Lake
Rock Lake
Whitefish Lodge
Whitefish Campground
Tillie's Pasture
Camp Douglas
Gas Car Shed
Iron Bridge
Rock Lake Station 1
McCourt Grocery
Shawna Lodge
Section House
Rock Lake Station 2
Ranger Cabin
Water Tower
Rock Lake Campground #2
Rock Lake Campground
Baulke's Point
Baulke's Store
SS #1 School
Men-Way-Tay Station
Stables
Barclay Estate
Chamberlain Rock
Rose Island
Jean Island
Perley Rock
Iron Bridge
Sawmill
Dam
Ranger Cabin
scale in metres
250 0 250 500 750 1000
Current Lease
Abandoned Lease
Current Landmark
Historic Landmark
Abandoned Rail Line
Highway
Road
Road Built Over Abandoned Rail Line

year of $5.50 to celebrate the Christmas season.[68]

The first regularly scheduled trains for the Ottawa, Arnprior and Parry Sound Railway (OA&PS) rolled through the newly minted Rock Lake Station on the new rails in January 1897.[69] In 1898, letters patent for rights of way and station-grounds were finally officially granted to the railway for nearly 30 acres in the vicinity of the station. The station location was ideal due to its close proximity to Rock Creek, where water flowing from Fisher Lake provided an ample supply for the thirsty steam locomotives.

During the building of the OA&PS railway, J. R. Booth obtained water and timber rights for 7,000 acres of land around the east side of Rock Lake. The area included the islands in the middle of Rock Lake (later named Rose and Jean Islands, after his granddaughters), and part of the west shore of Rock Lake. It also included Gordon Lake, where a boathouse was built for the family's fishing boat. Later, perhaps as early as 1903, Booth seems to have exchanged this vast acreage for patent title, or in effect ownership of 700 acres on the western shore of Rock Lake. Unfortunately, after Booth died he willed that all of his personal papers be destroyed, so the details of this transaction have been lost to history.[70]

In the late 1890s, the Booth/Flecks decided to build a summer residence on the property. Called Men-Wah-Tay Lodge, meaning "Place of Sunshine," the original house was featured in "Canadian Architect and Builder" magazine in 1900. The original architect was W. H. Watts.[71] In addition to the house, there was a stable with an attached blacksmith shop for making spikes, grinding axes, and fixing horseshoes. By the water on the north side was a single-slip log launching spot with a tall flagpole.[72] Close by was the Booth/Fleck personal private railroad siding and train station that he called Men-Wah-Tay Station. The original small shelter was replaced in 1920 with a one-room building on the curve (lakeside) just past the private siding that also housed the caretaker's residence. The station did not have any call letters, as Rock Lake Station did, because there were no telegraph facilities and it was not staffed by a station agent.

By 1904, Booth had tired of railways, or had deemed them to be unprofitable, and sold both the OA&PS and Canadian Atlantic Railway to the Grand Trunk Railway. Within a few years of the sale his railway line became a commercial gateway to markets in the United States.[73] This meant that large numbers of freight trains used the line, carrying goods, grain, and other products to and from points east and west.

By 1910, Rock Lake Station was a busy place, with up to six trains a day passing through, two of which were passenger trains. Over 120 loads of grain a day from the Canadian West would pass through during the summer. During the early years of WWI, the line was also used to transport troops to eastern ports.[74] In

---

67. John Ross Trinnell, ***J. R. Booth: Life and Times of an Ottawa Lumber King***, pg. 61.

69. The original Rock Lake Station sign still exists and is mounted at a cottage on Rock Lake.

70. Ottelyn Addison in her book *Early Days of Algonquin Park,* suggests that it was Fleck who obtained the water and timber rights not Booth and it was Fleck who exchanged the acreage in 1903 for the smaller amount of patented land. The author speculates is that Booth may have given the property to Fleck as a wedding present.

71. *Canadian Architect and Builder*, Volume 13, November 1900. For more details on the Booth/Fleck estate on Rock Lake see *Rock Lake Station* by Gaye I. Clemson.

72. The current Booth/Rock Lake trail runs between the old garbage dump and the stables.

73. For details as to history of the Ottawa, Arnprior and Parry Sound Railway, see *Over the Hills to Georgian Bay* by Niall MacKay.

74. Roderick MacKay and William Reynolds, *Algonquin*, pg. 45.

addition to being a transportation hub, where steam locomotives were refueled with water, Rock Lake Station had also evolved into a major camping and fishing destination. Tourists interested in escaping from the city for an inexpensive summer vacation would come from all over northeastern Canada and the United States. For women, the dress of the day was not the long dresses common to visitors to the Highland Inn at Cache Lake. Female campers wore breeches and high leather camping boots with colourful jackets and large hats. For everyone in the local area, the arrival of the train was a highlight of the day. Instantaneously the train platform would become a beehive of activity with people, produce, and equipment coming and going on and off the train.[75]

In 1915, the Ontario Legislature passed the Park Act that expanded the size of Algonquin Park to include eight new townships on the south and east sides. According to a map compiled and drawn by Ontario's Chief Geographer's Office in 1946, the two on the south edge of the Park (Nightingale and Lawrence) that included the Rock Lake area had been added in 1911 and the other six townships on the eastern side of the Park (Edgar, Bronson, Barron, Stratton, Guthrie, and Master townships) were added in 1914. Under the terms of Park Act of 1915, the Ontario Department of Lands and Forests took over administration of the area. Its regulations forbade anyone to locate, settle upon use or occupy any part of the Provincial Park unless approved by Park Officials.[76] In the short run the point was moot, as all of the settlers, i.e., the permanent residents of Rock Lake, were employees of the railroad and had built their residences on property patented by the railway. However, in 1915, the railway deeded much of that land, except that which was expressly needed for the train station, to the Crown. Those who decided to remain took out 21-year leases with the Park. The only exception is one piece of patent land at the south end of Whitefish Lake that was sold off by the Canadian National Railway and is in private hands to this day.

By the mid-1920s, Superintendent Bartlett's promotion of the Park as a tourism destination at the Canadian National Exhibition in Toronto and in newspapers and magazines in the eastern United States began to have an effect. Many of those who came to Rock Lake to camp got interested in obtaining leases on which to build fishing camps and summer cottages. Fewer than a dozen leases were taken out in the mid- to late 1920s, but by the late 1940s, Rock Lake was fully leased.

By the early 1930s, the Canadian National Railway, which had taken over the operations of the Grand Trunk Railway in 1923, was running only three passenger trains into the Park. In 1933, the main trestle at Cache Lake was condemned, forcing the train coming from the west to stop and turn around at Cache Lake. The train coming from the east would do the same at Lake of Two Rivers. To solve the problem, in 1933, crews began the construction of what became Highway 60.[77] The new highway officially opened for business in 1936 and during that first summer 3,809 cars were checked in through the West Gate. In the early years, the highway was really not much more than a trail full of crooked ruts. It had lots of low swampy places, sharp curves, and abrupt little hills and was maintained by a grader that would pass by three times a week. From Cache Lake to

75. Recollections from Robert Taylor, 2003 and 2004.

76. McCourt lease correspondence, 1916, Algonquin Park Museum Archives.

77. Gerald Killan, ***Protected Places: A History of Ontario's Provincial Parks System,*** pg. 64.

Whitney it was a bit rough but passable except after a heavy rain.[78] The trip from Huntsville to Cache Lake usually took one and a half hours on a good day, and as the Allan family from Rock Lake experienced:

> *"We were always intrigued by our mother's story of driving the new highway as it was being built—the base apparently being logs—with the car shaking and rattling so badly that eventually one of the headlights was shaken right out. The journey continued after a towel was wrapped around the light and it was wedged back in place."*

The route in from Ottawa was even more terrifying. As Hank Laurier from Canoe Lake remembered:

> *"We lived in Montreal and used to always go to the Gaspé for our holidays. But in 1935 our family doctor felt that mountain air would be better for my brother Carl's allergies so the family decided to send us to [Taylor Statten's] Camp Ahmek on Canoe Lake. That first year we went by train but in 1936, my dad Robert decided to drive us up to camp. It took nine hours to complete the 190-mile journey. The last 85 miles between Golden Lake and Canoe Lake was a single lane road negotiated at an average speed of 20 mph. We were constantly afraid that we might meet another vehicle coming the other way as we approached the crests of hills."*

In 1946, talk was in the air of building an access road directly into Rock Lake. The public demand for more recreation facilities was intense and the DLF was interested in opening additional public campgrounds in the Park. The Rock Lake beach was an ideal site. Initially the thought was to use the old CNR rail bed. However, the local Park Ranger, Stewart Eady, expressed concern that a bridge would have to be built at the south end of Lake of Two Rivers and that the rock cuts on the old railway tracks were too narrow to allow two cars to pass. Based on experience gained during his patrols of the area, he suggested that there was a sandy hill stretching all the way from Highway 60 to Rock Lake that would involve less distance and expense than using the old rail track line for the access road. The DLF took him up on his offer to blaze a trail to Rock Lake and a bulldozer did the rest.[79] This made Rock Lake access easy. Soon after, Rock Lake Campground No. 1 was built, and in the early 1960s, Rock Lake Campground No. 2 was added. Today the leasehold community numbers around 35 families and is incredibly strong and vibrant. They are located on the western shore of Rock Lake, along the Madawaska River and the southern part of Whitefish Lake, with a few scattered elsewhere on the lakes.

Lake Opeongo

Though not generally open for leases, there was at one time one lease on Lake Opeongo. John R. Bates was a Packard auto dealer from Johnstown, Pennsylvania, who had been coming to the park on fishing expeditions since the early 1920s. In 1930, he took out a lease on an island in the South Arm of Lake Opeongo. Soon after, the DLF decided not to allow any more leases in the area. Bates was well spoken of and considered a good straight, honest, and reliable businessman. In the eyes of the DLF, he was a first-class tenant of Algonquin Park. He had a 24-foot motorboat with an 80-horsepower Packard engine, which he loaned on several occasions to the local Park Rangers.[80] In 1968, Bates fell seriously ill and he died in 1970. Soon after

---

78. *The Raven*, June 1966 Volume 7 #2 (R.R). It wasn't until 1948 that it was paved.
79. Eady leasehold correspondence, 1947, Algonquin Park Museum Archives.
80. Bates lease records, 1930.

an inquiry was received from his wife, asking about the property on Lake Opeongo. To everyone's surprise, this Mrs. Bates was not the same Mrs. Bates who had spent many summers on Opeongo with John Bates. Apparently Bates had been leading a double life for decades. The real Mrs. Bates sold the lease back to the Crown and his island home was demolished. The island continues to bear his name. The site gained notoriety in 1988 when a marauding bear killed two campers who were camping on the site, one of only two fatal bear incidents in the Park's history.

Galeairy Lake

Just a short portage from Rock Lake is Galeairy Lake, a popular fishing and picnicking destination for the Rock Lake community. In the early years it was known as Long Lake and was one of those lakes that spanned the boundary of Algonquin Park, with the town of Whitney at the far west end. Squaw Point, located diagonally opposite Loon Island in the channel heading towards the Narrows, contains the only remaining leased parcel on the lake, a sharp contrast to the many parcels leased on Rock Lake. According to son Robert Miller:

> *"The Algonquin Park portion of Galeairy Lake has never known extensive active leases. My father, Rev. Roy Miller, a Presbyterian pastor from Pennsylvania, was first made aware of Algonquin Park by two fellow Presbyterian pastors, Rev. E. C. Good and Rev. W. Byers. Both with their respective wives were lovers of the outdoors and had camped in the area since 1928 and taken a lease with high school teacher Jim Knoh and Dr. John Walsh in 1933. With age, tenting became more difficult, so in 1946 my father obtained a lease and had built a simple three room cottage that we named Squaw Point. According to some local old timers at the time, it was a point where nomadic Algonquin Indians would leave their squaws before going to a trading post located across the lake in Francois Bay (now Purcell Cove)."*

Later a children's camp was established in 1950 in Forest Bay at the foot of the portage to Prottler Lake. Run by two returning Canadian servicemen from Toronto, Robert Telford and James Alexander McKenchnie, it only survived a couple of years and was forced to close when one of their campers allegedly came down with polio.[81] The DLF acquired the property in 1954, but the buildings weren't removed until 1966. Contrary to regulations, Welsh built a number of cottages on a single lease using components from buildings found at an abandoned logging camp in what is now Purcell Cove. Their lease was one of the first to expire and was acquired by the Crown in the mid 1970s. According to Robert Miller:

> *"Byers and Goods dismantled the buildings and floated them across the lake, log by log, where they were reassembled and used until after WWII at which time they were replaced with cottages built with conventional lumber. We would frequently get together with them on Sundays to share a potluck dinner, which largely featured bass and trout. My mother's specialty was baked lake trout with bread stuffing, which was delicious. These frequent Sunday 'pot luck' meals and the accompanying fellowship were enjoyed by all."*

---

81. Recollections from Robert Miller, 2003.

The North

Every July, the Algonquin Park Residents Association (APRA) holds its annual meeting at the Cache Lake Recreation Hall. Built in 1933 as a storage facility, its solid pine logs run vertically not horizontally, which makes the building seem much taller than it really is. According to the locals, the stones used for the huge fireplace were hauled in from Kenneth Lake three miles away. However, by whom and how long it took is unknown. The meeting attracts leaseholders from all lakes, with an important part of the meeting being a visit by the current Park Superintendent, who brings the members up to date on current activity in the Park. During the past few years, joining the meeting have been several of the leaseholders who reside in the far northeast corner of the park. Like so many other corners of Algonquin Park it was logging and railways that opened the area up to summer settlement. As recalled by Lyall G. Ireland, a Manitou Lake resident and one of the area's first visitors:

> *"All the timber in the area, comprising, in general, the watershed of the Amable du Fond, was under license to J. R. Booth, dating from the 1870s or early 1880s. The first and only cutting had been done by Booth, who took only the pine, mostly square timber. This entire cut was driven down the Amable du Fond to the Mattawa, then into the Ottawa River to Ottawa, and some of it into the St. Lawrence to Quebec, where much of it was loaded onto sailing ships for transportation to England for shipbuilding. Dams and log chutes had been constructed at the outlets of Long Lake and North Tea Lake and above the head of Kioshkokwi, and dams at the outlets of Manitou and Kioshkokwi, besides minor improvements on tributary waters. All of these were still in existence and in a fairly good condition when I first saw them, particularly the dams, which had been partly maintained by Booth against the day when the second harvest of pine and other floatable timber would be ready. The coming of the railroad ended the plan for driving the river again, and all the river improvements, except the Kioshkokwi dam, were allowed to rot away and disappear, not only the major ones but the minor ones on tributary waters as well. Booth did some cutting for a few seasons after the coming of the railroad, and, I believe, made one or two small drives down the river, but when Staniforth [Lumber Company] took over the limit all that ended, and now nothing of the river improvements are left. The disappearance of the dams and the consequent complete absence of control of lake levels is, in my opinion, one of the reasons for the regrettable, but undeniable, deterioration of the fishing."*[82]

In the north, the obtaining of leases was a bit different than in the south perhaps due to the greater presence and influence of the lumber companies. Lyall G. Ireland's experience in the early 1920s may well have been representative of the way leases were obtained in the north at that time:

> *"I had the good fortune to meet Archie McAdam, J. R. Booth's Superintendent [Walking Boss], when he had a gang repairing the Kioshkokwi Dam. Archie had one of his teams of horses take all of our camp equipment up to Manitou [where we were going to fish for a week]. Archie developed into a wonderful friend, and one night during the progress of a rousing good party at Peter's, I said longingly that I wished we could build a camp at Manitou, Archie replied, 'Well, why don't you?' This quite set me back, as I said that I had been*

[82] Excerpted from a 1959 letter from Lyall G. Ireland to his nephew, Bert Gillespie, describing the history of his lease on Manitou Lake called Camp Wabinash (meaning "High on the Hill").

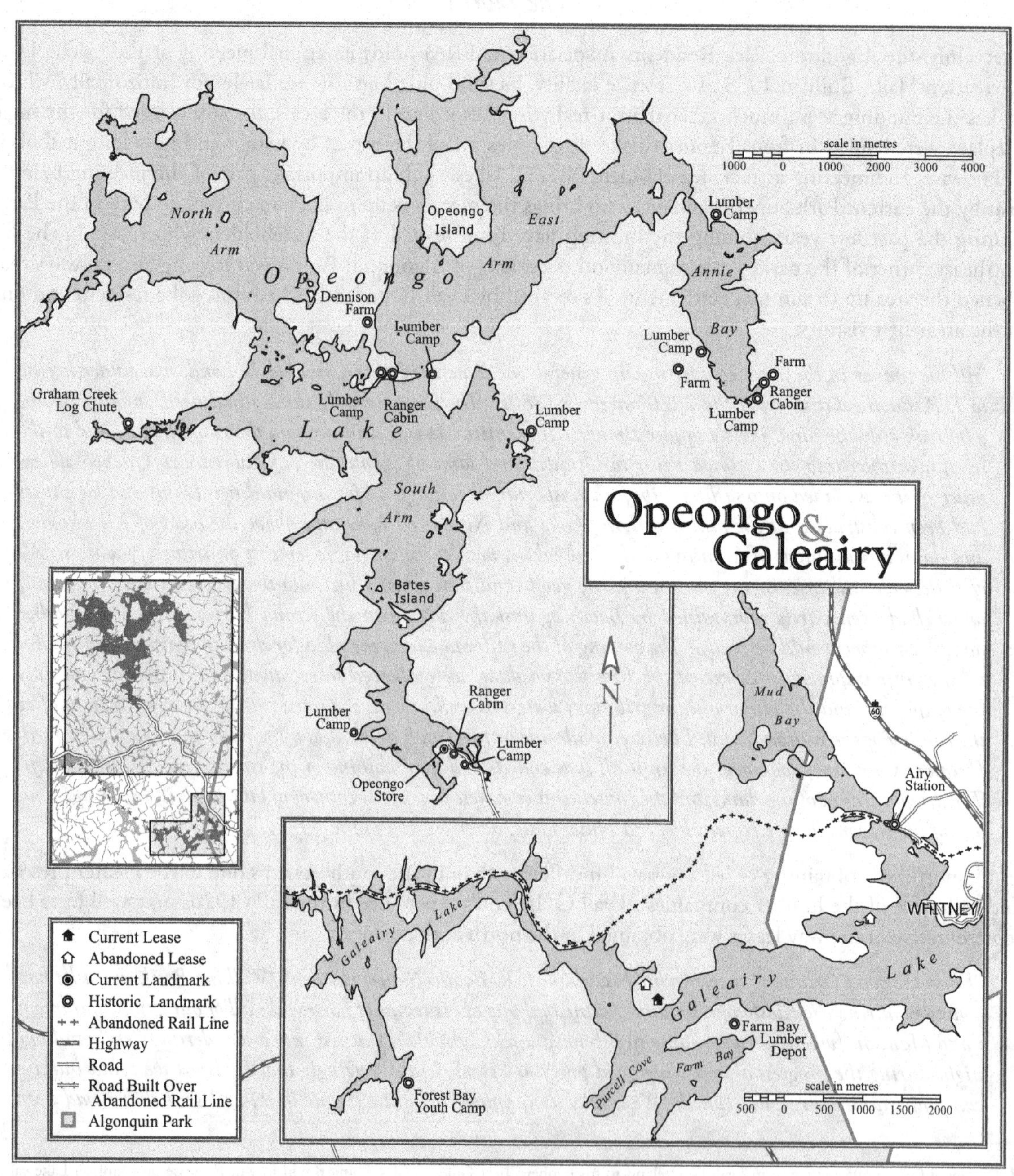

Opeongo & Galeairy
scale in metres
1000 0 1000 2000 3000 4000
North Arm
Opeongo Lake
Opeongo Island
East Arm
Annie Bay
South Arm
Lumber Camp
Dennison Farm
Ranger Cabin
Farm
Graham Creek Log Chute
Bates Island
Opeongo Store
Mud Bay
Airy Station
WHITNEY
Galeairy Lake
Purcell Cove
Farm Bay
Farm Bay Lumber Depot
Forest Bay Youth Camp
scale in metres
500 0 500 1000 1500 2000
N
Current Lease
Abandoned Lease
Current Landmark
Historic Landmark
Abandoned Rail Line
Highway
Road
Road Built Over Abandoned Rail Line
Algonquin Park

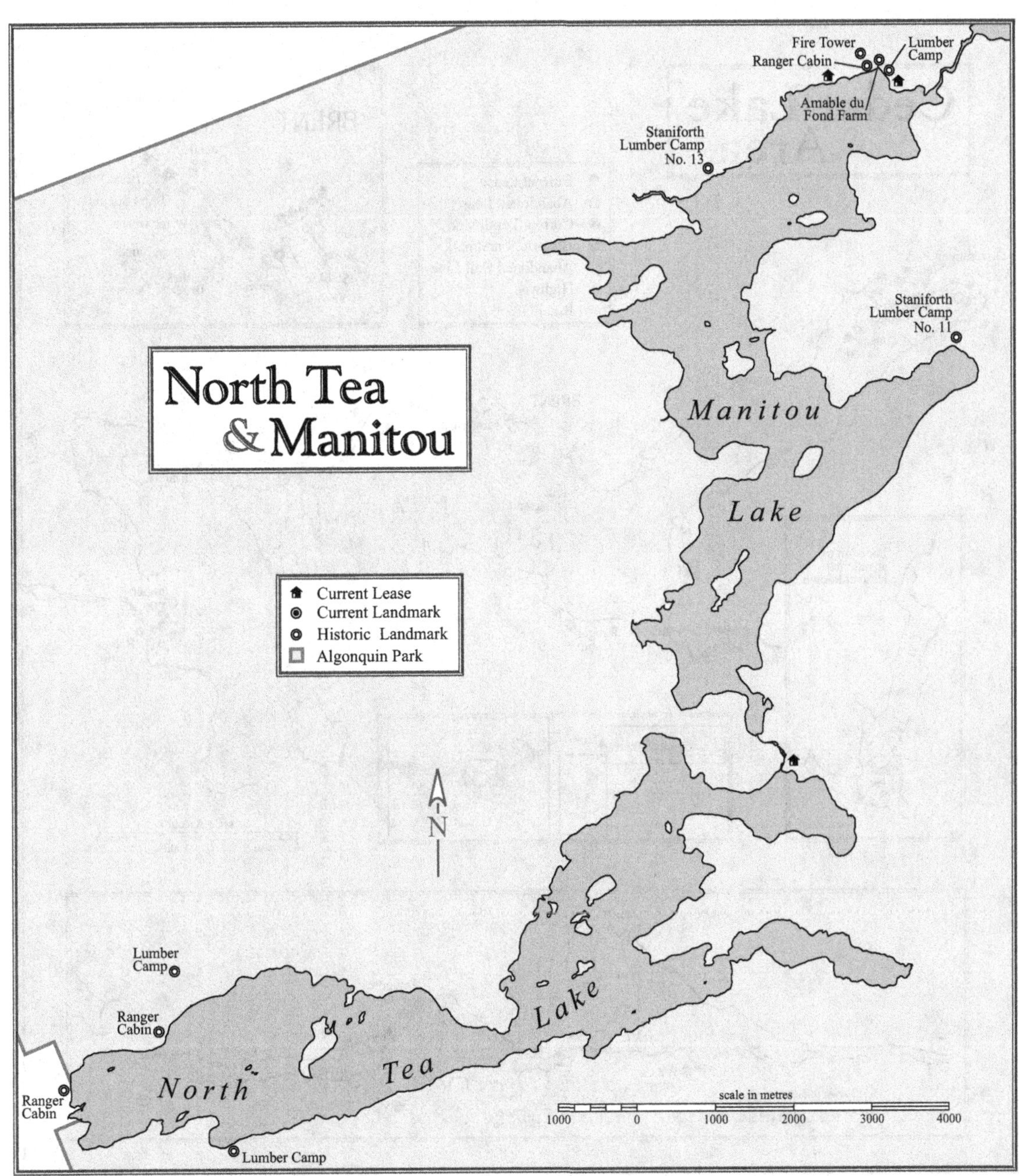
North Tea
& Manitou
Current Lease
Current Landmark
Historic Landmark
Algonquin Park
Fire Tower
Ranger Cabin
Lumber Camp
Amable du Fond Farm
Staniforth Lumber Camp No. 13
Staniforth Lumber Camp No. 11
Manitou
Lake
N
Lumber Camp
Ranger Cabin
Ranger Cabin
North
Tea
Lake
Lumber Camp
scale in metres
1000
0
1000
2000
3000
4000

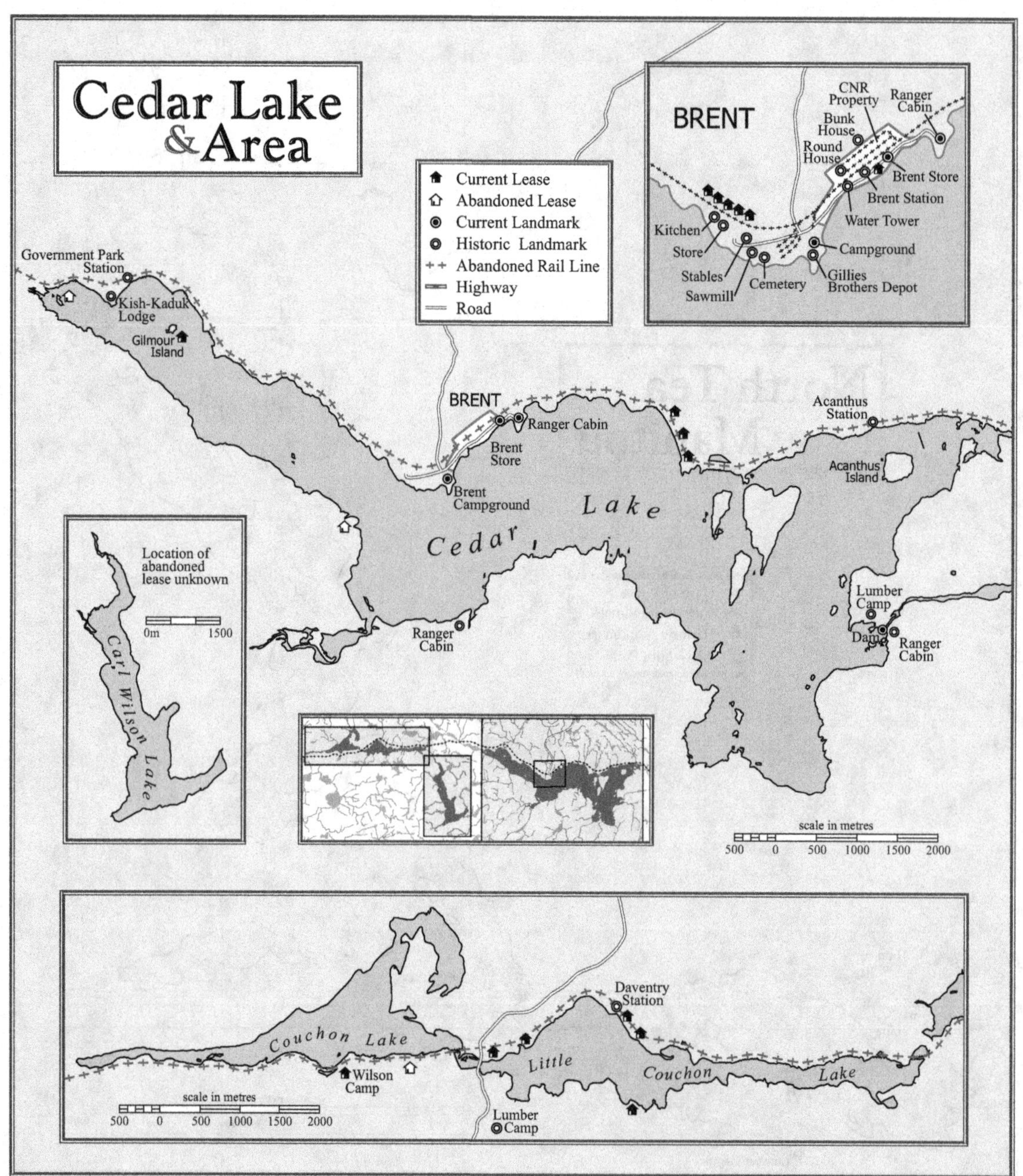

Cedar Lake &Area
Current Lease
Abandoned Lease
Current Landmark
Historic Landmark
Abandoned Rail Line
Highway
Road
BRENT
CNR Property
Ranger Cabin
Bunk House
Round House
Brent Store
Brent Station
Water Tower
Kitchen
Store
Campground
Stables
Sawmill
Cemetery
Gillies Brothers Depot
Government Park Station
Kish-Kaduk Lodge
Gilmour Island
BRENT
Ranger Cabin
Brent Store
Brent Campground
Acanthus Station
Acanthus Island
Cedar Lake
Location of abandoned lease unknown
0m 1500
Carl Wilson Lake
Ranger Cabin
Lumber Camp
Dam
Ranger Cabin
scale in metres
500 0 500 1000 1500 2000
Daventry Station
Couchon Lake
Wilson Camp
Little Couchon Lake
scale in metres
500 0 500 1000 1500 2000
Lumber Camp

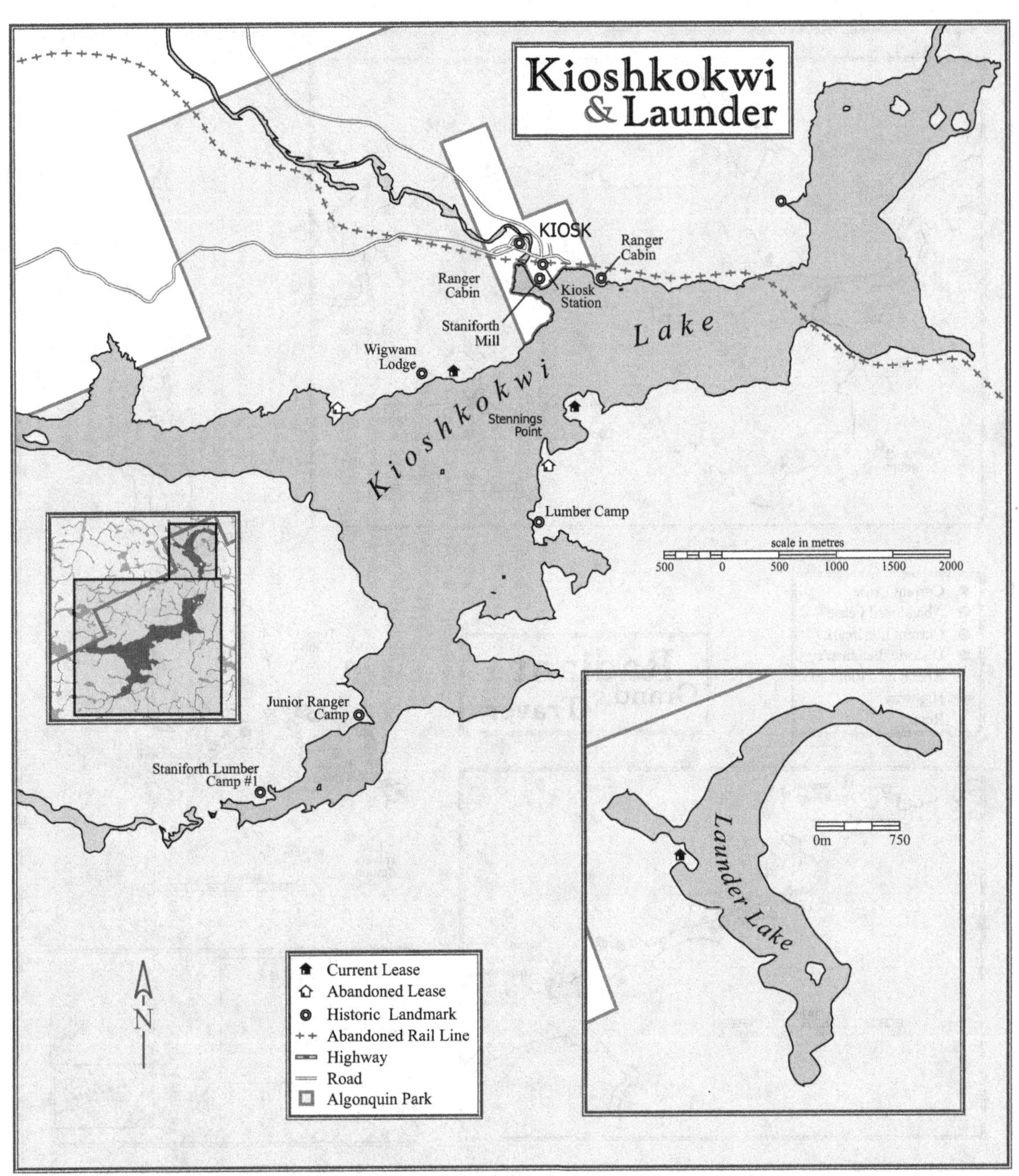
Kioshkokwi
& Launder
KIOSK
Ranger Cabin
Ranger Cabin
Kiosk Station
Staniforth Mill
Wigwam Lodge
Kioshkokwi Lake
Stennings Point
Lumber Camp
scale in metres
500 0 500 1000 1500 2000
Junior Ranger Camp
Staniforth Lumber Camp #1
Launder Lake
0m 750
N
Current Lease
Abandoned Lease
Historic Landmark
Abandoned Rail Line
Highway
Road
Algonquin Park

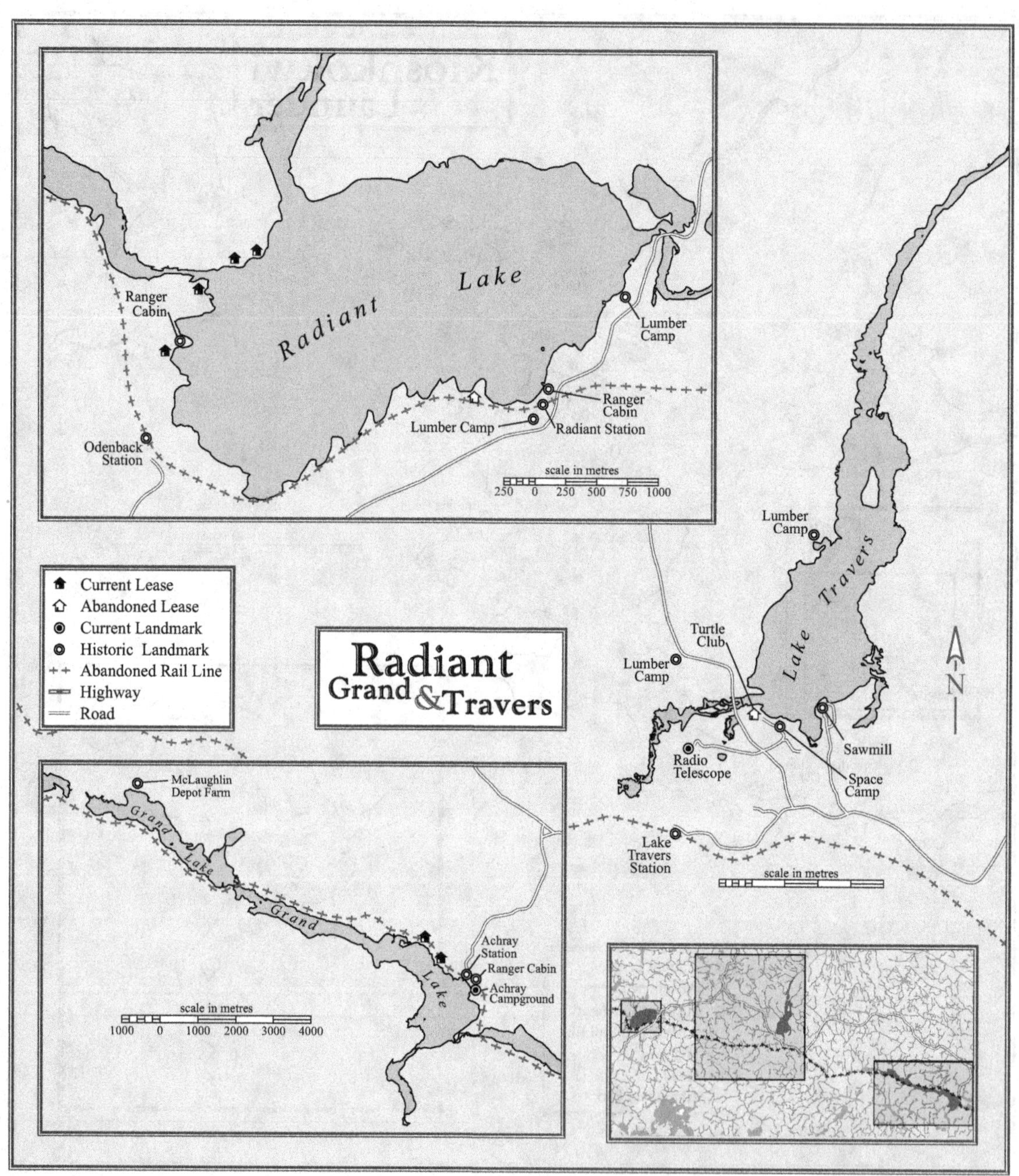

Radiant Lake
Ranger Cabin
Lumber Camp
Ranger Cabin
Lumber Camp
Radiant Station
Odenback Station
scale in metres
250 0 250 500 750 1000
Current Lease
Abandoned Lease
Current Landmark
Historic Landmark
Abandoned Rail Line
Highway
Road
Radiant
Grand & Travers
Lumber Camp
Lake Travers
Turtle Club
Lumber Camp
Sawmill
Radio Telescope
Space Camp
Lake Travers Station
scale in metres
N
McLaughlin Depot Farm
Grand Lake
Grand Lake
Achray Station
Ranger Cabin
Achray Campground
scale in metres
1000 0 1000 2000 3000 4000

given to understand that his company was opposed to the construction of any camps on its limits because of the danger of careless use of fire. He said that that was true in general, but that any rule could be suspended when justifiable, and that, in his opinion, this was one of those cases. He said that John Black, the Booth Company's General Manager at Ottawa, knew all about us and that he felt sure that on his [Archie's] recommendation Mr. Black would approve our building a camp. He said, furthermore, that he would go into Manitou with us and help us select a site that would be mutually satisfactory.

"Sometime after Archie returned to Ottawa, I received from Mr. Black one of the nicest letters I have ever received, saying that his company was entirely agreeable to our building at Manitou, that he would so signify to the DLF, that we were free to cut whatever timber was necessary, and that they would haul in whatever we needed in the way of lumber, stove, equipment etc. All of which illustrates the truth that almost all good things we receive in life we owe to our friends. I abhor the practice of cultivating friends for the purpose of using them, but it is true that the development of a real, unselfish friendship sometimes yields unexpected and unsought dividends. In due course, I made application to the Ontario DLF for a lease. With the endorsement of Mr. Black, the application received prompt and favourable action. I made a plan and bill of material, located a man in Bancroft who hired a couple of men, purchased and shipped material to Kiosk and made the safari in to Manitou. The job was finished and [the cabin] ready for use in the summer of 1922."[83]

A couple of years later, a second lease was granted on Manitou to Roy and Mira Gale. They had met Lyall Ireland on Kioshkokwi Lake a few years previously and become close friends. After they saw Ireland and his colleagues obtain their lease, they decided to apply as well, were successful, and built a cabin on their site soon after in the mid-1920s. Unfortunately, Roy was a victim of hay fever and asthma, and after his death, a number of years later, Mira sold the camp to a family whose children still own the lease.

Soon after Ireland got his lease, in 1923, Dr. Robert Pincock from St. Catharines, Ontario, took out a lease for a one-acre parcel on the north east side of nearby North Tea Lake. At the time, the only other resident was a ranger cabin nearby at the far west end of the lake. How the family ever got there is unknown, and in 1928, Dr. Pincock died suddenly, or as his wife, Jenny, said, "slipped away into the great beyond."[84] Jennie continued to visit periodically until 1941, when she sold it to a consulting engineer who wanted a hideaway where he could write a book. He would fly up a few times a year and would use it as a base to go hunting outside of the Park, but disappeared from the scene in the mid-1960s.

On Kioshkokwi Lake, the first leasehold was taken out by P. T. Hill in 1925. To the local Park Ranger, Hill was known as a "four flusher," or one whose 'mind was of the fluctuating variety, unsettled and in doubt of what he really wanted; one who would likely never have enough money to carry out his projects and was always on the look out for lambs with the necessary funds."[85] He had originally applied for a five-acre lease to establish on Manitou Lake, on the site known as Indian Farm, a "School for Campers." This was to be a camp for adults

83. Letter from Lyall G. Ireland to Bert Gillespie, 1959.
84. Pincock lease correspondence, 1928, Algonquin Park Museum Archives.
85. Hancock Lease correspondence, 1925, Algonquin Park Museum Archives.

where "people will be taught what to do and how to do it in the woods."[86] Hill had spent the previous 20 years camping and guiding in the Park and its vicinity. He initially had expressed interest in Sand Lake. Then he got interested in establishing a hunting lodge on the Bonnechère River. In 1919, he decided on a small lot where Camp Tamakwa is now, but due to financial circumstances dropped all of those ideas. Park Superintendent George Bartlett discouraged the Manitou Lake idea for a number of reasons, including:[87]

1) Difficulty in exercising supervision over camps in distant and isolated parts of the Park
2) The area contains some of the best hardwood bush, but the fire tower doesn't provide adequate fire protection
3) Manitou Lake hasn't been surveyed, nor has it been opened up for camps such as Mr. Hill proposed
4) Lack of usable buildings on the site except for a barn that is owned by Booth Company

Bartlett went on to suggest that a five-acre site near Kiosk site would be more suitable for him. Eventually, in 1926, it was agreed that he could lease the site near Kiosk and build a camp that he would call "The Wigwam." In its first few seasons Hill attracted a number of guests, but he died in 1929, at Kiosk, of a heart attack. In 1936, the lease was transferred to another family who had been leasing on the lake since the early 1930s. Today, their extended family occupies the three remaining leases on the lake.

Where the Amable du Fond River meets the lake, the J. R. Booth Lumber company had erected a barn and three buildings that were by 1936 mostly abandoned. According to a history of the area written by railway historians Doug and Paul Mackey, a lumberman named Sydney Staniforth came up with the idea in 1936 of trading a 100-square-mile limit of hardwood, pine, spruce, balsam, and poplar owned by his company, Fassett Lumber Company outside of the Park for the hardwood on J. R. Booth's limits in the Park.[88] Born in 1882, Staniforth had started in 1908 as an accountant for the Haskell Lumber Company of Pennsylvania, which had expanded into Canada in 1905. In 1913, he took over management of The Fassett Lumber Company, which had a base of operations near Fossmill, Ontario, south of North Bay. In 1934, a fire destroyed the Fossmill operation, so the principals decided to liquidate and reconstitute a new company, based in Kiosk, called the Staniforth Lumber Company. Concerned about the formation of a town within the Park boundaries, the DLF insisted that the agreement include a clause that no worker's family could be brought in to the Kiosk camp. Within months, a 70-member crew (mostly from Fossmill) was brought in and a sawmill was built at Kiosk. The men would stay in a bunkhouse and would go home to Fossmill on weekends. Their wages were $1.75 per day, six days a week, minus $.75 a week for room and board. Every week they would leave for Fossmill on the 4 a.m. Sunday train and would return on the 1 a.m. Monday train. Some didn't want to wait for the train, and would walk the 14 miles to Fossmill after the close of work on Saturday night.[89]

During the winter of 1937, the DLF allowed Staniforth to build a road at the head of Kioshkokwi Lake, below the falls, to haul logs across. The water apparently didn't freeze at that point, so there was no way of getting

---

86. Hancock Lease correspondence, 1919, Algonquin Park Museum Archives.
87. Ibid.
88. Doug Mackey, *The Fossmill Story: Life in a Railway Lumbering Village on the Edge of Algonquin Park,* pg. 175.
89. Ibid, pg. 195.

logs across unless the company put in a bridge. However, by the summer of 1937, the requirement that no families of workers be brought in seemed to have been forgotten, as Staniforth requested that the Department of Highways build a road into Kiosk. He wanted to build a town site near the mill. There was extensive correspondence as the Park sorted out whether or not Staniforth held any patent as opposed to timber rights (i.e., ownership) to land in the Kiosk area. Eventually "patents" dated 1888, which covered 144 acres including both the mill site and the potential town site, were found and a road was built into the area.

In 1940, the Staniforth Lumber Company established two lumber camps on Manitou Lake. By 1950, there was in Kiosk a planing mill, drying kilns, a veneer operation that was producing 10 million to 12 million board feet of lumber a year, a one-room schoolhouse that taught over 70 students, and a recreation facility. The town supported 186 permanent residents in houses and 60 workers who stayed in a local bunkhouse. Staniforth also built two cottages that he would use when he visited the area, one in 1944 and a second in 1951.

In December 1971, the Staniforth sons sold the company to Universal Oil Products and it became a wholly owned subsidiary, called Goodman-Staniforth.[90] Unfortunately, in 1973, the mill caught fire and burned to the ground. Ten acres of buildings and the lumberyards disappeared in just 90 minutes. Though the company wanted to re-establish a modern electric sawmill, Park Officials would not allow the firm to rebuild within the Park. With no local employment, over the next 15 years the community faded away. Residents lived in a state of uncertainty for a number of years until agreements were signed in the late 1970s that granted them 19-year Licenses of Occupation. Those wishing to leave could sell their homes to MNR. This occurred over the next few years, and by 1982 most of the town's occupants were gone.

On Cedar Lake, the first leasehold in the area was granted to Edwin Thomas, who applied for a two-acre parcel at the north end of Cedar Lake in early 1927. He wanted to start a lumber supply camp and stopping place for tourists that he named Kish Kaduk Lodge.[91] After some correspondence to obtain the correct survey language and avoid a local CNR right of way, a lease was issued later that year. Thomas, his wife, and his sister Minnie were originally from Manchester England, where daughter Rose was born in 1907. They came to Canada and settled in Kearney just before WWI. Thomas got a job with the Grand Trunk Railway and met Frank Wilkinson, whom his sister eventually married. Both families became "railroaders" and in 1914 lived in the double railway section house near the Highland Inn where the Wilkinsons' son Jack was born in 1912. The Thomases lived on one side and the Wilkinsons on the other. In 1914, Edwin became a section foreman and the family moved to Canoe Lake. As Rose Thomas recalled in a 1976 interview with Ron Pittaway:

> *"Everyone was so poor that even the mice would run across the floor with tears in their eyes. We lived in the Canoe Lake station house. It had living quarters upstairs. We had to carry everything upstairs: wood, water, coal, and the stairs were crooked. You went up one way and they turned to go up the rest of the way. One year we cut a hole in the floor to get the piano up into the living room. [The layout included] four bedrooms, a big living room and a big kitchen out back. The [railroad] office was downstairs with a big waiting room with slat seats that went all around the three walls. In those days, Tom Thomson used to put his paintings*

---

90. Doug Mackey, *The Fossmill Story: Life in a Railway Lumbering Village on the Edge of Algonquin Park.*

91. For more details about Kish Kaduk Lodge see Chapter VI.

around the room and dry them while he was waiting for the train."

During the war years, Edwin Thomas worked 10 hours a day, earning $1.39 per hour running two sections because the CNR was short staffed. He even learned how to change a rail by himself, which weighed on the order of 72 pounds a yard. Jack Wilkinson quit grade school at the age of 13, and joined one of the local winter logging camps. His job for $1.50 a day was to get out at 3 a.m. and feed the horses and look after them until 7 p.m. He could remember it being too frigid for sleigh-riding, and that icicles would hang from the horses' noses. He'd tie the lines up on the rack of the sleigh and around the logging chain, jump off and run behind so as to keep his circulation going.[92]

Over the next decade, a number of other leases were taken out on Cedar Lake; only a few of them remain today, most in and around the town of Brent. Through most of its existence, Brent was a CNR town and housed one of the company's major servicing facilities for steam locomotives and car equipment. In fact, as late as 1956, a steam engine maintenance staff was still based there, until the conversion to diesel electric locomotives, and improvements to train cars diminished the need for the facilities. For those whose jobs were on the Ottawa to North Bay route, it was a handy layover spot. Workers' families would come in by train at the end of the school year and spend most of the summer at Brent, creating quite a community. Two of the first leases in the area were issued in 1936 and 1938 to James Sereney and George Stewart, both of whom were CNR trainmen. They built cabins out of material salvaged from buildings abandoned by the local lumber company.

In its heyday, Brent was a pretty active place. It had a one-room schoolhouse where 42 children attended school during the day and where on Sunday church services were held. The teachers were always young people who'd stay a year or two. The church priest would come in from Pembroke and the Anglican minister from Mattawa. Residents would take the train to North Bay to do grocery shopping, although there was also a little store at Alderdale. Residents would send the storekeeper an order one week, and he would send the goods off on the next freight train. Residents would then send back the money owed on the following train.[93]

There was a general store that had been owned and operated for a long time by Gerry McGaughey. According to Smoke Lake resident George Garland, who used to canoe trip frequently into the area, the original proprietor was a fellow named Sandy Behan. According to a few local sources, McGaughey's family had owned a bakery in Pembroke, and he had been a bush clerk for the Gilles Lumber Company. His wife had chronic asthma so they had moved to Brent thinking that the clear Cedar Lake air would be good for her. He was a character who claimed that he had never been out of Brent more than three or four times, since he'd first moved there. According to Jake Pigeon, who now manages the former Brent facilities for Algonquin Outfitters, Gerry was a very tight-fisted and dour man. He would sit at the back of the store and scowl at people and give the odd grunt, while his daughter worked at the counter. It seems that canoe trips from the children's camps weren't very welcome at Brent in those days. One story recounted to Smoke Lake resident Don Standfield involved a canoe trip from Northway Lodge. Prior to the leaving on the trip, Pigeon told the girls that they couldn't be taken to dinner in Brent unless they wore their dresses. Not wanting to miss out on the fun, the girl campers

---

92. Thomas/Wilkinson interview by Roderick MacKay, 1976, Algonquin Park Museum Archives.

93. Interview with a Mrs. Chilson, a 1930s Cedar Lake resident, by Ron Pittaway in 1976, Algonquin Park Museum Archives.

brought their dresses in their packsacks:

> *"When we reached Cedar Lake, we camped across the lake and told them that Brent was over the hill beyond the lights that they could see in the distance. They hung their good clothes in the trees overnight to get all the creases out and then in the morning they all got fixed up in their dresses and clean blouses. We paddled across Cedar and then sent them into the store to ask Gerry when the next bus was going to Brent. He started yelling, and told them that they were in Brent already. Well, the front screen door opened and all of the girls came out screaming, with Gerry running behind. Of course we guides were outside, laughing our heads off. Luckily it didn't take Gerry long to see the humour of the whole thing and he was very nice to us and all the girls from then on."*[94]

Also in Brent in the 1930s, supporting both the local lumber operations and the train crews was George's Restaurant, owned by George Matheo Giacomel. His name must have been too hard for many to understand as most written records or oral conversations called him George Mathew. Either way, George was an Italian chap from North Bay who had set up his restaurant at the end of WWI. According to Smoke Lake resident George Garland, Mathew would provide meals for 24 cents each and loved to talk:

> *"He'd be working at the wood stove in the kitchen, bring dishes out to the table, while talking incessantly without stopping. You couldn't understand a word of what he was saying."*[95]

Once the CNR facilities shut down, most of the houses, which had been provided to employees at free or minimal rent, were torn down, though some were sold by the CNR to people who kept them as cottages. Today there are 10 leases on Crown land and a number of others that sit on patented land owned by the CNR.

Only a few leases still exist in the northeast corner of the Park. On Little Couchon Lake, one lease was issued in 1932 to a Dr. W. J. Stevenson, a longtime fisherman in the area and apparently a friend of Herbert Lennox and Clifford Chase, who were members of Parliament at the time. Across the lake, near Daventry Station, were several other leases, one of which is today owned by two sisters whose grandfather had obtained the lease in 1947. Getting to their lease was not an easy proposition:

> *"In the 1940s and 1950s my father would go fishing in May and then again in late July/August and stay till late September. Friends that came to visit us always came in by train from North Bay. The train would pass by between 2 a.m. and 3 a.m. about 100 yards from our cabin. My father would put out a red flag near the tracks when he ran out of scotch. The train would stop and the CNR guys would come out and ask what he wanted. In return my father would provide the occasional fish and beer to the train workers. They'd go to Ruby's store to get extra things and kept an ongoing list of what was at the cottage and what was needed. All of our furniture was bought through Eaton's catalogue. Later after regular train service stopped in 1964 it would take a whole day to get in and another whole day to get out. From the main highway we would drive 25 miles on dirt road. We would pick up the keys to the gate that blocked the road from a guardhouse. Near*

---

94. Interview with Jake Pigeon by Don Standfield, 1991, Algonquin Park Museum Archives.
95. Recollections from George Garland, 2003.

the railway trestle at Daventry Station by the lake we would park and then take our little boat to the camp. Then as today we had no electricity, no running water and no TV."[96]

For nearby Radiant Lake, records are even more obscure, but indicate that there are four remaining leases on the lake. At one time Radiant Lake was a stop on the CNR rail line. According to John Robins, a University of Toronto English professor, who loved to fish in Algonquin Park and visited the area in the 1940s:

"The inhabitants of the town of Radiant consisted of a Park Ranger, a Fire Ranger, five section men, two wives, one sister-in-law and three children. In addition were a dozen or so log buildings belonging to a lumber company and the Park Ranger shelter hut."[97]

Due to the fact that so few settled there, those who leased in the north had much more exposure than those in the south to the Park Rangers. Lyall G. Ireland's recollections of those that he met during his early decades in the Park provide some very interesting insights into the kind of people who took on what was at times a difficult life in the Park. As he shared with his nephew in 1959:

"When I first visited Manitou, and for several years afterward, the Park Ranger was Jim Sawyer. Jim was one of the original group of Park Rangers, most of whom had been trappers and hunters in the area included in the Park before its dedication. Preservation of wildlife was one of the principal objectives of the Ontario Government, and it was felt that this objective would be better served by having these men as employees, presumably working in the interest of conservation, than on the outside, probably working against it. As you doubtless know, the abundance of fur-bearing animals, particularly beaver, in the Park is a constant temptation to carry on illegal trapping, and every year the Park Rangers catch some of the people involved in it; I am sure they don't get all of them. Jim was of the old school of woodsmen, a big and very powerful man. We met him one day coming up the long portage carrying a full pack of provisions surmounted by a bag of potatoes, over his canoe. He was highly skilled in every branch of woodcraft, could make anything or do anything in the woods. The only tools he needed were an axe, a hatchet (he always called it a 'tommyhawk'), an auger, an awl, a drawknife and a jackknife. Jim was skillful at bark canoe building. For his own use he made 12-foot, one-man canoes, and had a fleet of them parked at convenient places throughout his beat. He made a 15-foot canoe for [fellow leasee] Bert Hawke, which Bert took to Brantford, where he used it on the Grand River. He also made mine, and I watched him build it in his 'shipyard' under the old elm tree by the beach. This was I think in 1922, perhaps 1923. Jim was a wonderful friend; he went on many trips with us, including those to Tea Lake, Lost Dog Lake, Brown's Lake and Long Lake, on some of which your mother went. To travel with Jim was to receive a liberal education in everything concerning the Park. I have even slipped up in a canoe with him to a beaver house, and heard him converse with the beavers. The name of the Camp, 'Wabinash,' Algonquin for 'High-on-the-Hill,' was given it by Jim.

The North Tea Lake Park Ranger in my early years was Tom Wattie, a dour (protective shell only) Scot, but a good friend. At that time the shelter was at the west end of Tea Lake, close to where the creek, which drains Round Lake, enters Tea Lake, and not far from the beginning of the trail to Lost Dog and Brown's Lakes. Tom

---

96. Recollections from Sara Stroup, 2004.
97. John Robins, *The Incomplete Anglers*, Second Edition, 1998, pg. 21.

had a mutual admiration association with the neighbourhood skunks. To sit on the porch with Tom while four or five skunks in full possession of all their faculties accepted potato peelings and other tidbits from his fingers was a severe test of self-control. Tom had a number of expressions, which I enjoyed; one in particular I especially liked. He never spoke of autumn as 'fall'—it was always 'the fall of the leaf.'

The Park Rangers at Kioshkokwi Lake were Peter and Telesphore Ranger. Peter was the more active of the two, Telesphore being of a more meditative or contemplative nature. He could sit and contemplate a job of work without moving, longer than almost anybody. At long intervals Telesphore would begin developing plans leading to a major project—washing. For days beforehand he would talk about it, gradually working himself up to it. Finally the great day would come; Telesphore would arise when 'dawn's left hand was in the sky,' and Peter would discreetly find something to do elsewhere. Finally, at about 10 a.m., the enterprise was complete, and there would appear on the line, for each brother one pair of socks, one suit of long-handled underwear and one flannel shirt. By then Telesphore was in a state of complete exhaustion, and required several days of complete rest to recover his customary vigor—in a manner of speaking.

I think I should like to make mention of one of the most pleasant of my recollections of my early years at Kioshkokwi—the memory of Mrs. Peter Ranger and her children. She was a sweet and gentle lady, and her children were proof of her devotion and careful training. She had few of the accessories of urban life, but nevertheless made a comfortable and happy home for her family. The Rangers had a cow for a few years. Peter was very fond of my corned beef hash, so each trip, on the last day, I would make up a big batch which we would take to Peter's along with any surplus provisions, and have a dinner party for all hands. On one of these occasions Mrs. Ranger provided the dessert, and timidly apologized for having nothing better to offer us—freshly made wild strawberry preserves, and real cow cream, thick enough to stand by itself. Hah!

Another of the old Park Rangers, of whom we were very fond, was Frank Robichoud. He was at Manitou for a while after Jim Sawyer was gone and then at Tea Lake after the new shelter was built at the Tea Lake dam. Poor Frank had a tragic end. He died alone, from a heart attack, in the shelter at Three-Mile Lake, on a cold winter night. His body was found several days later by a search party, which, I think, included Peter, frozen stiff, his ears and nose gnawed by mice. Frank was one of the real old timers, having worked for Booth in the square timber days, during which he worked all winter out of the camp at the head of Moose Bay.

Another of the old Park Rangers, whom I knew very well and liked and admired, was Mark Robinson. Mark worked as a Ranger because he loved it. He told me once that he was an unusually lucky man because he was paid for doing what he loved to do. He wrote extensively and well about the Park and its flora and fauna. Many of his articles, illustrated by his own photographs, appeared in the Globe, and, I think, in the old 'Saturday Night.' Mark served many years in the Cache Lake, Joe Lake and Canoe Lake area and later at Brent on Cedar Lake. He was Chief Park Ranger for a few years and was Acting Superintendent for one year. On several occasions he visited us and spent a day or two with us—always red-letter days for us. His knowledge of the Park and everything in it was comprehensive and accurate, and he loved to talk about it."[98]

[98] Recollections from Lyall G. Ireland, 1959.

Lakes and Locations

Highland Inn with Tent City Post Card 1908

Highland Inn Post Card c1915

Highland Inn Dining Room 1914 APMA #52

Highland Inn Aerial 1943 APMA #751

Postcard of Highland Inn View From South of Train Station c1915

Postcard of Park HQ and Superintendent's Residence on Cache Lake c1910s

Northway Front Lawn and Gardens c1940s APMA #499

Democrats Heading Off to Nominigan Camp and Minnesing Camp From the Highland Inn c1920s APMA #261

Post Card of Nominigan Dining Room c1910s APMA #5956

Northway Lease 1936 (Fomer Nominigan Camp) APMA #482

Minnesing Living Room c1950s APMA #766

Post Card of Minnesing Lodge c1920s

Cache Lake Trestle 1896 APMA #154

John Bates Sitting on the Bow of His Boat Chatting With Park Officials on Opeongo Lake 1930 APMA #321

(left) Railway Turntable at Cache Lake APMA #5608

Last Train Through Algonquin Park 1959 APMA #5886

Hepburn Island on Cache Lake 1894 APMA #77

Climbing Skymount Tower at Cache Lake (date unknown) APMA #6641

Smoke Lake Fire Tower 1923/24 APMA #87

Brent Store on Cedar Lake 1978 APMA #4978

Mail Delivery at Kiosk 1921 APMA #17

Indian Farm on Manitou Lake 1913
APMA #1850 Findlay Collection

Gerry McGaughey Inside Brent Store 1979 APMA #4982

Ranger Cabin Between Manitou and North Tea That Was Burned in the 1950s APMA #219

Beautiful Rock Lake View Greer Collction

View From MacKay Dock of Lake of Two Rivers
MacKay Collection

View of Little Couchon Lake in the North
Alger Collection

Wilson Camp on Couchon Lake
Stroup Collection

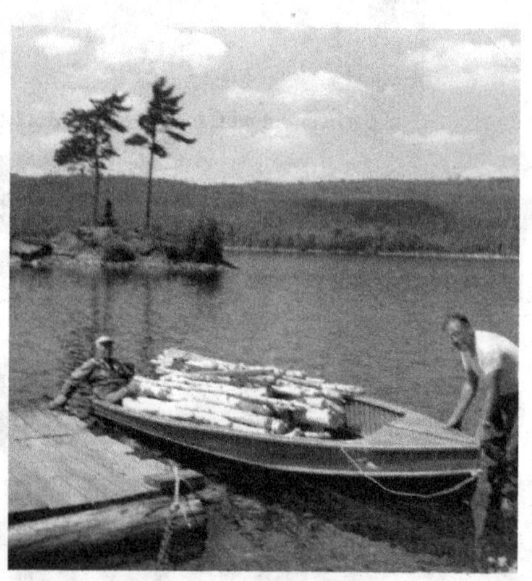

Recycling Birch From a Fallen Tree For Cottage Furniture Wilson Camp Arthur Wilson (L), Howard Wilson (R), (Couchon Lake) Stroup Collection

Chapter 2

Living in the Forest

I have been working on collecting leaseholder heritage stories for several years now. Though I now know a fair bit about how the park was settled, I have little insight into the character of these people. It's suggested that I seek out longtime resident and former Camp Tamakwa alumnus Michael Budman. I call Michael and he invites me down for drinks at his retreat on Bonita Lake. Across a small bay from Blueberry Island, one of the primo blueberry picking sites in the area, his Bonita Lake retreat used to be the homestead of Jack Coons, an electrician by trade and 20-year maintenance supervisor at the Taylor Statten Camps. In 1994, Jack decided that living in the Park year-round was getting difficult, so he and his wife Verna moved to Emsdale just north of Huntsville and Michael Budman and his wife Diane Bald took over the lease. Like many of his generation, Jack was a builder and fixer of just about anything so his lease site became a collector's heaven. Jack was likely to have at his fingertips just about any tool or piece of equipment that any one might need.

I step out onto the dock on the backside of the property and admire the winding chip-strewn trail that leads to the house. The field that was once the home of several old cars and motors of various types is now a beautiful area of natural grasses. Jack's workshop is now a lovely rec hall with an open space large enough to hold a dinner party for 20 or reception for many more. Just behind the rec hall is a beautiful fire pit and barbeque area complete with wooden chairs made out of stumps for easy outdoor entertaining. The main house has been completely restored and remodeled and is used as a base for winter camping trips by school groups organized by longtime Smoke Lake resident and outdoor ed teacher Linda Leckie and photographer Don Standfield.

Michael meets me at his rec hall and offers me a beer from the nearby fridge, which I gladly accept. Michael has an infectious way of being that draws you in and doesn't let you go. It's been over 40 years since I've spoken with him, so we start by sharing stories about our days as camper and staff at Camp Tamakwa in the 1960s. He remembers me as a 10-year-old girl with white-blond hair and blue eyes. Our major frame of reference is the fact that my father and Lou Handler, the owner and founder of the camp, were good friends. In the 1960s, my father shot the camp movies that Lou used as marketing devices to encourage folks from Detroit, his home base, to come to the camp. Lou Handler was another giant of a man. Known as "Unca Lou" to all campers, he'd been a boxer in his youth, loved kids, had a smile that would light up the sky, and warmth that knew no bounds. As children we were constant visitors for Friday night dinners at the camp. Some of my fondest memories are of driving back in our boat along Bonita Narrows in the moonlight. A movie called "Indian Summer," written by fellow camper Michael Binder, was shot at the camp in the 1990s. The actor playing "Unca Lou" does a pretty good job of capturing his character.

Born in Detroit, Michigan, Michael is now a leading Canadian businessman, a retailing creative genius and part of Canada's fashion elite. He operates in a world that I can't even imagine. The story of his adventure from his roots in Algonquin Park is fascinating. Budman and Don Green first met in 1963 at Camp Tamakwa on Tea Lake, which marked the start of their lifelong love for the Park. In 1972 after having moved to Canada, they opened a small shoe store in downtown Toronto, selling the Roots negative heel shoe. From those "roots" they expanded into leather goods and later clothes and over time built a network of retail stores across Canada. Today their "Roots Canada" chain of 150 North American stores is an integral part of Canadian culture. Their brand of high quality leather goods, apparel, footwear, bags, accessories, and Olympic team uniforms are world famous.[99] *In the process their brand has become a mainstay of Canadian culture. It seems now like no Canadian in their right mind would be caught dead without at least one or two articles of Roots clothing and their success at designing leather goods and uniforms for Canadian, American, and several other Olympic teams is legendary. To me it's a bit incongruous, given that two guys from Detroit started the ball rolling so long ago.*

But no matter how hard I try, to me Michael will always be the handsome canoeing instructor with the wild hair who taught me how to paddle a canoe in what I call the "Omer Style." This beautiful form of paddling, now accepted as a national standard, was invented by Omer Stringer. It involves changing one's centre of gravity and using the shoulder and upper arm to paddle in such a way that the canoe glides cleanly over the surface of the water and the paddle moves in a fluid circular motion. When mastered, it enables nearly perfect control over the movement of the canoe and the paddle for executing Figure 8s, inside and outside turns, parallel paddling along an edge of a dock, and the precision stroke known as the "running pry." Omer Stringer was the youngest son in a family of 16 children raised on Canoe Lake. His father Jack was an Algonquin Park Ranger. He and my mother were friends, as they both had attended teacher's college at the same time in the mid-1960s. In fact, if I recall correctly, I got my first and only starring role as the bow person in one of his early films for the Ontario Safety League's Water Safety Program. Omer would 'whimsically maneuver his craft like no other, able to perform exciting acrobatic stunts, while effectively conveying the essential message of canoe safety.'[100] *One of Omer's more famous canoeing skills was a showstopper. Without fanfare, Omer would run at full speed down a dock, leap into his canoe and without skipping a beat, start paddling away. In the middle of demonstrating paddling methods, with great ease and without stopping, he would deftly move to the front of the canoe where he would do a headstand on the seat without losing balance or tipping over. His book, The Canoeist's Manual, and his many films established him as the genuine master of Master*

[99] Excerpted from Roots Founders biographies, provided by Roots Canada.
[100] Article by Elaine Ziemba, www.carryingplacecanoeworks.on.ca/html/omer.html

Canoeists. He was posthumously awarded the 1988 Friends of Algonquin Park Directors Award.

Michael was and still is a stickler for perfection, so I would spend hours and hours doing the same stroke over and over. First on the dock, then in a canoe beside the dock and eventually from the canoeing dock out across the bay and back, regardless of the weather. In those days, and I have no doubt it is the same today, he demanded excellence in everything. At the time it was very frustrating, but when a stroke finally came together it was worth every minute. Though I was unaware of it at the time, those hours of practice created strength in the upper arms and shoulders that enabled a power stroke that years later was extremely helpful both in obtaining a Master's in Canoeing in my late teens and in solidifying my first major romance. My boyfriend of the time, whom I'd met at Taylor Statten Camps, commented in passing one day that one of the great joys of his life was watching the rippling of my arm and shoulder muscles as I paddled. Even today, I view it as one of my most precious compliments.

Michael and I settle down in his Muskoka chairs and start to talk about the impact that Algonquin Park has had on our lives and the role that leaseholders have played in its development over the last 100 years. We muse about how one has to be a certain type of person to have any sort of longevity as an Algonquin Park resident. To go to all of the trouble that it took to get here in the early days, you had to be passionate about wanting to be here. If you haven't got the passion, the hauling of groceries, equipment and supplies in by boat gets very old, very quickly. More importantly you have to be self-sufficient, and committed to generally doing things yourself. With the closest town (Huntsville) over 50 kilometers away, you can't just run over to the corner store to get something that you might have forgotten. This was especially true in the early days, when driving Highway 60 was very intimidating. You have to love the outdoors and sometimes even obsess about the environment and your willingness to go to bat for it. You also have to be comfortable working within the framework of a tough set of regulations and interpretations of regulations and accept it all with grace.

Leaseholders also have to be self-entertaining and enjoy the simple things of life like a paddle at sunset, a hike in the woods, or card games and puzzles on rainy days. Those who really wanted the comforts of the city in the forest usually ended up hating Algonquin Park. Those who want to water ski, or drive a fast boat, which did chase a few second-generation leaseholders away in the late 1970s, don't stay. Residents also have to be tolerant of the sometimes foolish behaviour of day visitors and novice wilderness adventurers. Those who decide to picnic on your dock and leave behind a mess of beer bottles, or think it might be fun to feed the bears, or go out on a lake in a thunder and lightning storm. You have to not mind picking up the trash they leave behind on hiking trails, or putting out fires that aren't extinguished correctly, or rescuing them when they accidentally dump their canoes because they have too much gear or aren't sitting in them properly.

But for those of us who have been here, watchful, for a long time, and have seen all the changes that the Park has gone through over the last 100 years, are very mindful of how critical protecting it is and the important, though small, role we play in doing so. We are an integral part of the historic fabric of the Park. I paddle off down the lake and think about Michael's comments. In many ways, I think he's right: Algonquin Park leaseholders are made of a unique sort of cloth. It's time to investigate in more detail the typical lifestyle of Algonquin Park cottagers.

Living

Omer Stringer in action
www.nashwaakpaddles.com

A skullfull inside turn
www.nashwaakpaddles.com

Michael Budman (L) and Dan Green (R), founders of Roots Canada
www.rootscanada.com

A headstand to illustrate balance
www.nashwaakpaddles.com

Lou Handler
www.camptamakwa.com

Tamakwa Shore Line 1974 APMA #2152

Profile of a Typical Algonquin Park Cottage[101]

Rory MacKay describes his cottage on Lake of Two Rivers

Most Algonquin Park cabins are fairly primitive in their plan and furnishings. This is often intentional as most leaseholders consider their cabins their hideaways. In the case of my cottage, a wooden stairway at the western end leads through a screen door and wooden door made of half-log siding into the kitchen. The kitchen in the early years was furnished primarily with a coal oil three-burner stove and lighting was by coal oil lamp. Dishes and utensils were stored in various containers of tin or wood, some of the latter having been made from orange crates turned on their ends and covered with oilcloth. A washstand stood in a corner, under a small window in the west end of the cabin. On the south wall of the kitchen was a window. One half of the two parts of the window opened sideways; the other swung on hinges at the top and was hooked to a beam above when it was open.

The kitchen was separated from the living room by a partition of quarter-inch plywood. A bright green table and chairs occupied a place beneath another window on the south wall, similarly arranged with sideways and upward swinging halves. A day bed occupied the partition wall and a wooden rocking chair sat in front of a window in the northern wall of the room. Two or three coal oil lamps lit this room at night, and a coal burning Quebec Heater stove, which was used to burn wood as its fuel, fended off the cool evenings of August. The floor was linoleum. A door in the south wall led to a small outdoor porch, or what might be called a deck today.

Off the living room to the east were two small bedrooms, added after the original construction, separated by another quarter-inch plywood partition. They were sufficient only for a bed and a nightstand. Each had a coal oil lamp and a window in the east wall. The view from one window was dominated by the trunk of an immense hemlock tree.

The aforementioned porch was used as a sitting location, unscreened. It was a shady location, being protected from the sun by the hemlocks. The two posts that led to the stairs were topped by carvings of bears, about a hand's length tall, one standing with paws raised, and the other sitting on a log with eyes covered by its paws. The porch also served as a place under which to store lumber, nails, stovepipe, and a cold storage area. This was a tin-lined wooden enclosure with a tin-lined wooden door. Ice could be placed inside a container within the "cooler" to keep perishables a bit longer than without this arrangement. There was another small "cold cellar" partly built into the hillside, just outside the kitchen door.

---

101. Recollections from Rory MacKay, Lake of Two Rivers resident, 2005.

Typical Leaseholder Cottage Lifestyle

Building a suitable cabin on a lake in Algonquin Park is not and has never been an easy task. It is a task, though, for which every resident has an extensive and often enthralling tale. In the early years of the 20th century, avid fishermen would pick sites on various lakes that they would use as yearly campsites. After a few years, they would build a small shack in which to store a canoe, life jacket, and paddles. In those days, all cooking was done outdoors over an open fire pit, with pots, pans and other cooking utensils hung on nails hammered into a board between two white pine trees that the loggers had most likely left behind. Many would eat on dapple-gray and blue tin ware with a wooden spoon and a penknife as utensils. Foodstuffs would be kept cool in a sunken pit, covered over and weighed down and latched so that the bears and raccoons couldn't get into it, or in a nearby stream. Then as much as a decade or more later, these early settlers would obtain an official lease.[102] At first a small sleeping cabin, called a bunkee, would usually be built either from scratch or from a pre-fab kit. Later a larger living space with an indoor (rather than outdoor) camp kitchen would be added as the family grew.

Today the typical Algonquin Park cottage is a 50-year-old, two- to three-room cabin painted green or brown, or unpainted with one or two out-buildings for sleeping, with neither hydro nor running water, and accessible only by boat. Most blend in to such a degree that their visual presence on lakes adjacent to the highway has no significant impact on the appearance of "wildness" of these lakes.[103]

Of course, these cabins did not go up overnight. Many settlers began as campers. For instance, when the Graf family came to Algonquin Park in 1938, they set up a high-wall 10-foot by 10-foot tent, dug a hole behind a log for an outhouse and another hole in the ground to hold a lidded copper wash boiler that they used for a refrigerator. Ice was packed around the boiler to keep it cold. They rarely saw a canoe or heard a motorboat.[104]

> *"To keep things cold, most leaseholders eventually graduated from pits dug in the side of a hill to an icebox. Initially those in the Canoe Lake and District area got ice blocks from an old log icehouse at the Portage Store. As more and more cottages were built on Smoke Lake, local caretaker Jack Hamilton built a log icehouse at his cottage, which is now the site of the Smoke Lake parking lot."*

For refrigeration, the Kase family up on Brulé Lake cut ice out of the lake every year in the winter and had three coolers. One held the soft drinks, another the beer, and a third was for vegetables, meat, and milk. For heating they had three stoves, including a kitchen range and big box stove in the living room. During the years the family lived on Brulé Lake full time, the province of Ontario would provide lessons for the children's schooling each week. Mrs. Kase would oversee the childrens' work and mail it to Toronto. The teacher would go over it, and send it back for review and correction.[105]

---

102. Collinson brief to Provincial Parks Council, 1986, Algonquin Park Museum Archives.
103. William Brice note to William Davis, 1975, Algonquin Park Museum Archives.
104. Graf correspondence, 1938, Algonquin Park Museum Archives.
105. Interview with Edmund Kase by Roderick MacKay, 1976, Algonquin Park Museum Archives.

Things were primitive then, as they still are for most leaseholders, and it was only the peace, grandeur, and beauty of the Park that made putting up with such rustic conditions not just acceptable, but desirable. Both then and often still today, water for cooking was carried in buckets or hand-pumped up to the cottage. As Rory MacKay from Lake of Two Rivers recalled:

> *"Water was provided from the lake, pumped up hill by a hand-operated cast-iron pump, painted red, through one-inch diameter galvanized pipe. At the top of the hill there was a galvanized tub with a lid, and a tap at the bottom. Clothes would be washed nearby with square washtubs and a washboard, wrung by hand and hung on a line between trees."*[106]

For most leaseholders, fireplaces provided the only heat, though some installed oil space heaters. Two great stories about these monstrous space heaters come from both Rory MacKay on Lake of Two Rivers and the Matthews clan on Canoe Lake. As Rory shared:

> *"Our large double-burner oil space heater was purchased second-hand in Pickering and brought to the Park in the trunk of my father's Pontiac car. It was unloaded at the highway and carried in through the bush over the hill behind the cottage. As the story has it, my father was entertaining the Greek consul, John and his wife Dory, their friends Marcos and his wife Greta, and a Mr. Rosetti, who was the Greek Ambassador to Canada. (I have no idea how he came to meet them). John, Marcos, and my father hauled the space heater while Mr. Rosetti supervised enthusiastically. The space heater made staying at the cottage in the winter more possible, and it is certain that through the mid- and late 1950s and into the late 1960s there were frequent visits when snow was deep on the ground, including an annual trip to the cottage immediately following Christmas Day, with arrival home in Toronto usually on New Year's Eve.*
>
> *We would arrive in the late morning and snowshoe in. The space heater would be lit, and while the cottage was warming up a space was shoveled for the car off the road. This usually took considerable time. Water was obtained by chopping a hole in the ice with an axe and pickaxe. A walk on the lake might follow, or an excursion down the road, to check on the river mouth. All this activity was by design, as it took many hours for the cottage to fully warm; while after a few hours some of the air was warm, one could still see frost on the metal table legs and the beds had a cold, damp feeling to them. My mother recalled that it was easier to look after my brother Niall and I up there in the wintertime, because there were no bears about and the lake was frozen and we couldn't fall in. It is my impression, and this may make me sound like an old-timer, that in those days the winters were colder and there was considerably more ice covering the lake than of late. One might think that we spent lots of time burrowing in snow forts or making snow angels, but my father discouraged that sort of thing. He had helped conduct research on men in winter conditions in northern Saskatchewan after the war and always impressed upon us boys the importance of staying dry when it was cold."*

The Matthews furnace project was a perfect example of what some neighbours thought was a completely insane idea. Their Canoe Lake cottage was really two log buildings placed end to end in a slight V-shape in

---

106. Recollections from Rory MacKay, 2005.

order to form a triangular-shaped bathroom in the centre. This design made it difficult to heat. As recounted by the family:

"One day in the fall, the Matthews brothers (Graham and Bill) were at lunch in downtown Toronto and noticed a group of houses being demolished nearby. Curious, they got out of the car for closer inspection and among other goodies they found a nearly new oil-fired, forced-air furnace. The foreman said, '$100 and you can have it all!' That included all the wiring, the thermostat, all the ductwork and the 200-gallon fuel tank, along with everything else that wasn't nailed down. They gave him a deposit and went back on Saturday with a trailer to load it all up. It was then stuffed into one side of one brother's double-car garage for the winter.

The next challenge was to figure out how to get all of it to the cabin site. Graham spent most of the winter building a barge out of two-by-fours and plywood. In the spring, the barge was loaded onto the trailer and various furnace parts were placed onto the barge in a relatively balanced way. Early in June, they took off for the cottage with this huge load wrapped in plastic and the trip went without incident. They backed the trailer into the water and the barge floated free and clear. With a little adjusting of the load, they started the outboard and away they went across the lake. The one-mile trip from the Portage Store went smoothly, except for some strange glances from fellow cottagers. The prize was unloaded stowed away temporarily, and they began excavating for a new room at the rear of the main cottage. The first few wheelbarrow loads went relatively easily but as they worked further into the bank, they ran into major rocks and an enormous amount of dirt, as the bank got steeper. Some of these boulders would only yield to the pressure of a small winch. Finally, they had a level area cleared and began constructing a building, which took shape relatively quickly. Before it was completely closed in, they manhandled the furnace into position using rollers and the brute strength of all the warm bodies they could find. The enclosure was finished and the stovepipe was installed.

Now the whole family had to get involved. Daughter Marnie, then 12 years old, was elected to crawl under the lowest part of the original building and dig out a trench for the ductwork, which would serve that area. This involved lying on her belly and digging with a shovel as she moved forward. What a nasty job this was, but after eating a great deal of topsoil, she completed her assignment. Meanwhile son Dave was disposing of the dirt from Marnie's excavation, while little Pete was the head 'gofer' delivering cokes and beer as required and wife Mary Lou was keeping everyone's spirits up with offerings of food. Eventually all the parts were in place and the floating dock was towed back to the Portage Store to pick up four barrels of furnace oil that had been delivered from Huntsville. Each contained 45 gallons of oil and weighed about 300 pounds. With brute strength they towed the barrels across the lake and moved them as close as possible to the fuel tank. They then pumped the 180 gallons of oil into the fuel tank with a hand pump! They completed the electrical work, hooked up the thermostat and turned it up to the desired temperature. After a momentary pause while the fuel oil got to the burner, it burst into life, which brought smiles of great satisfaction to everyone's face! The Matthew clan is glad to report that it is still functioning normally and they have never had a service call after 35 years of use!"[107]

Dead trees and driftwood, left over from the logging days and the raising of the water levels by the creation of the dams, were cleared out from the shoreline and sand beaches appeared. Occasionally signs of other

107. Recollections from Matthews Family, 2003.

inhabitants were uncovered, as the Hayhursts on Smoke Lake discovered when they decided to move one of the sleeping cabins:

> *"We were digging holes for posts to set the cabin on, but our shovels kept hitting logs as we dug. Eventually we excavated enough to see the outline of what looked like an old Indian longhouse! We also found nearby a sunken dugout canoe filled with rocks. We speculate that the site may well have been an ideal campsite for traveling bands of Indians generations ago."*[108]

Recollections of getting to the Park in those early years were many and varied. George Garland's first visit to Algonquin Park was in 1931, just as the smoke was still settling on the remains of the second Mowat Lodge that had burned down that spring. He and his parents were going up to visit his brother and took the night sleeper train from Toronto to North Bay. The sleeping car they were in was detached from the train at Scotia Junction at 6 a.m. in the morning. The family stepped out to have breakfast at the station platform hotel, which allegedly served the worst food in Canada. The sleeping car was then attached to a mixed train and rolled into Canoe Lake station at about 10 a.m. No meal service was provided on the train. The express train came in on Tuesday, Thursday, and Saturday, stayed overnight at Cache Lake and went out Monday, Wednesday, and Friday. In addition, there was a freight train Monday and Friday, so there was actually a train coming in five days a week. One of the exciting parts of the run in was the high trestle over Tonawonda Creek between Ravensworth and McCraney where the train had to proceed very slowly, at between five and 10 miles per hour.[109]

The trains bringing campers into the camps would generally consist of 24 sleeping cars that sometimes had to be taken across the trestles near Cache Lake half at a time because of the enormous load. From Canoe Lake Station, a boat named "The Street Car" would transport goods and people from the station to Taylor Statten Camps, Camp Ahmek and Camp Wapomeo. It was a long narrow boat with glass windows down both sides. Often the evening train was late, so camp staff waiting for the train would have to hang out at the train station until midnight. If there was mist on the lake, getting back down Potter's Creek and across to the camps without incident was very difficult.

Kay Graham, a Smoke Lake resident, remembers her summers in the Park on Cache Lake as a teenager:

> *"In the 1940s, we drove from Toronto to Kearney where our car was left for the summer. After a night in Kearney we caught the train to Cache Lake. The Highland Inn eventually closed but the store remained open and we could get fresh milk and bread. The rest of our supplies for two or three months (mostly canned goods and dried milk) were shipped in. My father was an avid fisherman and provided our only source of fresh protein. Occasionally visitors would bring us fresh meat and vegetables and fruit with them."*

For years, Valerie Young Argue and her first husband would take a train to Huntsville. After a night at the Empire Hotel, they would either take a cab to the Smoke Lake landing or hitch a ride with the lumber company trucks that frequently went by.[110] For the first few years the Renwick, Gray, and Harshman families

---

108. Recollections from Hayhurst Family, 2003.
109. Recollections from George Garland, 2003.
110. Recollections from Valerie Young Argue, 2003.

all shared their three sites, each using it for three weeks.

"We didn't have a car, so we always had to find someone with whom to hitch a ride to Algonquin Park. We couldn't afford two of everything [one for our house in the city and another for the cottage], so would have to bring blankets and teapot, etc. back and forth from Toronto. Initially there was no real parking lot at the landing so we would follow a path in from the highway. For years we had a canoe that we would cache in the woods. In 1940, Charlie Musclow built us a cabin but we couldn't afford glass windows and for years we were open to the elements."[111]

Gordon Willson describes his first Smoke Lake experience in the late 1940s:

"Early the next June, my mother, accompanied by my sisters, drove me to Union Station in Toronto where I was set aboard a train to join my Dad in the Park who had journeyed there some days earlier. At Scotia Junction, the plan was that I would board another train bound for Algonquin Park. I had just turned ten years of age a few weeks before. The train was composed of a steam engine, tender, baggage car and one passenger car in which I was the only passenger. The train creaked toward the Park leisurely, stopping now and then, sometimes it seemed for extended periods of time. During one particularly long stop, near sunset, at a shack beside the track, in the middle of nowhere, I walked to the head of the train to find the engineer and fireman and two others enjoying a smile and a game of cribbage. It seemed to be an enthralling game as my presence did not seem to have any effect. The train finally squeaked to a stop at Joe Lake Station sometime after midnight where Dad was waiting. Eventually we got to our canoe and paddled off into a starry black night.

Across Canoe Lake, we then threaded our way through the fallen forest of Lake Bonita and Smoke Creek and sighted down the length of Smoke Lake by the early cool light of breaking day. I do not recall the last leg of the long journey, reaching for Molly's Island where we camped for more than a week. I built a pirate ship with driftwood, fishing line and other found things, which fitted the imagination. We launched the model with fanfare and good wishes for a fine voyage. North it sailed until it disappeared from view around Ranger's Point – its birch bark sails seemed to billow strangely as it was carried away in the breeze stern first. On overcast or cool days, we fished on Dad's favourite trolling ground along the shoal running north from Nominigan toward Hangar Bay. A pan-fried freshly caught trout meal seemed to be a part of food fare most days. At Park Headquarters, Dad looked into available cottage lots. We visited the Portage Store, not yet officially open for the season. On another day we visited the Smoke Lake hanger and were shown around by the Park Superintendent. Over the days, we visited many potential cottage sites, sometimes picnicking on them when the bugs were tolerable. Toward the end of our two weeks, we canoed to the northwest arm of Smoke Lake to look at lots previously not visited. Opposite the old highway, west of the Nichols, the shoreline was heavily mined with fallen trees. Captured in this log jungle was the model pirate ship we'd launched over a week before."

---

[111] Recollections from Nancy Gray, 2004.

Getting to and from leaseholds was and still is a constant problem on some lakes. For most people, the distances from highway parking areas to cabin sites was so far and over such difficult terrain that, except for the very hearty, walking in each weekend was not a feasible proposition. To get to their cabin on Smoke Lake, the Savages blazed a short hiking trail from the Smoke Lake Landing that they would use in the spring. They would then get their canoe, paddle to the landing, load up all of their gear and return across the lake in all kinds of weather. This same process would be done in reverse in the fall after close up.

The Savage family would arrive in June with provisions for the summer, digging a huge hole four-and-a-half feet deep to put the boxes in to keep them cool. There was a fresh spring in the bay that produced a cold channel of water out into the lake, which was where the family would get fresh water. Every spring James Savage would dig down a bit and install a wooden four-sided box, which would fill up and provide 45-degree water all summer long. Brooks Transport would bring in meat once a week. Every once in awhile they'd pressure-cook three or four roasts of beef, pack the meat in jars, and place them in a hole dug in the ground to keep them cool. Using the three-burner coal oil stove, it would take over an hour to heat the stovetop oven up to 350 degrees. Mrs. Savage was constantly making jams, pies, and other goodies with the blueberries and raspberries that would be picked. One winter James and a friend came up and brought in a Quebec heater that they dragged over the ice. They then spent several days building it, but the morning they intended to leave there had been a thaw and the lake was covered with inches of water. They had to wait until dark when the lake froze over again. As Bea Lawford from Smoke Lake recalled:

> *"Every June, we would give Eaton's a big food order, which would be delivered to the Smoke Lake landing. The cookies and the oranges would be carefully given out to last the summer. Visitors would know to bring fruit, vegetables and meat when they came for a visit or holiday. 'Before we had a motorboat, we would lash two Peterborough canoes together and transport everything across the lake, in the evening or early morning when the lake was likely to be relatively flat. When there was a strong southwest wind, it is very difficult to get from Ragged Bay into the main part of the lake due to the crosswind."*

And Kay Graham echoed:

> *"For us, one of the most exciting days at Smoke Lake was the year the propane refrigerator came down the lake and was installed in a back porch to go with the two-burner propane stove that we already had in addition to a wood stove that was in the kitchen. Originally a small Quebec heater provided the heat in the living room but later a large stone fireplace was built and the Quebec heater removed to the sleeping cabin."*

In 1947, the Source Lake access road stopped at the top of the hill before the railway bed, and everything had to be carried through the bush to the end of the lagoon. Leaseholders were able to obtain land-use permits for small strips of land near the Source Lake landing, where a few erected boathouses. As Brian Maltman remembered in 2004:

> *"There were no motor boats, so our fridge came in across two canoes, and the wood stove was dropped off by the train, assembled out at the railway tracks, and carried in on poles."*

For a few years in the late 1930s, Charlie Musclow, owner of Musclow Lodge on Tea Lake, and later Everett Farley on Canoe Lake, played the role of water taxi drivers for the Canoe Lake District, as did Johnny Baulke in the Rock Lake/Whitefish Lake area and Ken Unger on Cache Lake. Some leaseholders would leave boats in hidden caches tucked away in the forest near the highway or near boat landing spots, and others asked for permission to leave boats near the Park Ranger facilities. As Raymond Wiltse of Smoke Lake wrote in 1942:

> *"We do not wish to impose unduly on the splendid cooperative spirit of the Park Rangers, but find that some assistance is necessary with conditions as they are and wonder if we could leave our boat near the Smoke Lake Hangar."*

One year, one Smoke Lake leaseholder arrived in late June and took the wrong boat from the landing, finding out later that another neighbour had borrowed his, which had looked very similar. There was even a rumour that one of the local guides from Canoe Lake would "borrow" leaseholders' boats and charge a fee to take visitors on fishing expeditions from the Smoke Lake Landing to the Ragged Lake Portage.

It was even more difficult getting to Rain Lake. By 1957, there was no train service except for an infrequent freight train. Ralph Bice asked if the DLF was going to put a road on the railway bed, but was advised that they "though the DLF was going to secure title to the old right of way, road access would be closed at the Park boundary and would not be available to leaseholders in the vicinity of Rain Lake."[112]

In 1955, the Canoe Lake Landing was completed and a plan was announced for the Canoe Lake access road to go directly to the highway. The portage to Smoke Lake was routed to the south of the new road "thereby removing the hazard of canoeists going along the highway."[113] The Smoke Lake leaseholder parking area and garages were to be moved so that Canoe and Smoke Lake parking could be at the same turn off the highway. Congestion at the Canoe Lake Landing, however, continued to be a problem due to the number of canoes and trips launched from there. The suggestion was made by the leaseholders, and eventually adopted by the department, that the sandy beach at the bottom of Portage Bay be developed into a canoe-launching site.

In 1959, the CNR tracks to Brulé and Rain Lakes were removed, making it very difficult for the few leaseholders on those lakes to get to their property. Mrs. Gould wrote that year to ask if the Brulé trestle was still standing. They were expecting to take a train to Huntsville and then the mail bus or a taxi in from there. Their backup plan was to ask the son of Park Ranger Jack Gervais if he could swim across the lake where the trestle had been, get their canoe and paddle it back over to them. If none of this worked she wanted to know if the DLF would be willing to fly them in, a request that, of course, was refused. A few leases were located close enough to the highway that road access was feasible, though some leaseholders were very uneasy leaving their cars by the roadside where they would be "at the mercy of every transient who came by."[114] After repeated requests, approval was granted in 1956 for a public access road running from Highway 60 to Little Joe Lake. The owners of Arowhon Pines and the Taylor Statten Camps agreed to manage it jointly. Since it was an open public road,

---

112. Bice leasehold correspondence 1957, Algonquin Park Museum Archives.
113. Canoe Lake and District Leaseholders Association minutes, 1955.
114. Lake of Two Rivers leasehold correspondence, 1930s, Algonquin Park Museum Archives.

it also enabled easier access for the 34 leases located at the north end of Canoe Lake and on the Joe Lakes.

Eventually, especially on the bigger lakes, as the number of leaseholds increased, this "hiding stuff in the bush" strategy became impractical. The leaseholders asked if they could use the Camp 2 recreation hall as a storage facility during the week. After some consideration, Park officials agreed to build garages at several access points including both Canoe and Smoke Lakes, and make them available to leaseholders. Unfortunately, the demand for the garages always exceeded supply.

On Lake of Two Rivers, a grass airfield was built in the 1930s as a depression relief project and some leaseholders with airplanes would fly in. Floatplanes could of course land directly on the lakes, and many did. Art Hollingsworth on Source Lake used to fly in and land on the lake. He had two sons who became fighter pilots in the military and would occasionally fly low over the lake and wave their wings at their father as they flew by. Bob Fowler on Cache Lake was a test pilot in Toronto and would keep his Otter plane anchored in the bay. According to Bob, flying in was easy, but not so flying out, as you'd have to taxi all over the lake to get the right launching spot given wind speed and direction, and the fact that a floatplane could kick up quite a wave. George Elms on Rock Lake used to fly his "Seabee" amphibious plane to Rock Lake and tie it up to a floating barrel just off his dock.

Though used regularly, the Lake of Two Rivers airfield presented some challenges that needed to be kept in mind. When asking about the conditions at the airstrip in 1946 for friends arriving by airplane, Lester Graf from Smoke Lake was advised that "they should experience no difficulty in landing, but it would be as well to circle the field low to locate any deer, which might be feeding there."[115] Rick Rigby at Cache Lake would arrange to be picked up by flying over the lake and dipping the wings of his plane over the cabin. Someone would boat over to the parking lot and drive to the Lake of Two Rivers airstrip to pick him up. Upon one landing, a wolf ambled up to the plane and sat there watching to see what this giant creature would do or if anything interesting inside it was moving. Rigby had to wait until the wolf moved on before disembarking from the plane. In 1970, the airport was closed and now is allegedly the best blueberry patch in the Park.[116]

Though under the watchful eye of the local Park Rangers, their relative infrequent use made Algonquin Park cabins ready vandalism targets in the spring and fall. As a leaseholder on Lake of Two Rivers advised in 1950:

> *"The glass in the storm door was broken and the inside door was forced open, both the doorframe and lock being broken. The only things taken were a new axe, two bath towels, and four sets of playing cards. The person or persons entering did not light a fire or remove the shutters from the windows. They lit an oil lamp and smoked up the chimney, but it could not have burned more than half an hour as there was very little coal oil used. The cottage had the appearance of someone breaking into it and looking for some specific thing, and they were apparently in a hurry."*[117]

Sometimes visiting fishermen needed a place to stay due to accident or foul weather. Though sometimes the

---

115. Graf leasehold correspondence,1946, Algonquin Park Museum Archives.
116. Richard Eldridge and Orville Osborne, ***Cache Lake Reflections,*** 1995, pg. 91.
117. Cottle leasehold correspondence, 1948, Algonquin Park Museum Archives.

unexpected visitors left a mess, most of them were grateful for shelter and removed nothing from the premises. In the 1940s, Manley Sessions on Smoke Lake got very creative and set up a booby trap in a lamp post on his dock that was designed to drop a pail of cold water on an unsuspecting visitor. Unfortunately, one "culprit" was the Park Superintendent, who had stopped in to see Sessions. As he told the Park Superintendent:

> *"You will agree that it's an efficient piece of apparatus for dousing a caller. I'm glad that your experience was limited to shock only, as few others have not had quite such a narrow escape as yours."*[118]

Occasionally the thieves got organized, as they did in the 1930s, when a ring based in Whitney raided a number of cabins on Whitefish and Canoe Lakes. On Canoe Lake, Hannah Gillender and Annie Krantz, who had a site at the north end, were broken into nine times in 13 years. The extent of the group's activities first came to the attention of the Park authorities in the fall of 1934, when Dr. Seybold on Whitefish Lake advised the DLF that his cottage had been broken into, obscenities had been written on his windows, and a number of items stolen.[119] It later turned out that other neighbours including the Andrews, Jamieson, McCallum, and Blatherwick families had also been broken into and items stolen. When asked if there was anyone in the area who might have been harbouring any resentment towards him, Dr. Seybold recalled an incident several years previously when he'd hired a guide and former Fire Ranger named Ruddy to take him on a fishing trip. Seybold hired him without asking the price of the guiding services, only to discover upon departing on the trip from the Rain Lake train station that Ruddy wanted $5 per day. Seybold indicated that he thought the regular rate was $4 and asked another guide at the train station if this was so. The other guide confirmed the $4 rate and also advised Seybold that if Ruddy asked for more he could lose his guiding license. Ruddy accepted the $4 rate but was "mad clear through."[120] The DLF replied that:

> *"The Provincial Police immediately investigated, but there was not much to go on except that the culprit wrote on your windows and seemed to know your name. A regular patrol has been kept on the cottages except when the Park Rangers are out chasing poachers and the job was done in their absence. We found in Jamieson's cottage, also broken into, an almost new 16-foot canoe, which Jamieson says, does not belong to him. Did you have a canoe of this description in your cottage? We have it at the ranger's cabin at Rock Lake. They also have a line on a 15-foot canoe, which is outside the Park, and which we think might be the one you had stolen two years ago. This is in the hands of trappers and until we can be sure of our ground and see it quietly or catch them with it we cannot just be sure whether it belongs to the persons who are using it or if it was stolen. I am very sorry about these occurrences and assure you that we are doing all we can to stop them."*[121]

Park authorities diligently worked the case, and in early 1935 the Park Superintendent announced that the robberies had been solved with the arrest of Michael Worankie, who:

> *"Turned King's Evidence and today gave Provincial Constable Porter and Chief Park Ranger McCormick all the information pertaining to the case, and who was involved in the disposal of the stuff taken from the*

---

118. Sessions leasehold correspondence 1946, Algonquin Park Museum Archives.
119. Seybold leasehold correspondence, 1934, Algonquin Park Museum Archives.
120. Ibid.
121. Ibid. DLF did later seize the canoe from the trappers, who claimed that a tourist had given them it. A reward was given to Ranger McCormick who passed it on to the party responsible for its recovery and who wanted his identity kept secret.

cabins. The hiding place is being looked over this afternoon and the stolen goods will be taken to Rock Lake and kept until claimed next summer. Warrants have been issued for the arrest of two other men involved, Steve Worankie and Michael Lavallee. They have been involved in nine robberies since last fall, and we believe yours will be traced to their activities. All the men are from Whitney, Ont. The clue that led to these cases being solved was some printing on the window of Dr. Seybold's cottage.[122]

A greater problem to many leaseholders, especially in the 1950s and 1960s, was vandalism of the animal sort. It was conventional practice in the early days for residents to establish garbage dumps in the woods behind their leases. When use of the Park was modest, these dumps were of little attraction to wildlife. However, in the early 1950s, recreational use at the various campgrounds along Highway 60 increased dramatically. The resulting garbage dumps required to service these new users, as well as improper storage of food containers attracted a new kind of bear. It didn't take long for these foraging bears to begin to terrorize cottagers and damage property. One leaseholder was so afraid that he asked if he could get permission to keep a firearm as self-protection:

"On the afternoon of Monday Oct 19th, 1953 while I was packing my car to return to Toronto, a big black bear approached my cottage. He was not in any sense afraid of me. In fact, instead of running away from me he walked toward me, presumably thinking I wanted to feed him. I assure you, I had no desire for close contact with this creature, and I returned to the cabin. He stayed around for a considerable time and finally went north, across the highway. Fortunately at this time there weren't any tourists feeding deer on the road. Otherwise I am afraid a regrettable incident might have occurred. This bear seemed to think it quite all right to walk up to me. Whether or not he would harm a person I don't know, but it is a most uncomfortable feeling to have a bear look at you and quietly walk towards you, instead of away from you. In this situation I was completely defenseless."[123]

Of course his request to keep a firearm was denied and he was advised to call a Park Ranger if the bear reappeared. A dramatic increase in the bear population followed, and several years of very poor berry harvests didn't help the situation. As Park Superintendent George Phillips reported:

"I have seen more bears from the air this Spring than I have in my thirty years with the Department I suppose this partly explains why bears are troubling more people. The only advice that I can offer is for you to buy some large firecrackers and if a bear comes along, light and throw it as close to him as possible. If we put a Park Ranger out to guard the people of Algonquin Park who complain about bears, our men would do little else. I hope you have no further trouble with bears, but I am afraid that for those of us who persist in living in Algonquin Park, trouble from bears will be as real as tax bills."[124]

In the 1950s and 1960s, bear incidents were frequent and very frightening for those involved. On Rock Lake, Mary Eleanor Riddell Morris had a three-legged bear that would make the rounds of cottages and campsites all over the lake, including a nightly walk by her screened in sleeping porch. Park Ranger Stewart Eady finally

---

122. Seybold leasehold correspondence, 1934, Algonquin Park Museum Archives.

123. Humber leasehold correspondence, Algonquin Park Museum Archives.

124. DLF correspondence, 1953, Algonquin Park Museum Archives.

had to shoot it. On another occasion, Mary Eleanor's 15-year-old son Rob had caught a fish and decided take it down to a young couple staying on the nearby campsite. As he paddled up to their campsite, he found the couple enjoying their dinner and admiring the sunset, totally unaware that just behind them was a huge bear standing on his back paws. Rob told them to move slowly to their canoe and to get out. All three ended up at one of the neighbouring cottages. The poor couple was in such a state of shock that neither could speak. Later in the week, the bear crashed through the dense bush on the other side of the bay, swam across the lake and was shot near Whitney soon after. In another bear incident, a leaseholder was trapped in his cottage by a rogue bear that had already been tagged and removed three times my Park officials.[125] A bear invaded the Pultz cabin on Smoke Lake, even though they had boarded up the windows and doors and removed all of the summer supplies. The bear tore off three shutters and a storm door, broke a window and even a bed inside. In the fall of 1955, a bear tore a 3-foot by 4-foot hole in the end wall of the Taylor's cabin on Cache Lake.

Unfortunately, Park officials of the day weren't very supportive of leaseholder bear concerns. The Park Superintendent at the time was even quoted in the ***Toronto Star*** as suggesting that "cottagers bothered by hungry bears have only themselves to blame. They leave food inside, along with dirty pots and plates."[126] Many leaseholders took offence, and one advised him in no uncertain terms that such statements were "untrue, and not a fair statement to release to the public."[127] Things came to a head in the fall of 1953, when more than 100 foraging bears were shot during the last few weeks of the summer by Park staff in Algonquin Park. Unable to find food, the bears broke into cottages and cabins. The resulting publicity damaged the Park's reputation as the province's leading game reserve.[128] More than 40 cottages at Cache Lake were damaged and Park Rangers feared more damage to others at Smoke Lake. The local District Forester noted that there were more bears that year than he had seen in 25 years. He blamed the hot summer, which destroyed the animals' food supply.[129] Alas, things didn't get better in the summer of 1954. Though concerned about damage, of greater concern was fear of safety for children and visitors to cabins. On Cache Lake it was especially bad, as reported by one leaseholder:

> *"I would like to draw to your attention that on three occasions since the 24th of May this year, and as late as last Saturday night, we have been visited by bears. They seemed to take great delight in smashing the windows. We have had this place for the last six years and have had no problems until last fall when there was considerable damage done to one of the buildings. I felt at that time that it was only a temporary thing, and probably would not occur again. While I do not appreciate the damage to the building and the inconvenience of replacing glass and windows, I am particularly apprehensive concerning the safety of children on the property from time to time. At the present time one of my relatives is using the cottage and there are five children staying there for the next two weeks. I understand that the bears also broke into other cottages on our side of the lake so we are not alone with this problem. I would appreciate it if the Park Rangers stationed at Smoke Lake could lend some assistance in eliminating this nuisance. I am an old time camper in the area, having traveled by*

---

125. Recollections from Mary Eleanor Riddell Morris, 2003.
126. ***Toronto Star*** article, summer 1953, found in the leasehold records, Algonquin Park Museum Archives.
127. Sellery leasehold correspondence, 1953, Algonquin Park Museum Archives.
128. Gerald Killan, ***Protected Places: A History of Ontario's Provincial Parks System,*** 1993, pg. 77.
129. Sellery leasehold correspondence, 1953, Algonquin Park Museum Archives.

canoe through the Park over the past 31 years, so am also interested in protecting the wildlife there."[130]

As the Park Superintendent wrote in 1954:

> *"The bears have created quite some difficulty in the Park over the past year and you will appreciate that this is a difficult situation to cope with as in all probability the damage is caused by one or two bears rather than the larger number. These marauders prowl at their leisure and can be here today and many miles away tomorrow. It is therefore difficult to dispose of the marauder unless he is caught in the act. Although we appreciate the fact that a bear is a strong and vicious animal, if molested, the general feeling is that they are no more harmful to man than their many associates who prowl the woods in their diurnal rounds. At the present time we have snares set on Cache Lake in an endeavour to quell the destructiveness, which is taking place. Our past experience has found that they will scamper for shelter when a human endeavours to give them a scare. Our Park Rangers will dispose of any that we are able to discover and we hope that with the disposition of garbage via incinerators this year that this situation will be cleared up to the satisfaction of all concerned in the near future. It is our belief that if a resident is strictly in constant fear of these animals they should not be left alone as the appearance could be detrimental to their health from the sudden shock and experienced fear. Although bears are not to be disregarded it should also be noted that we have not experienced any deaths from these animals since 1881."*[131]

Not all bear incidents were destructive. Some were very amusing and most leaseholders had one or two bear stories that were used to make everyone laugh on social occasions. A visitor to a Cache Lake family one year was picking blueberries at the clearing near the third trestle. So was a bear from the same bush, and they almost backed right into each other.[132] Kay Beckett from Canoe Lake saw a figure, apparently wearing a fur coat, standing upright at his front door. He assumed it was Mr. Farley, the local postmaster, whom he knew had a fur coat. He opened the front door and encountered a bear, which was just as surprised as he was. Later that summer Beckett decided to install gutters and downspouts. He dug a trench to hold tile to carry the water away, and had installed and filled over about 20 feet. The next morning, he saw that someone had dug up the tile and strewn it around the area. During the day he reinstalled the tile and added another 30 feet. The following morning, Kay found that most of the tile had again been dug up, and wondered if this was perhaps vandalism rather than a practical joke. After reinstalling the tile, he kept a vigil and was rewarded as a bear soon ambled onto the property, sniffed along the filled-in trench, and began to dig up the tile. Kay scared off the bear, and decided to discourage it from further digging. He reburied a tile with one end of a clothesline tied to it, and fastened an assortment of pots and pans to the other end, which he threw over a nearby tree limb about eight feet off the ground. Sure enough, the bear later returned and diligently set about removing the offending tile. During this process, the clothesline fell from the tree. The resulting clatter of pots and pans so frightened the bear that it left and did not return, apparently believing that drain tile was less of an evil than the clangor of pots and pans.[133]

---

130. Bryant leasehold correspondence 1944, Algonquin Park Museum Archives.
131. Cochrane leasehold correspondence, 1954, Algonquin Park Museum Archives.
132. Richard Eldridge and Orville Osborne, ***Cache Lake Reflections,*** pg. 52.
133. Recollections from the Becket family, 2004.

Barbara Newton on Cache Lake loved card parties and would invite up her city friends for a couple of days of bridge. One time a bear got onto the front porch and began playing with the ice chest, hoping that it would open. The bridge-playing ladies stayed up all night placing bets on whether that old bear could get inside the ice chest. The stakes got pretty high, but the bear was unsuccessful. In the morning Barbara tiptoed warily to the dock and blew her emergency whistle and got rescued. Unfortunately, that was the last time that she was able to get her friends to come up for cards.[134]

On Canoe Lake, Marg Hogg kept telling her husband Les that she could hear noises on the roof every morning. He figured it was just raccoons or squirrels and didn't think much of it. So she went out one morning to have a look and it turned out to be a young bear. It would sit on the roof, close to the stovepipe where it was nice and warm, and watch the sunrise over the lake. Smart bear![135]

Anti-bear strategies became a common subject of conversation at annual leaseholder get-togethers. Lennox Beauprie on Cache Lake had one good idea. He was a good craftsman and built cabins, canoes and paddles. To discourage the bears, he put turned-up saw blades on the windowsills. A lawyer friend visiting the Browning lease on Cache Lake put up a notice one summer: "No Bears! Swift and Strict Reprisals."[136]

The best bear story, though, was the one told by Islay McFarlane from Canoe Lake. One fine summer day, Islay had gone to get groceries at the Portage Store. When she got back, she got out of the boat and went inside the cabin to find a dumped sugar bowl, and a cookie jar in pieces on the floor. She slowly approached the kitchen area in time to see a huge black bear go storming out the back door. On closer inspection, Islay discovered that it had gotten into the fridge and attacked the fat jar, which had spilt over everything. In a panic, Islay phoned Jim Stringer, the local lake handyman, and asked if he had a gun. She was afraid that the bear would come back again and wanted to be ready if it did. Jimmy allegedly called the Park Headquarters and got permission from the Ministry to shoot the bear if it did return. He headed over and a little while later, sure enough, the bear did come back. As soon as he saw it, Jimmy picked up the gun and chased it down the path yelling, "Fresh meat! Fresh meat!" He came back awhile later saying that he had shot it and buried it out back in the woods. A tall tale, perhaps, as it is hard to imagine the diminutive Jimmy being able to dig a hole big enough to bury a huge black bear. Nevertheless, Islay rewarded him with dinner and a strong drink.[137]

In the 1960s, bears continued to be a big problem for leaseholders. One experiment at the time was for each leaseholder to build an incinerator and burn their garbage. Alas, the smell of burning steak bones made things even worse and would attract the bears from miles around. The Adaskins on Canoe Lake had an old stone incinerator out their back door destroyed by a bear one summer. Murray heard a noise out back and upon investigation saw a huge bear's rear end sticking out of the incinerator. Murray banged a pot to scare it away, and the bear got so frightened that it totally smashed up the stone incinerator. Several decades later, Cliff Nelson, husband of Adaskin niece Tamar, was reading a book on the dock when he heard a red squirrel going

---

134. Richard Eldridge and Orville Osborne, ***Cache Lake Reflections***, pg. 67.
135. Recollections from Betsy Hogg Cook, 1999.
136. Richard Eldridge and Orville Osborne, ***Cache Lake Reflections***, pg. 79.
137. Gaye I. Clemson, *Algonquin Voices, Selected Stories of Canoe Lake Women*, 2002, pg. 161.

crazy. He turned around to see a bear on his upper deck observing him. He called out and the bear took off into the bush. A few minutes later the bear reappeared down the shore. It then jumped in the water and swam across the entrance to Whiskey Jack Creek. The Nelsons discovered to their horror that, not only could bears swim very fast, they were very buoyant. The bear looked like a huge black raft as it raced across the channel. Once the handling of household garbage at the public campgrounds, tourist resorts, and children's camps was managed more aggressively, and "pack-out" regulations for interior campers and leaseholders implemented, the bear problem diminished considerably. Today one hears of the occasional foraging bear around the public campgrounds, but few have been seen by leaseholders for decades.

Despite the bears, summers in Algonquin Park were for children wonderful. As Rory MacKay shared:

> *"As soon as school was over it was cottage time. As was the custom of the time, my mother would spend July alone at the cottage with my brother Niall and I, and my father would come up on weekends from Toronto, usually arriving late Friday and leaving early evening Sunday. Though a self-described city girl, my mother's bravery was tested one year when late at night her solitude was interrupted by a fearsome noise of unknown description just outside her bedroom window. A courageous investigation by flashlight revealed that a porcupine was the source of the strange sounds. It had climbed the front steps and couldn't figure how to get down. During July we would go on nature trails, took part in conducted hikes, explored the nearby woods, canoed, and played with children at other cottages nearby. All, including parents and children, became close friends. Rainy days were a challenge, but solved with a solution assembled by my mother. An old suitcase was converted into a rainy day chest. Inside were crayons and paper, puzzles and colouring books, and all sorts of entertaining diversions, which the children were permitted to play with only when it was raining. In August my father would came up for the full month and we'd all would go off on canoe trips, often to nearby lakes including Rock, Pen, Louisa and Welcome. In the mid-1960s we ventured to Crotch Lake and Shall Lake on the Opeongo River and eventually discovered the Barron River Canyon. These trips fed a lifelong interest in archeology and park history."*[138]

My own experience on Canoe Lake was very similar and, as I wrote in my book, ***Algonquin Voices:***

> *"If wind and the weather was cooperative, each day's outdoor activities would include swimming, sailing, canoeing, hiking, hiking to various landmarks or picnicking anywhere there was an open rock or clearing. On rainy days there would be a slew of puzzles, card or board games to keep us fully occupied. Many families had small 1 or 2-horsepower motorboats that we kids would use. Once you were 10 years old these small boats were the ticket to lakeside independence. It meant that we could drive ourselves over and back to a friend's cabin and explore the mysteries of the lake without parental supervision. Occasionally we'd run out of gas or*

---

[138] From 1972-78, Rory was employed as a seasonal interpretive naturalist at the Algonquin Park Museum. Many years and much research later, Rory wrote a text on the history of the Park to accompany photographs by William Reynolds. The book was called *Algonquin,* and it was published in 1993, the centennial year of the Park. Three years later Rory published with the cooperation of The Friends of Bonnechère Parks a history of the Bonnechère River called *Spirits of the Little Bonnechère.* His brother Niall had an ongoing interest in the Ottawa, Arnprior and Parry Sound Railway. As children, he and Rory had been frequent visitors to the Algonquin Park Station at Cache Lake when picking up their mail from Sally Yaskovitch, who ran the Algonquin Park Post Office. After many years of archival research and walking of the former railroad bed, Niall wrote *Over The Hills To Georgian Bay,* which was published in 1981 with many subsequent printings.

have some other mechanical problem, which taught us all a lot about keeping safe and managing in a crisis. One downside, though, was that we'd be constantly leaving our belongings at each other's cabin. One year there were so many things left at the Hoggs' cabin that Mrs. Hogg hung them all from a huge T-shaped piece of wood mounted on the boathouse wall. Everyone who drove or paddled by would check and see if anything that belonged to them was there. In this way, most items got returned to their rightful owners in no time flat."[139]

---

139. Gaye I. Clemson, *Algonquin Voices: Selected Stories of Canoe Lake Women,* 2002, pg. 151.

Winans Sisters and Friends Building a Fire 1908

Post Card of a Typical Fishing Party c1905

Marge Burnett (seated) Eating a Meal 1928

Irene Winans (stirring) and Elizabeth Burnett, Mother of Robert Burnett Cooking Dinner Outdoors 1934

Helen Winans (standing) and Marge Burnett (sitting), Resting While on a Hike

Winans Sisters Breakfasting on the Point Cache Lake c1920s

Photos from Burnett Collection

Park Gate 1950 Matthews Collection

Source Lake Landing Dernoga Collection

(left) Tere Dernoga Heading to the Cottage From the Source Lake Landing 2005 Dernoga Collection

Camp Two at Smoke Lake During Highway 60 Construction 1935 APMA #3591

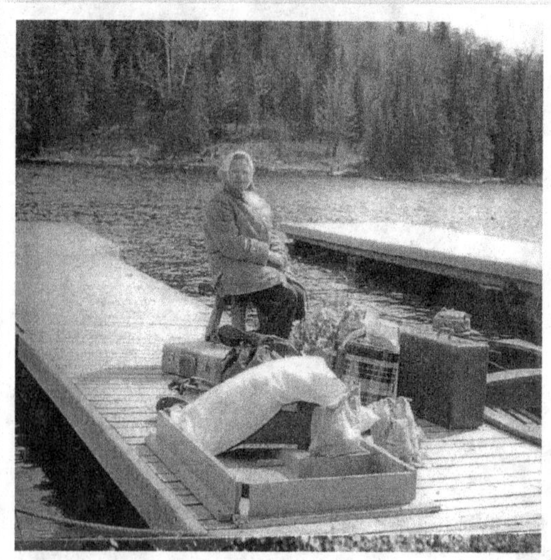

Grandma Waiting for the Clemson ferry at the Portage Store Docks 1950s Clemson Collection

Heading Out From the Canoe Lake Landing 1996 Clemson Collection
L to R Gaye, Taylor, Kris (foreground)

(left) Sandy Point on Smoke Lake
(L to R) Robert, Gaye, Isabel (mom) Clemson
c1963
Clemson Collection

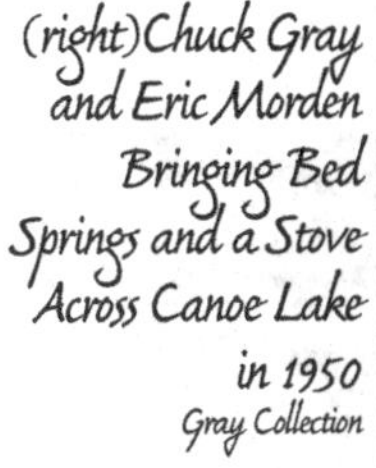

(right) Chuck Gray and Eric Morden Bringing Bed Springs and a Stove Across Canoe Lake in 1950
Gray Collection

(both above)
Art Work on Manning Cabin Walls 1998
Clemson Collection

Summers Alone at the Cottage c1950s
(L to R) Rory, Elizabeth and Niall MacKay MacKay Collection

Frank Braught's Famous Guest Book Gray Collection

Sharpe Family Skiing Sharpe Collection

(both above) Cold Storage in 1920s Burnett Collection

MacKay's Red Water Pump MacKay Collection

Irene Winans and Friend Caroline Derier Building a Chair in 1920 That is Still in Use Today Burnett Collection

26 OVERLOOKING CACHE LAKE FROM HIGHLAND INN, ALGONQUIN PARK, ONTARIO

View of Cache Lake From the Highland Inn Date Unknown But Guess it was From the 1920s Clemson Collection

Postcard of the View of Canoe Lake Looking North From Portage Bay c1970s Clemson Collection

Douglas Young at Camp Ahmek c1920s
Young Argue Collection

MacKay Cottage Just After Construction c Early 1950s
MatKay Collection

Douglas Young (right) and Helper Building in Their Smoke Lake Cabin
Youn Argue Collection

Valerie (Young) Argue, Camping c1943, Before the Cabin was Built on Smoke Lake
Young Argue Collection

Haliday Cabin c1950s

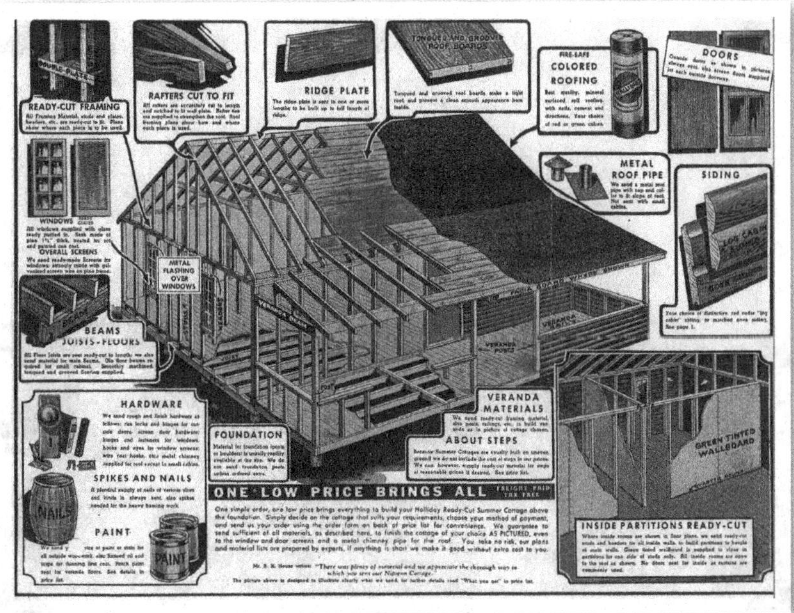

Haliday Cabin Detail c1950s

All photos this page from Alger Collection

Sawing Logs for the New Alger Cabin on Little Couchon Lake c1940s

Polling a Raft of Logs to the Alger Site Bought from the Local Saw Mill

Building the New Alger Cabin c1940s

Chapter 3

Cottage Rules of Engagement

It's a gorgeous summer afternoon in early August. A slight breeze blows from the southwest and I am about to settle into reading **Protected Places**, *Gerald Killan's history of Ontario's provincial parks system, when my phone rings. On the line is a voice and a name I don't recognize. It seems that a resident of Tea Lake has heard about my project. Her mother, Midge Rasey now over 80 years old, has a manuscript describing the trials and tribulations of building their cabin in the late 1940s. Her mother wants to deliver it to me personally and wonders if they can drop by. Of course I say yes and wait for their arrival. With the help of her daughter, Midge, a slight woman who looks so frail that she might break at any moment, climbs up to my cottage on the ridge with her story clutched tightly in her hand. Suddenly the details of her experience that I found in the Park archives come back to me. She was married to a Methodist minister, who took out a land use permit and later a lease in 1949. The family built a pre-fabricated cabin and all was well until 1971 when her husband died unexpectedly without a will. Because of the nature of park regulations and the challenges of having no will, it took a painful five years to arrange for the lease to be transferred to her and her two children.*

Two months later, I get a call from Grace Fraser Hancock. Her parents, Karl and Grace Fraser, had taken up two leases on Kiosk in the early 1930s. Later friends joined them and took out a lease nearby, as did a brother-in-law. At one point there were four leases in the extended family. We spend a wonderful hour as she recounts story after story about her experiences in the North. A few days after our conversation, I get an email from another woman, Ann Sinclair, whose mother settled alone on an island in Cedar Lake across from Kish Kaduk Lodge in 1930. Like Grace, Ann is another who comes from a stock of fiercely independent women, braving the wilds on her own.

To top it all, the next issue of Cottage Life Magazine contains a story about 78-year-old Mary Gardner Russe and 82-year-old Vivien Hannon, two longtime residents of Cache Lake who have been paddling around

Algonquin Park for almost 70 years. Mary and Vivien are just two of the Cache Lake cottage matriarchy of strong, independent, and vocal females dedicated to keeping their cottages simple and rustic.[140] *I realize, as I did once before, that it is the voices of the women that resonate the most with me. My first two books on Algonquin Park leaseholding,* **Gertrude Baskerville The Lady of Algonquin Park and Algonquin Voices: Selected Stories of Canoe Lake Women,** *are not an end, but just a beginning. I redouble my efforts to uncover more about these remarkable women and bring their voices to life.*

Building Regulations

In an effort to attract leaseholders, the DLF in 1923 went to considerable expense to survey and lay out the most suitable parcels for summer resorts around the key lakes near the Park's five railway stations. Alas, leaseholders didn't always like the decisions that the surveyor made and would ask for parcels to be expanded, contracted, or any myriad of changes to their shape. Leasing land in Algonquin Park has never been easy. It has always required abiding by a collection of park regulations and interpretations of regulations that governed many aspects of life. In hindsight, it's a wonder that anyone chose to stay. Many found the rules too cumbersome and left for Muskoka and other locations outside of the Park. In the early years, Park officials were very accommodating, but by the 1940s began to insist that every potential leaseholder who wanted a parcel that wasn't on the 1923 approved parcel map pay for a formal land survey, at considerable expense. Most of the time, great effort was made to find compromises that would enable the leaseholder to obtain what they wanted, but still be in keeping with the regulations. As Park Superintendent Frank MacDougall wrote in a letter to DLF Deputy Minister Walter Cain in 1934:

> *"The parcels surveyed in 1923 simply represented the opinion of the surveyor of what constitutes a summer resort parcel and while in the main include all the likely spots, there are unsurveyed tracts that seem to appeal to the tourists. Tourists in many cases wish to have their places on a cliff or other height of land, which often look to the surveyor to be unsuitable. The fact that these tourists so select such areas means that what we might consider to be the more desirable sites are still available for sale."*[141]

However, what became over time a challenge was that the interpretation of these rules often changed. Not surprisingly, this resulted in occasional tensions between DLF staff and local residents. One incident in 1925 concerned the use of a team of horses owned by DLF that was stationed at Cache Lake. At the time, the DLF often made their team of horses available for use by Algonquin Park residents at a cost at the time of about \$1.50 or \$2 per day, which was deemed to be about \$1 less than the market rate. That year one of the Park Rangers found a group of leaseholders cutting ice down by the shore. The horses were standing belly deep in the cold water, with the temperature below zero. As he wrote in frustration later:

---

140. *Cottage Life* magazine, August 2004, pg. 90.
141. Whiddon leasehold correspondence 1934, Algonquin Park Museum Archives.

"As soon as the horses came out of the water their legs were covered with frozen balls of ice. I gave instructions to the stable man to use hot cloths on the horses' legs as soon as they were returned to the stable. Had this occurred in Toronto, the Humane Society would have fined and perhaps sent the [offenders] to jail. They borrow our wagon, in fact wear it out more than we do, borrow our sleighs and other equipment. Nine times out of 10 the articles are never returned until we go and get them. Our team is a great convenience here and on many, many occasions residents, including those at the Highland Inn and Bartlett Lodge, make use of the team in an emergency. I know that it would cost at least $48 to bring in and return a team to Eganville. No liveryman in Ontario will hitch up a single horse for a dollar and a half a day let alone a team. They are being utilized at the present time in hauling wood and ice for the three camps, hard hauling and hard on the horses and a dollar and a half does not pay for the wear and tear."[142]

Since its founding, one of the most important responsibilities of the Park was its role as a wildlife refuge. Poaching was a serious issue and a crime in Algonquin Park. Even as late as the 1930s, one of the main responsibilities of a Park Ranger was to be constantly on the lookout for potential poachers, especially in the winter. In 1926 Lennox Irving, head of the Barnet Lumber Company, advised the DLF that:

"On or about 28th May three trappers entered and ransacked our cottage on Brulé Lake. I would ask you to take such proceedings as you deem advisable to protect our property from such depredations and prosecute those who have done such a mean thing."[143]

He was advised by the Park Superintendent that:

"The poachers evidently deemed it unwise to travel the road to Brulé Lake Station so they broke into your house to get a canoe to get quickly across the lake. They were seen at that [but we were unsuccessful] in heading them off. You know that the handful of Park Rangers have a slight chance to watch 250 miles of border line and at the same time traverse toward the interior of this big Park. It is my candid opinion that we have done pretty well in bringing some 14 fellows to justice this last season and not one was fined less than $100 or three months at Burwash. In the fall we captured one of this same gang who broke into J. C. William's cottage and Taylor Statten's camp. In this instance we recovered the Hudson Bay blankets belonging to the camp and a canoe taken from Mr. Williams of Canoe Lake. A Park Ranger must travel a long beat and while he is away 10 or 15 miles, it is an easy matter to break into a cottage and get clear away. We are doing our best to protect our tenants in the Park, but you must know that a Park Ranger cannot sit on a doorstep all the time to watch one cottage."[144]

Leaseholders were also not excused from such close scrutiny. One known poacher in the Park was Dan McElroy, originally from Scotia Junction, who was the first trainman for the Grand Trunk Railway at Cache Lake. He had camped on the lake for years and later took out one of the early leases. Later it was discovered that he allegedly had a side business, trapping and smuggling furs. He was told to give up his lease or he'd be arrested. He immediately sold his cabin in 1924 and disappeared from the Park.[145] In another episode, Laird

---

142. DLF correspondence, lease files 1925, Algonquin Park Museum Archives.
143. Irving leasehold correspondence, 1926, Algonquin Park Museum Archives.
144. Irving leasehold correspondence, 1926, Algonquin Park Museum Archives.

Saunderson recalls the time in the 1950s on Source Lake that her parents built a chicken wire cage with logs at the front of the cottage to keep her brother, Duarte, from going in the water. The Park Rangers visited and questioned her parents closely to verify that they weren't trapping or keeping animals.[146]

Another regulation related to firearms, whose possession and use was prohibited. The only known exception was made in 1932 for Gar Northway who did not like the idea of his wife being up on Smoke Lake in the winter time without some sort of protection, though from what is not clear. He was given permission to keep a firearm for personal use.[147]

In 1935, questions were raised about the interpretation of the liquor regulations that at the time allowed only one bottle per person to be brought or shipped into the Park. As the use of alcohol was a major source of entertainment in those days, one presumes that the policy had originally been established to curb drunkenness and other abuse. As noted in my 2005 book ***Rock Lake Station***, poor Mrs. Merritt, who had settled at Chalet Camp on Rock Lake, had previously run afoul of these regulations in 1933. She was under a doctor's care for a stomach ailment and the doctor had prescribed for her a quantity of ale to be taken daily. Her brother Murton Seymour had arranged with the Brewers Retail in Huntsville to ship to her via train one case of ale every week to 10 days. Unfortunately his shipping instructions were not followed and all five cases that Mrs. Merritt was expected to need during her stay at Rock Lake were shipped at once. These arrived at the Algonquin Park Station at Cache Lake and were immediately seized by the Park authorities. Mrs. Merritt was advised that she needed to immediately come to Cache Lake Park Headquarters, along with her resident permit and the doctor's prescription, sign for the cases herself, and provide an explanation. This was impossible for Mrs. Merritt as neither the train nor the jitney service was in operation and paddling the long distance along the Madawaska River to Cache Lake wasn't feasible. After a flurry of correspondence and telegrams between Seymour, Merritt, and Park Superintendent MacDougall, MacDougall made an arrangement with the local station agent, a Mr. Needham, and advised Mr. Seymour:

> *"Each time our gas-car goes down to Rock Lake that the car driver [will] be permitted to carry one case, so that Mrs. Merritt will receive her ale without having to come up and get it and also allow the Park Regulations to be complied with. One case was taken down the first of this week, and the remainder is being delivered as often as the car goes by. There being no train service between Algonquin Park Station [on Cache Lake] and Rock Lake, you should route future shipments from the East. The use of our gas-car for carrying express to Rock Lake in this instance was only given as a courtesy by the CNR in order to assist Mrs. Merritt and not as a regular procedure."*[148]

Another alcohol-related situation occurred at Nominigan in 1933. As mentioned previously, Gar Northway loved to entertain and Nominigan was constantly filled with guests coming and going. It was discovered by Park officials that often these guests would leave behind unused bottles of alcohol, which meant that Northway

---

145. Richard Eldridge and Orville Osborne, ***Cache Lake Reflections,*** 1995, pg. 14.
146. For more great stories about Park Rangers pursuing poachers in the Park, see ***Rock Lake Station*** by Gaye. I. Clemson, 2005.
147. Northway leasehold correspondence, 1932, Algonquin Park Museum Archives.
148. Merritt leasehold correspondence, 1933, Algonquin Park Museum Archives.

had more than his one bottle per person allotment. After some discussion, it was agreed that it would be left to the good judgment of the leaseholders if some alcohol got left behind after guests have left that results in having excess of the stated regulations.[149]

Another important DLF regulation was one that stated that leaseholders were only allowed to have one parcel of land in their name. This policy encouraged a few families to lease several lots in the same area, one in their name and a second in the name of their spouse. This enabled extended families to share the same general location, though they did have to build a cabin on each separate lot.

The most critical regulations, and those that over the years often proved most controversial, were the various Park building regulations. A key one, at least as far as the DLF was concerned, was the requirement that within 18 months of obtaining a lease, leaseholders build improvements worth at least $500 on their sites. In the early days it was very common for leaseholders to camp on a site for many years, build a cabin and apply for a lease after the fact. By the 1940s, though, most leaseholders took out a lease first and built afterward. Though not always enforced, to meet the spirit of the regulations a respective leaseholder was required to submit for approval a plan and a detailed description of what was going to be built. This included not just new structures, but any change of any kind to dimensions such as the adding of a verandah, replacing a dock, and so forth. Some Park Superintendents had strong opinions as to the design of the cabins and their colour schemes. As Park Superintendent Millar wrote in 1925 concerning a cabin to be built on Cache Lake:

> *"The proposed two-story cottage to be erected is more pretentious and elaborate than any other building on Cache Lake. Mr. Hall and his family are of the most desirable type of tenants and I would respectfully urge an early consideration of the plans, as they are most anxious to have the cottage near completion before the snow flies. I must say that it is a source of pleasure to me to see so unique and so pretentious a building being erected on Cache Lake. It will be an ornament to Cache Lake. Some of the cottagers might well feel ashamed with their cottages or shacks stained with the cheapest and dirty shantyman's red colour. The colour scheme adopted by the dept as a standard is white with green trimmings which fits in so well and harmonizes with the woods and rock background in Algonquin Park."*[150]

In a 1926 letter to the DLF Deputy Minister concerning plans submitted for a cabin on Cache Lake, the Park Superintendent wrote:

> *"You might note that of plans recently submitted, these are of a much more elaborate type of houses than the general run and I am pleased to see and know that a higher standard of bungalows is being established."*[151]

And in a letter to Brulé Lake resident Lennox Irving, the Superintendent wrote:

> *"I received your pen and ink sketch of the plan which is in the course of construction on Barnet Island on Macintosh Lake. Permit me to congratulate you on the plan submitted. It is a big advance on the style of cottage usually erected in the Park. I am continuously urging a much higher standard and am pleased to say*

149. Northway leasehold correspondence, 1935, Algonquin Park Museum Archives.
150. Hall leasehold correspondence, 1925, Algonquin Park Museum Archives.
151. Cache Lake leasehold correspondence, 1926, Algonquin Park Museum Archives.

that there are half a dozen cottages on Cache Lake of recent construction, which are a credit to the builders. Some years ago, any old thing appeared to be good enough for Algonquin. A shanty hastily thrown up and stained a dirty old shantyman's red would answer the purpose. But now I insist on a more costly house and every new house must be painted white with green trim, or some attractive, lively inviting light shade, such as cream or light fawn colour. There are too many good houses, which have been ruined by the application of creosote stain or shantyman's Red, but it is the desire of the DLF to get away from the dull, dingy, dreary looking aspect of such colouring, reminding one of old coal sheds."[152]

Sometimes, due to events beyond a leaseholder's control, it was impossible to meet these deadlines. This was especially true during WWII, when both basic supplies and workmen were in short supply. Some leaseholders ended up not having the heart for the task and gave up. As Fred Chapman from Smoke Lake wrote in 1947:

"I have had so much difficulty in trying to line up someone to build my cabin on Smoke Lake. For some reason, which I am unable to understand, all persons who have contracted to build me the cabin have asked to be excused, and last year I had things so far advanced that I purchased the necessary lumber, windows, door frames, shingles, etc. and they are now on site. I am completely tired of the whole affair and in my present frame of mind, believe that the best thing I can do is to sell the material on site and give up my lot."[153]

On Smoke Lake, Al Gordon wanted to build a log house of the large white pine "squared timbers." In the spring of 1950, he purchased a building made of square timbers called Brady House in Haliburton County. He arranged for it to be dismantled and the logs moved to Smoke Lake. At the time, he was a forestry student attending university in New Brunswick, so he arranged for a local contractor to move the timbers to a main road from where they could be hauled to Smoke Lake. On his return from New Brunswick, he came to Smoke Lake to find no timbers and upon inquiring from the contractor found out that an illness had prevented him from completing the job. The following winter, the logs got moved to the main road in Haliburton County, but the trucker who was to bring the logs to Smoke Lake broke the contract and failed to transport the logs to the Park. Eventually, the following fall, Gordon contracted with another trucker and to assure the job paid him in advance. Once again, when he came up in the spring, there were no timbers. This time he immediately drove to Dorset to complain to the trucker and was promised a delivery date of early summer. Finally the timbers arrived and Gordon then spent his honeymoon tumbling 20 16-foot timbers into the water and booming them across Smoke Lake to his site. At one point the boom broke and dozens of Smoke Lakers went all over the lake helping to round up the logs. He hired Felix Lucasavitch and his brother to transform this two-story house into a one-story cabin. Felix taught him how to use a broad axe properly and later gave him one of his broad-scoring axes.[154]

Many bought prefabricated cabins and bunkees from companies such as the Halliday Company from Hamilton, Ontario. Rory MacKay's family's experiences on Lake of Two Rivers provide some interesting insight:

---

152. Taylor leasehold correspondence, 1927, Algonquin Park Museum Archives.
153. Brooks leasehold correspondence, 1947, Algonquin Park Museum Archives.
154. Gordon leasehold correspondence, 1950-1953, Algonquin Park Museum Archives and recollections 2003.

"Though now only one remains, the cottages of the MacKay family lie along Highway 60 at the kilometer 35 marker, on the rocky north shore of Lake of Two Rivers. Park records show that sometime in 1947, my grandfather, the Reverend James MacKay, and grandmother, Grace, took out a lease. My grandfather and father had camped on Whitefish Lake in 1942 and at Lake of Two Rivers in 1947 and 1948. They enjoyed the lake with its natural setting and after deciding that leasing was a more viable financial option, chose a site on Lake of Two Rivers. One may question that decision today, based on current government intent to remove the leases from the Park, but at the time my grandfather was assured that the twenty-one year leases would always contain the renewal clause for another twenty one years, and that indeed the government wanted leaseholders to occupy their place within the Park. So, like many others who responded to the government advertising from as early as the 1920s to take up lots, my grandfather (and a few years later my father) decided on Algonquin. As Chief Park Ranger of Algonquin Park at the time, and the resident Park Ranger on the lake, Tom McCormick was the contact person for the individual parcels of land. My grandfather had looked at a site in 1945 and apparently Tom McCormick had penciled his name in on that lot, even though a firm decision to take it had not been made. Conversation with the Chief Ranger had relieved any concerns that a lease would be anything other than as good as permanent.

My grandfather's cabin was known in the family as the 'Little Cottage,' was built on the west end of his lot. My father's cabin became known as the 'Big Cottage,' and was built on the east end of his lot. The two cottages were separated by what Park records refer to as a bumper lot. In the earliest years, access to the two cottages was by a path amongst balsam, birch and bunchberries from a parking lot, shared with our nearest neighbours. The parking lot sat adjacent to an access road or cart trail, which ran from the highway to the foot of the lake at the Madawaska River. This road had been built in 1948 or 1949 along an old skidding trail used by a lumber company, which had cut the area some years previously.

The 'Little Cottage' was a prefabricated cottage delivered by train to Algonquin Park Station at Cache Lake, transported in kit form by truck to kilometer 35 on Highway 60 and then carried in to the building site. For some reason, the plans for the cottage as sent were found to be unsuitable and were modified to suit our needs. This entailed cutting long boards shorter, putting shorter boards together to make longer lengths, and custom building all the window frames. This made maintenance and putting up of shutters quite a game in later years, as nothing ever fit right as the cottage aged. The brush was not cleared right to the lake, as efforts were made to have their cottages blend with the landscape and not be too visible from the lake.

The first cottage on the 'Big Cottage' site was a Halliday 'Bunkie Junior,' which was likely put up in 1950. It arrived in seven sections and three men from Whitney were hired to assist in carrying it down to its site near a flat rock and a cedar tree. Only ten feet by ten feet in area, it served as living room and bedroom for the family. Nearby was a table and two benches covered by an awning made of a groundsheet, which provided shelter for cooking and eating on rainy days. Later a proper sized cottage with two bedrooms was constructed on this original site and the 'Bunkee Junior' was moved a short distance west and uphill. The new cottage had a large living room dominated by a substantial fireplace built by a local stonemason from the rock behind the cottage. Only the three large horizontal stones that made the mantle-piece were from elsewhere. The cottage itself was of frame construction, with half-log siding and sat on a foundation of stones and cedar posts with an enclosed crawl space beneath. Across the front of the living room was a verandah with large windows overlooking the lake. The windows, each about three feet wide, swung upward and could be fastened to chains suspended from the ceiling. This afforded a breeze through the screens without having swinging windows in the way. A kitchen area was added several years later.

In 1958, a second sleeping cabin was added. It was another Halliday Bunkie Junior, located west of the first Bunkie on the same hillside. In 1961, permission was given by the government for an addition to be built onto the original cottage that both a kitchen space and an indoor bathroom with flush toilet. In 1962, the government purchased a small section of our lease for highway widening. While blasting rock, a rounded rock projective pierced the roof through shingles, sheathing, insulation, and the white-tiled inner ceiling of the cottage. Unfortunately it wasn't discovered until the following spring, by which time several small animals had moved into the cabin. The family retained the rock for a number of years, but eventually it became misplaced. In 1965, permission was obtained to build a road that gave us access to the highway by our own roadway. Thereafter a small sign showing the name MacKay was all that identified the laneway."

It was also very common for leaseholders to build their cabins themselves regardless of whether or not they had any skills in the work. In 1945, Carl and Hank Laurier on Canoe Lake decided to build a "do it yourself" Quonset hut. Neither had any building experience, so the hut was not properly squared or leveled and consequently it barely lasted the first few winters.

On Smoke Lake, the Young family camped on their point for the first few years in the mid-1940s. In 1949 they bought a prefab vertical pine cabin that was loaded on a rented truck and brought up to the Smoke Lake Landing. They then lashed two canoes together and paddled the pieces of the building down the lake. With the help of two hired workmen from Whitney the cabin was assembled in a week. Also on Smoke Lake, the Bolt family had to haul their lumber and windows straddling two canoes up Smoke Creek, which at that time had just been cleared of old deadheads. It was a perilous journey, with canoe gunnels just clearing the water line. In the case of the Raseys on Tea Lake, their prefab cabin components were dropped off by the side of the road at the Smoke Creek bridge. Luckily it was late August and nearby Camp Tamakwa wasn't in session, so Lou Handler, owner of the camp, offered up the camp barge to transport the house lumber to their site on the west side of the lake. As Midge Rasey recounted in 2004:

"We had ordered a small, 14-foot by 20-foot pre-fabricated house to be delivered on the day of our arrival, which of course didn't arrive until several days later. My husband Herbert and foster son Bob worked with the tape measure and level to build the foundation for the house. Our pre-fabricated company recommended cedar posts for the foundation, but though we tried to shore up the foundation with cement blocks, they were not sufficient to level the grade. The three kids ended up lugging stones of all shapes and sizes to Herbert, from sturdy flat ones to large fill-in ones that even made Bob groan to carry. Finally, with many small stones precariously balanced to 'fill in,' we managed to nail down the foundation beams. The next morning, Saturday, August 27th, dawned brightly with mild weather. We could do no more until we moved the pieces of the house to our land. The fellows went over to Camp Tamakwa hoping to be able to use their barge. If Bob and Herbert would help haul the sailboats into winter storage, Mike Lundy, the then-Camp Director, and two friends, agreed to help carry the 20-foot sides and the 14-foot ends of our prefab down the hill and

onto the barge, haul them through the channel, across the lake to our place, unload them onto the rocks, then carry them up the hill and deposit them in the spot where they would be erected.

At last, Bob and Herbert were able to start the construction. The men laid all the joists onto the sills, only to find the company had not sent enough for the 16-inch centres they had advertised. The only option was to space them unevenly. Many of the flooring boards were quite warped from the previous day's torrential rains, but the fellows did their best to force them into shape. We knew the house wasn't going to have a good floor because the cracks were too big, but with our unskilled labour, we did the best we could. As it turned out, the company had sent us a few extra pieces of flooring, and we would use them eventually for patching over the years. Once completed, we moved all of the loose lumber, gable ends, inside partitions and small pieces from the barge. Next to our tent were our roof rafters, roof sheeting, and trim, siding lumber, and odd unknown pieces. We hadn't the foggiest notion of where it was all supposed to go, but eventually we assumed all would become evident as we hammered the puzzle's pieces together. The grade level didn't look too steep when the site was cleared for the building's placement; but now, with the flooring on, we noticed how high the front of the house really was. We gathered some large stones to bolster the unsteady foundation and to also provide a mound-like step from which to climb in the front door.

The next step was attaching the sides and ends of the house. We arranged the cedar posts as rollers, and with much grunting and groaning, heaving and resting, we got both 14-foot ends up the hill and ready to lift onto the flooring. I am sure it was from different motives, but the fellows and I each had extra strength. I never knew I could tug, pull, shove, hold heavy things and lug the way I did with those two men. I thought I'd be limp and aching from so much exertion, but I had no adverse affects from it. We then worked at clearing a large path from the barge to the flooring for everyone to walk while carrying large sections. With the help of the men from Camp Tamakwa, it didn't take very long for the five men to carry the four heavy sides of the house off the barge, up the hill and lift them onto the floor to be attached. Those three dear men were jewels. They helped long enough to get all sides fitted, joined and nailed solidly into position. Suddenly it dawned on someone that the room partitions were still outside leaning against a tree. Carefully one corner was pried open a wee bit and the partitions were warily slithered inside and the sides were once again fused solidly into position. We now were enclosed and protected on all sides.

Then Bob and Herbert started to build the roof. Neither one had experience and therefore no skill in this type of labour. They set the rafters, spliced the ridgepole together, and started putting on the roof boards. They were cedar, but they were grade five lumber. They got about half of one side on when the rain came. They tried to keep working, but it was pouring so hard and the wind was whipping at the nails in their hands that eventually they had to stop. The majority of the next day was spent putting on the roof boards and then the roofing, with Herbert directing the children and me as to what to fetch hold and carry. The sun seemed to be rapidly moving westward. By now we had learned the black night would pounce on us at any moment. The roof wasn't quite finished along the ridgepole, but we decided to spend the night in our own cabin anyway. It was the best gift the kids and I could have given them. We all lay huddled on the battered, bear-torn mattresses on the floor, wrapped in our sweaters and blankets against the cold, gazing through the open spaces I the roof, watching the stars wink at us, as the moonlight blessed us. Thankfully, it didn't rain during the night and we were awakened by the sun's warm smile. The fellows finished the ridgepole section and put on all the roofing we had. Unfortunately the company had not sent enough. It was the middle of the afternoon when we finished clearing away the brush and heavy logs in the front, so our water line would look neat.

Later that day the Murrays canoed over. He had told Herbert he'd come and donate his expertise on stair building. Because of the slope of our land, the front door entrance was shoulder height. Herbert and Bob had constructed a small porch, but gave up trying to figure out how to make the stairs. By now we were getting weary of the entrance pattern: back up–run–step on the piled up rocks–jump up and fling your body on to the porch. The twins of course had to be lifted up and down. By the end of each day, even the fellows were calling more often, 'I need a boost.' To have Toronto's young architect's advice and help with the stairs was awesome.

Bess and I sat in the warm sun watching these two brilliant men walk around pondering the pros and cons of the land's topography, the appearance of a side entrance vs. a front entrance and exactly what materials were immediately available without going to Huntsville. Jim started figuring the ratio of treads and rises and began explaining to my two the what, when and whys of the project, so they could visualize the progress as they went along. Herbert, Bob and Jim each worked assiduously cutting and hammering. One section was ready to be fitted to the porch, but that set of steps leaned precariously. Bess and I turned our chairs to face the lake, so our dear ones would not see up quietly chuckling. Not being quitters, the three again rose to the challenge and before dark brought it to fruition. We had real steps by which to enter the door. The kids ran up and down them a few times to make sure they were like the ones at home. There were no stars or moon to keep us company that night. Being cowardly, we all went to bed on the floor with our raincoats on.

The next morning the fellows began clearing a large area of all tree limbs, branches, rocks, stones and other foreign items that were on the sand between two tall trees at the edge of the lake. This project naturally led into clearing the sunken logs from the waterfront area and soon the kids were swimming in a nice beach area. Herbert then took one of the long, thick ropes that had been tied around our possessions on the trailer, picked up a blown out tire that we had, and threaded the rope through it. Each fellow then tied an end onto a huge branch of a tree standing near the water and the tire was soon off the ground swinging enticingly into the kids. Their squeals and jumps of anticipation pleased the givers as they watched them sit on it together for their first ride. Soon they were pumping the swing out over the water and dropping off into the lake.

With that completed, my two carpenters decided they'd lace some logs together, secure the 4-foot by 6-foot platform by nailing an X underneath from leftover lumber and anchor it to an old stump about 45 feet from our ancient, stone point It made a marvelous combination of breakwater, dock and sunbathing spot."[155]

Another problem for cottage builders was to find a flat section on their leases in a landscape full of rocks and steep hills. Archie and his brother, E. O. Ewing, and Archie's son Dick ferried by canoe $800 worth of lumber to their cottage site in the early 1950s. The Ewing lot was on a fairly steep slope and the three had to excavate a slot cut into the hill to fit in the building. As their nephew Terry Hutchins shared in 2004:

"Archie was a forester, furniture maker and skilled carpenter and Uncle E. O. was a professional builder

[155] Recollections from Midge Rasey, 2004.

whose credits include Toronto's old Palace Pier as well as some apartment buildings. They knew what they were doing. As a result, the cottage hasn't shifted an inch in over 50 years. They picked a great location. The climb up the hill is worth it. It's like living in a tree house with spectacular sunset views."

Other leaseholders chose to buy logs from nearby lumbering companies and arranged for local workmen to build their cabins. For Esther Keyser, the 1938 construction of her cabin was more simplistic as she used the Park Ranger huts as her model. Labour rates at that time were $.75 an hour and 90 feet of pine clapboard cost $3.60. With a local workman's help, her one-room cabin with a front porch, two windows, and a door was built in no time. Inside was a small wood burning stove, a small table with two benches out of white pine, and a bed with a frame that she'd filled with fragrant, freshly cut balsam boughs. By the steps that led to the porch she dug a hole and arranged rocks covered with dirt to make a cool place for storing perishables.[156]

Popular and very talented builders in the late 1930s were the Lucasavitch brothers and Charlie Musclow.[157] As W. Gibson Gray wrote to Frank MacDougall in 1939:

"I have just written to Mr. Charles Musclow of Canoe Lake affirming an oral agreement made at Ahmek last week between Mr. Musclow and myself. I personally am very well satisfied with the type of work that Mr. Musclow does and I am informed by Mr. George Chubb that Mr. Musclow's proposition is quite reasonable and at the same time practical. Mr. Musclow proposes the construction of a spruce cabin on my lot with the dimensions to be 20-feet by 12-feet with a 6-foot screen verandah. The roofing will be exactly the same as that used on the new dining hall at Camp Ahmek (a shingle with small stone on tar) and the flooring for both the cabin and the verandah will be tongue and groove flooring. The three windows and the doorways will be obtained from Mr. Hutchison of Huntsville. Mr. Musclow informs me that if I pay the required price to the Park he is competent to cut the necessary logs and that he would like to do so in December or January. It is proposed that the logs be cut then and that they be peeled in March or April and that the building be finished by May 15th. I am unable to forward a sketch or blueprint to you because neither myself nor Mr. Musclow has one; suffice it to say that the cabin will be to all intents and purposes a replica of the cabin he is at present building at his own place. The cabin will be oiled immediately and I feel sure that it will be a credit to the Park."[158]

After the 1954 Park policy change that halted all further leaseholding in the Park, Park officials were much more diligent in keeping track of leaseholder building projects. To make the point, in the fall of 1954, a formal letter from DLF went to all leaseholders advising that:

"Any construction in the Park which does not have the written approval of the Park Superintendent is in violation of the terms of the lease and could result in the cancellation of the lease. Forthwith any improvements must be confined to the minimum necessary to provide comfortable occupancy for the unexpired portion of the term of the lease and one renewal."[159]

---

156. Esther Keyser, ***Paddling My Own Canoe,*** pg. 88.

157. For a detailed story of Charles Musclow and his adventures in Algonquin Park, see ***Gertrude Baskerville: The Lady of Algonquin Park, pgs. 14-23.***

158. Gray leasehold correspondence, 1939, Algonquin Park Museum Archives.

159. 1954 letter from the Park Superintendent issued to all leaseholders, Algonquin Park Museum Archives.

Park officials would inspect most properties every year and sometimes would discover the addition of other structures that had not been approved. Driving this was a need to legally clarify with each leaseholder that for the purposes of future repossession by the Crown or expiry of the lease, any improvements were deemed to have no value.

"Just recently our Provincial Land Tax Inspector noted that you have begun erection of a large summer cottage on the above-noted parcel, in addition to the small log cabin, which has been there for some time. Our files indicate that no permit was issued to you for this larger building. The necessity for such was pointed out to all leaseholders in our literature sent to them some time ago. It specifically stated that no buildings were to be erected before plans and descriptions had been approved by the DLF. Kindly let us have plans and details of your cottage as soon as possible so that we may give you our letter stating that you will not be allowed compensation for this when your lease eventually expires or when you might enter into negotiations with the Department of Public Works for acquisition of improvements on your parcel."[160]

Lease Transfer and Other Rules

A leaseholder could also get in deep trouble with DLF officials by cutting down trees without permission, as Kate Hart found out in 1928 when she wanted a verandah around her newly built cottage on Cache Lake. The contractor she hired cut down several large pine trees, to the consternation of Park Officials, who made her pay for the trees at a cost of 1.5 cents per linear foot for those under six inches in diameter and three cents per linear foot for those over six inches in diameter.[161] Generally however, Park officials were pretty accommodating when it came to building, as Reverend Charles Zorbaugh discovered on Rock Lake in 1933 when his best-laid plans ran into trouble:

"No doubt you will remember that I engaged Jim Hyland last fall to put up a log cabin for me. As it turned out Jim was unable to do the job so his son Rory undertook it. Perhaps you have heard what sort of a job he did. He must have been drunk all the time. It is absolutely impossible to describe to you the miserable product of his efforts. In the first place, there is no foundation. The bottom logs are already slipping. He evidently picked up odds and ends of logs to throw together and cover with a roof. There aren't two logs the same size in the structure. As a result there are six and even more inches between some of the logs, These places are filled in with odd pieces—just shoved in as chinkers. I don't believe that there are more than three full logs in the building that run the length or width of the building (20 feet by 12 feet). The structure is a conglomeration of odd sized pieces. It really defies description. As Ranger Bowers said, there isn't a real log in the whole thing. Of course I am greatly disappointed. The only thing I can do is have the cabin torn down and salvage what I can in the way of logs and lumber. I can save the doors, the lumber in the floor and roof and possibly part of the roofing. It will have to be rebuilt from the foundation up. Ranger Bowers is going to try and find a reliable man to do the job for me. It will mean building a new cabin and will require new logs as the present logs are not matched and even a magician couldn't build a cabin out of them.

---

160. Lease correspondence, 1956, Algonquin Park Museum Archives.
161. DLF correspondence, 1925, Algonquin Park Museum Archives.

I realize that to build a new cabin I will require more logs (counting those already used) than such a building would ordinarily require. I am wondering if under these unusual circumstances you would permit me to replace the cabin, charging me only for the logs used in the original structure. I am fully aware that this is a rather unusual request and would never suggest it under other circumstances. But the logs now standing are honestly worth nothing and I know that you would agree with me that they were picked up with no reference to their value.

If you think perhaps I am exaggerating I wish you would call Ranger Bowers on the phone and ask him what he thinks about it. Of course I realize fully that this whole affair is my own tough luck and that you may consider my request unreasonable. If so please do not hesitate for a moment to say so. I think that you can see my end of it however. The cabin has to be torn down. Additional logs will have to be found. New materials will have to be purchased and labour incurred to erect the cabin. In other words practically all that I have sunk in it so far is just so much throwaway. Quite naturally I am not anxious to pay for twice as many logs as I actually use. But if the present logs were good, and only the workmanship bad, I wouldn't make this suggestion. Since the logs are not good, most of them cannot be used in erecting the new cabin. I assure you that if you see fit to grant this request it will be greatly appreciated."[162]

Sometimes individuals got carried away with their requests to Park officials for exceptions to the regulations. In the early 1950s, residents often would travel from Radiant to the interior to fish by riding on the logging company trucks operating in that area. Later, when the logging firms left the area, they asked if they could ship in a jeep by rail and leave it stationed there permanently for use over the logging road. Needless to say, this arrangement was not approved by the DLF. In fact, Park officials advised that they would insist that lumber companies fire any men caught even taking a fishing rod on one of their trucks.[163]

Another key element of the 1954 Park policy change was that except in the case of transfer to a spouse, son, or daughter, a lease first had to be offered for sale to the Crown before it could be sold. Upon inspection, if the property was deemed to be of little or no value to the Crown, the seller was free to sell the property and the Crown would transfer the lease to the new property owners. If the Crown desired to acquire the parcel, a request to purchase was submitted to the Ontario Parks Integration Board. Upon approval, Public Works would undertake negotiations with the seller and purchase the property at an agreed-upon price. In this way, over the course of the next 30 years the Crown was able to reacquire over 100 leases. Along with three leases that expired, and weren't renewed and one expropriation, the number of family leases had dropped to just over 300 by the mid-1980s.[164]

But whatever the reason, once a lease was terminated, leaseholders had one year in which to remove all improvements from the leased property. If they choose not to remove the improvements, they reverted back

162. Zorbaugh leasehold correspondence, 1933, Algonquin Park Museum Archives.
163. Mudge leasehold correspondence 1953, Algonquin Park Museum Archives.
164. The only known expropriation was of the Webb cottages on Canoe Lake to make way for the Portage Store staff cabins in 1967. However according to both official and unofficial correspondence, there was considerable pressure applied to get some of the leaseholders to voluntarily sell their leases especially on Smoke Lake to enlarge the Smoke Lake Landing parking lot and at the east beach on Lake of Two Rivers.

to the Crown. The cabins plus any remaining contents were then dismantled and usually burned. Beautiful stone fireplaces were left standing as reminders long after the cabin sites were reclaimed by the forest. Most of these fireplaces are still standing today on these abandoned lease sites and are a constant reminder of what was widely perceived by many in the community as a brutal way to return the sites to their natural state. It was one thing to dismantle or burn abandoned shacks, but quite another to destroy perfectly beautiful log cabins such as those of Gillender and Krantz, the Farleys, the Colsons, the Webbs, and the Cousineaus on Canoe Lake. In the case of the Herr lease on Cache Lake, the Park Rangers:

> *"Dragged the cabin down onto the ice and set fire to it. Eventually it opened a hole in the ice and the whole thing fell through and the ice crept back leaving a little ring of carbon where the edge of the remaining ice touched the burning cabin."*[165]

Occasionally some cottages were also assessed for their historical and cultural value. The official position was that if a cottage possessed historical qualities, then Park officials would seriously consider preserving the structure for its historical interpretation.[166] However, the definition of historical and cultural value wasn't clear. Very few old log cabins, even if in good shape, were considered to be historical structures worth preserving. The only known exceptions were the Recreation Hall on Cache Lake that was maintained by the Cache Lake Leaseholders Association and the Turtle Club on Lake Traverse. Two that were the most painful and heartbreaking for leaseholders was the destruction of the Booth/Fleck/Barclay Estate on Rock Lake in 1955 and of Nominigan on Smoke Lake in 1977. In the case of Nominigan on Smoke Lake, the parcel was one of the first leases to expire under the 1954 regulations. As was previously mentioned, an attempt was made to preserve the main house, its logs dismantled and transported out of the Park but it was never rebuilt. The Booth/Fleck Estate (700 patented acres on the east shore of Rock Lake) built by A. W. Fleck, J. R. Booth's second-in-command who had married his daughter Helen Gertrude, was acquired in 1935 by Fleck's great-grandchildren Ian Barclay and Joan Barclay Drummond. Facing considerable expense with the upkeep of the great house and pressure from Park officials, who wanted all patent land to be returned, the Barclays reluctantly sold the property back to the Crown. There were suggestions that the estate might become a luxury resort and even other rumours that it would be converted a senior citizens retirement residence, but the Fire Marshall's office wasn't supportive of the idea.[167] Soon after, it was burned to the ground. As poignantly noted by Helen Beaton, who had arrived on Rock Lake in 1950:

> *"[We heard that] the beautiful Barclay summer residence with triple boat house/recreation room with its gorgeous huge fireplace all now emptied [was] slated to be burned that coming winter. [We] found an open window, crawled through and took a look inside. It was such a crime to burn the beautiful wood in the walls, the staircase, and the floor. We saw one small lonely footstool, which had been left behind; saved it from the torch, and have it still. After it was all over, some of the boathouse fireplace stones lying in the water were lovingly collected and safely embedded in our fireplace."*

---

165. Richard Eldridge and Orville Osborne, ***Cache Lake Reflections,*** 1995, pg. 61. It's important to remember that in those days, burning was the conventional way of getting rid of unwanted structures, versus today's environmentally friendly practice of dismantling and hauling to a landfill site.

166. For details on the history of the Barclay Estate, see ***Rock Lake Station*** by Gaye I. Clemson.

167. Camp Douglas correspondence, 1955, Algonquin Park Museum Archives.

So ended the Booth, Fleck and Barclay dynasty on Rock Lake. As Joan Drummond said in 2004 with tears in her eyes:

"So many marvelous memories. Amos the Indian teaching me how to paddle the birch bark canoe, walking on the gunnels, tipping it, righting it, and getting on board again. Learning of the edible plants and roots in the woods, the moss on the trees, telling you which way was north, the marvelous bass fishing in Gordon Lake. I became an expert frog catcher, and 'dew wormer,' never cringing about baiting and releasing fish, much to the delight of my brother, who would not touch either. (Shades of my grandmother!) It was from Billie that I learnt that a good spit on the bait always caught more fish too! I often took my small pup tent and went off on my explorations, down to the end of the lake by the huge rock cliff, or half way to Gordon Lake, where I discovered some Indian caves and drawings. Sitting on top of Booth Rock for hours waiting until the cloud formation was just right to take pictures with my Brownie box camera. The great baseball games we played at the Rock Lake Station beach and field area where we used cow dung as bases. The Sunday services at the Baulke house where we really 'rocked and rolled' under the tutelage of house Baulke, the deaconess, who played on the old pump and roller organ. But above all I remember the magnificent northern lights, the majesty of the huge pine trees, the blue of the lake, the haunting call of the loons and the mournful cry of the wolves. I still to this day get tears in my eyes when I remember my beloved Rock Lake, the nearest place to heaven that I will ever be."

The capital budgets for the repossession of leases by the Crown was not large and there were some disagreements internally as to how aggressive the Crown should be. As the District Forester noted in the mid-1960s:

"It appears to me that the outcome of this policy could result in a reduction in the number of parcels acquired through the simple expedience of the lessee asking a higher price than he expects to receive. The lessee is then free to arrange an assignment at his own price. It is most unfortunate expropriation proceedings are not possible in situations of this nature. There is every expectation the acquisition price will grow rather than decrease with time and it would seem it would be cheaper to acquire the property now if there is only some machinery to do so."[168]

However, the Chief of the Parks Branch replied:

"The Department of Public Works is prepared to pay the going rate in an area, but if the leaseholder is able to obtain a price beyond this amount, it would seem reasonable that he should be allowed to do so."[169]

This resulted in a number of leases being transferred either because the property was deemed to be of no use to the Crown (a campsite, for example) or was too expensive to repurchase. But by the 1970s, MNR officials took a much harder line:

"As I have opined before, if a leaseholder isn't interested in keeping his lease for himself or his family it should revert to the Crown. These leases provide an ideal hideout for various kinds of unsavory characters who create

168. Letter from the District Forester, 1966, Algonquin Park Museum Archives.
169. Ibid.

problems for me. I don't need any more."[170]

As indicated previously, the 1954 Park policy change allowed for the transfer of title to a spouse, son, or daughter, but the administrative requirements to actually do so were often very complex. For a number of leaseholders, the conventional practice at the time was to put the lease in the wife's name so as to protect it from loss should the business affairs of the husband run into trouble. Don't forget that this was an age when few women were knowledgeable of financial matters. A perfect example happened to one wife in the late 1940s:

> *"[My former husband] gave me to understand that the lease was put in my name when we chose this location in 1937 to protect him from any possible future creditors. He has repeatedly since that time told me that the lease is only a piece of paper saying I am responsible for the rental charge annually but that he himself is the owner of what stands on the land such as buildings, improvements and equipment. He also has said that our motorboat is exclusively his property. Is this true? He refuses to permit me to have use of the parcel for part of each summer and tells me I am not in a position to make demands whatsoever. Also, at one time, prior to [our separation], all monthly letters and correspondence were addressed to me. Suddenly all information regarding fishing, timber cutting and Park activity generally ceased. I have often wondered why, but presumed the Park had discontinued printing monthly letters for leaseholders. Has my former husband requested they be sent to his business office directly? I would be obliged to you if you would give me any information you have regarding this point. If it is in order would you prepare copies of all correspondence and information generally that has transpired since that year up to the present time so that I may have a better knowledge of all matters pertaining to this property."*[171]

Of course, the DLF didn't want to get in the middle of this marital disagreement and suggested that she consult a lawyer and get advice as to what her rights were in the situation.

If a leaseholder died, as is still true today, a number of forms had to be completed and submitted along with a copy of the deceased probated will. The worst possible situation was the death of a leaseholder without a will. Over the years there were many situations where widows were faced with what must have seemed like overwhelming difficulties in sorting out the change in title. Some continued to pay the annual rent and didn't worry about officially changing title until the time came for renewal of the lease. Then things could become very messy, especially if the leaseholder was a resident of the United States. In general, prior to 1954 most of these untidy situations were solved in a way that was acceptable to both parties. After 1954, the DLF became much less flexible and as a result a number of leaseholders lost their leases or gave up due to their inability to meet the Crown's requirements. In the case of one leaseholder on Tea Lake, who died without a will, it took over six years to sort out the issues around transferring title from the husband to his wife.

Even after extensive review of the lease records, there appears to be no solid evidence of concern about leaseholders and their role in the Park. How or why leaseholders later became such focus of concern in the

170. Letter from the District Forester, 1970, Algonquin Park Museum Archives. It is unclear as to what sorts of unsavoury characters were being referring to. The author speculates that by the early 1960s many of the children of original leaseholders had come of age, right in the middle of a time of extreme societal change. Unsavoury characters could well have referred to anyone with long hair who wore multicoloured shirts and bell-bottomed pants.

171. Correspondence from an Algonquin Park leaseholder, 1945, Algonquin Park Museum Archives.

1950s is unclear. It is true however that leaseholders as a group were generally not a quiet bunch. As will be discussed later, leaseholders were generally aware of the importance of the Park preservation and conservation movements. However, as is still sometimes true, legitimate expressions of concern about the Park environment by leaseholders were seen by some as merely self-serving. In 1938 for example, there was a rumour that a "short cut" road was being planned to run from Algonquin Park Station to Kearney through the western part of the Park. The idea of such a road caused great consternation among many leaseholders. As Edmund Kase on Brulé Lake wrote:

> *"The road in question would cut right through one of the most beautiful and unspoiled sections of the Park. It is very easy to spoil nature's handiwork and very difficult to locate areas as beautiful, as peaceful, as unspoiled as the western section of the Park. I think there must be other ways of meeting the legitimate demands of the fishing public and other means of providing work for the unemployed."*[172]

And as Cameron Hillmer wrote in 1950:

> *"On Source Lake I have a lease, which is just two lots away from the new road, and wharf which you constructed last summer. When the road was put in last summer, the bulldozers evidently unearthed large boulders, logs, limbs and particularly tree trunks, which are now strewn all around the parking area, beach and wharf. Consequently this area is quite unsightly and I am wondering if it would be possible for the department to tidy it up and at least cover up some of the stumps and boulders. The road that you have put in is certainly excellent as is also the small wharf and with a little cleaning up it will certainly be one of the nicest lakes in the district."*[173]

172. Kase leasehold correspondence, 1938, Algonquin Park Museum Archives.
173. Hillmer leasehold correspondence, 1950, Algonquin Park Museum Archives.

Cabins, Cabins, Cabins

(above) Powells on Canoe Lake 1998 Clemson Collection

Canoe Lake's Wilson Family Outside Their Cabin 1940s
Wischnewski Collection

Taylors on Rock Lake Taylor Collection

Hall, Browne, Jones and Lewis Cabin on Source Lake
2005 Dernoga Collection

Typical Cabin Interior King Collection

Mudge Camp on Radiant Lake APMA #3479

Bates Cottage Front Stoop on Opeongo c1930s
APMA #1425

Burtwell Cabin on Cache Lake c1930s APMA #4836

Strike Cabin on Manitou 1946 APMA #6638

King Lease on Cache Lake APMA #6465

Alger Cabin Site c1950s on Little Couchon Lake
Alger Collection

(all above) Building the Pepler Family Cabin (Tynhead) and Outhouse on Rock Lake Sharpe Collection

Miller Cabin on Lake Galeairy 2000 Miller Collection

Watson Cabin on Rock Lake Greer Collection

Rouse House on Whitefish Lake c1940s Greer Collection

Baulke Cabin in Winter Greer Collection

Taylor Cottage 1921 Greer Collection

Shawna lodge c1910 Taylor Collection

Merritt Chalet Camp Greer Collection

MacBeth Cabin on Rock Lake c1940s
Hugerman Collection

All photos this page: MacKay Collection

(left)
Relaxing in Front of Garnhams
(L to R) Grace Jull, Agnes Humber, Doreen Grant 1960)

MacKay "Big Cottage" 1950 Lake of Two Rivers

(left) Jim MacKay Cottage c1950s

MacKay Cottage Interior 1980 (Dismantled in Late 1980's When Lease Expired)

Taylor Clemson Waving from MacMurchy Cabin Deck on Canoe Lake 1998
Clemson Collection

Winans/Burnett Cabin on Cache Lake Burnett Collection

Left: Cache Lake Recreation Hall
1937 APMA #3337

Eady Cabin on Rock Lake
Taylor Collection

Merrydew now Manning Cabin 1998 (originally built c1910s)
Clemson Collection

Armstrong-Whithey Cabin on Canoe Lake Clemson Collection

Jeffery/Hagerman Cabin 1970 on Rock Lake Hagerman Collection

Matthews Homestead on Canoe Lake c1950s Clemson Collection

Lloyst Cabin on Canoe Lake c1940s now gone

Loudon Cabin Lake of Two Rivers
Loudon Collection

Chapter 4

Supporting Multiple Use In a Natural Environment Park

I am reading a series of briefs from the various leaseholder associations and come across one written by the Smoke Lake Leaseholders Association in 1966. The words jump right off of the page. I am shocked to realize that even though nearly 40 years have passed since these notes were taken, little has changed. The notes read:

> *"The question is essentially of reconciling the objectives of maintaining an area of unspoiled wilderness, and of providing recreational facilities for a great number of vacationers. On one side are those in favour of complete wilderness, and on the other, those desiring more facilities for highway travelers, but the leaseholders find themselves caught between the two."*[174]

This struggle has still not been put to rest even after all these years. For example, in the summer of 2004, fireworks erupted in the Toronto Star newspaper as a result of an opinion piece written by one of the co-directors of the Peaceful Parks Coalition. The intent of the piece was to raise concerns about the use of RVs in public campgrounds, the implication being that Ontario Parks, especially Algonquin, should be banning such vehicles completely, not accommodating them. The author's concern was that sleeping in tents, cooking on campfires, sitting at picnic tables and making do with only the bare essentials was no longer part of the Ontario Parks camping experience.[175] *In the summer of 2005 the CPAWS-Wildlands League, the Ontario Chapter of the Canadian Parks and Wilderness Society, expressed concern (also in the Toronto Star) lamented the fact that there were more logging roads than canoe routes in the Park and asked Premier Dalton McGuinty to review the practice of logging in the Park and develop a plan to phase it out.*[176]

---

174. Smoke Lake Leaseholders Association brief, 1966 pg. 1.
175. Opinion piece by Anna Maria Valastro, Co-Director, Peaceful Parks Coalition in the Toronto Star newspaper August 2004
176. Toronto Star newspaper article by Janet Sumner Executive Director of ***CPAWS***-Wildlands League, the Ontario Chapter of the Canadian Parks and Wilderness Society ***"Algonquin No Place For Logging"*** August 2005

I decide that its time to visit my part time summer neighbours John and Sandy Churchill. John's uncle Don MacMurchy, was one of the founding fathers of the Algonquin Park Residents Association (APRA). The MacMurchy lease is just across the narrows and is a local landmark because swimming across to their dock was and is a 'right of passage' for all Clemson children and visitors. The Churchills and MacMurchys share the same great grandparents with the nearby Matthews clan who reside just a ways up the west shore of the lake. My memories of the MacMurchy family are fond as their children were about the same age as my two brothers. Unlike our dock, the MacMurchy lease gets the morning sun and has a wonderful protected cove with a small sandy beach facing northward - though when a strong wind hits in late summer or fall, it can be bitterly cold. As children, we would often paddle over and spend the morning at their place and then return to ours in the afternoon when the sun was overhead. Lunch would be spent at whomever's mom suggested the most appealing menu.

Unfortunately Donald MacMurchy and his wonderful wife Marylou, died in the 1980's at far too young an age. I'm hoping that his nephew John Churchill will be able to give me some insight into the role that his uncle played during one of the Park's most turbulent times. As I paddle over, in what turns out to be quite rough water, I recall an event that I'd totally forgotten. I was about 12 years old I think. Don and several of his Matthews cousins were hauling over large empty oil drums on a raft of some sort. I can't recall where the raft came from nor what the oil drums were fore – though I did find a rusted one out behind our place and believe that at one time they were used to incinerate our garbage. There was a very strong north wind with whitecaps of at least 2 feet. As the group ventured past our dock the water suddenly built up along the front of the raft. Within a few seconds the bow of the raft disappeared under the waves and the oil drums rolled off the front into the water and sank like stones.

I approach the MacMurchy dock and quickly haul up my canoe as John and his wife Sandy bound down the path to meet me with a cup of coffee in hand. Sandy is a science and geography teacher and has spent the last few summers at Taylor Statten Camps as the resident ecology staff member. John is a large animal veterinarian and has from time to time used his skills to help with lame, sick or injured horses at nearby Camp Ahmek. Their dock is the perfect spot, to share a cup of coffee and soak up the morning sun. I explain my mission and am quickly told that, in his city life, MacMurchy was a human resources manager for one of Canada's big oil companies. Hard working and quiet, he had the reputation of being a great mediator. This it turns out was an important skill in the early days of the Algonquin Park Residents Association (APRA). Each lake had its own perspective and opinions, so his intuitive ability to integrate many conflicting viewpoints and keep the group marching towards the same goals was invaluable.

John jumps up to refill our coffee cups and returns with a blue booklet that I've never seen before. The title on it reads; "Algonquin Park – A Park for People and the accompanying photograph was a shot taken from this very spot. The booklet is in fact a report and set of recommendations presented to the Minister of Natural Resources in late 1969 by APRA officers Don MacMurchy (President, from Canoe Lake), Dr. Iain MacKay (Vice President, from Lake of Two Rivers), D.G. Matthews (Treasurer, from Canoe Lake) and (Orville Osborne (Secretary, from Cache Lake). The contents of the report were the work of a team of residents who together represented over 1,000 years of association with and knowledge of the Park and echoed what was spoken at an APRA meeting nearly 20 years later:

"Perceptions of the Park", the APRA president at the time said, "reside on a continuum. On the extreme

right are those who want to capitalize on the land for immediate profit, and on the extreme left are the protectionists who would put a fence around the Park and only occasionally let the general public peer in. Leaseholders, play an important role in helping balance between these two extremes. We try to be a group of reasonable people who use and contribute to the Park in a positive way. We know it more intimately that probably any other group, and have done so for over 100 years."[177]

I head back across the lake anxious to delve into this new discovery of our community's past and its contribution to Park development.

The Impact of Logging on Multiple Use

In 1967, the then DLF Minister Rene Brunelle announced a new classification system for Ontario's provincial parks. The idea was that each park would be classified as either a Primitive, Wild River, Natural Environment, Recreation, or Nature Reserve park. Algonquin Park, an area of outstanding scenic, natural, and historic significance was to be classified along with Quetico, Killbear, and Pinery Parks as a Natural Environment Park, and was to be set aside for recreation and education.[178] Commercial logging would be allowed to continue in Algonquin Park, but recreation would be recognized as the dominant use. Within each Natural Environment Park there would be five zones to be used for planning, development and management purposes namely primitive, natural, historic, multiple-use and recreation. Long-range plans would be developed for each Park so that its development and management would be in harmony with the purpose of the park class to which it belonged.[179] After a preliminary discussion document was released in 1968 to extensive comment and suggestions, the Algonquin Park Master Plan was approved in 1974 with a wide range of new policies. Most were very positively received and supported by leaseholders. However, the day-to-day challenges of leaseholding continued to involve striking a balance between three competing influences—logging, car camping and day visitors.

One of the issues that the Park summer residents had to manage in the early years of their Park experience was the complex and sometimes tenuous relationship with loggers. Though cognizant of the need for effective forest management and logging's economic value to the local communities, there was from time to time, unease on the part of leaseholders about the actions and impacts of loggers in the Park. Though by the late 1930s logging camps were no longer present in most of the areas where there were leasehold communities, they still were a nearby presence. The most troublesome issue early on was the logging camps' perceived indifference to the impact on cottage property of constantly changing of water levels in the lakes. Rock and Whitefish Lake and Lake of Two Rivers residents would often find in the spring that their docks or shorelines had been substantially damaged by excessively high water that was being used to manage the spring log drives

177. Recollections from Don Lloyd, the then APRA President in a 2003 speech.
178. Gerald Killan, ***Protected Places: A History of Ontario's Provincial Parks System,*** 1993, pg. 166.
179. Ibid, 1993, pg. 167.

down the Madawaska River. In the spring of 1940, for example, William Pretty came to his cottage on Rock Lake only to discover that his diving board had been entirely swept away, and several logs of his protective breakwater had been wrenched out of place. He wondered as he wrote that year:

"I am positive that the break up of the ice did not cause this for it was for this purpose that the break-water was built and has withstood the annual break up for the last six or seven years. I wonder if the lumber company has driven logs through the area and caused the damage."[180]

Another year, on Rock Lake, a local lumber company allowed its pigs (used for food in the winter) to run wild in the woods. As Reverend Zorbaugh wrote to the Park Superintendent:

"I am writing to make a complaint to you concerning the nuisance to which we were subjected at Indian Clearing on Rock Lake last summer, and which was continuing to disturb us and threaten damage to our property when the boys came away the middle of September. I refer to the drove of pigs, large and small about 20 in number, running at large through the woods [belonging to a local lumber company]. These pigs were an infernal nuisance to us while we were in camp, and stayed in our neighbourhood in spite of our best efforts to drive them off. With their rooting they can tear up a yard and leave it looking like a battlefield of Flanders. We have a root-house we constructed with vast labor and pains, and this is likely to be torn down in ruins by these confounded pigs while we are away. If the company wants to keep pigs, let them keep them in a pen and not in our clearing. Will you kindly let me know what relief and protection lies in your power to give us under these circumstances."[181]

Occasionally mistakes would be made. In one situation, a lumber company cut down two trees at the back of one leaseholder's parcel on Cache Lake. Park officials insisted that the company clear up the resultant debris and also cut up any of the trees left as firewood and pile it for the leaseholder's use.[182] On another occasion a lumber company, was going to build a road into Cache Lake, and intended to take out any large logs that they saw on nearby leases. However, the Park Superintendent insisted that the right of way for the road be changed to a bay west of the leaseholders. As he wrote to the leaseholder involved:

"I hope it won't make an eyesore. The company's intentions were all right, but the log makers in a few hours often get where they should not."[183]

On Lake of Two Rivers, Burt Moore, the proprietor of soon-to-be-built Killarney Lodge and a prolific letter writer, had an especially difficult time with a lumber company over the years. From timber cutting to water levels to noisy camp whistles, Moore saw it all and complained extensively. For example, though the company did have timber rights to the lake, their selective cutting took out over 280 trees cut on his lease, including 87 cedar, and 193 birch, spruce, pine and balsam. During the spring of 1935 and 1936, the company raised the level of the lake considerably, which caused significant flooding of the low-lying parcel upon which Moore was going to build Killarney Lodge. The first year, much of the wood that he had cleared the previous fall was lost

---

180. Pretty leasehold correspondence, 1940, Algonquin Park Museum Archives.
181. Zorbaugh leasehold correspondence, 1931, Algonquin Park Museum Archives.
182. DLF correspondence, 1937, Algonquin Park Museum Archives.
183. Ibid.

and considerable amounts of rubbish drifted onto the site. Even worse, by 1938 he had had to pull out over 150 stumps of trees that had been killed by high water in previous years. As Moore reported:

"I am not complaining any more, about what has been cut on the point that was done before I took my lease, but I cannot see why I have to be cleaning up damage that has been done each year over the high water nuisance that can be easily remedied and not cause a hardship to anybody."

In 1938, all leaseholders were advised that a lumber company had received a timber license to cut hardwood in Peck and Livingstone Townships. Needless to say, leaseholders were alarmed and concerned about the impact. As Mrs. Hamilton from Tea Lake wrote at the time:

"We are anxious to know how this will affect our place. Will the lumber company cut all the decent sized trees on our lot? What steps are being taken to protect the cottages of leaseholder and the trees on our lots? It seems rather a shame that the beauty of the Park has to be marred by lumber operations."

She was advised that a 500-foot strip of land was being reserved along the shorelines of Smoke, Canoe, Bonita, and South Tea Lakes, and on 500 feet on each side of the highway so that both the scenic beauty of the lakes and the leases would be protected.[184] In 1939, the Wiltses on Smoke Lake noticed that logging operations had begun at the south end of the lake and expressed concern to the DLF about the impact of these logging operations. A Park Ranger inspected the vicinity and indicated:

"No clearing [of trees] will be made on the point [near the Wiltse lease], nor will there be a road or skid way near there. The logging company however will have a road leading onto the lake from the bay north of this parcel and there maybe a skid way cleared either in the bay to the north or in the bay to the south. With the reserve area around the lake, there will be no cutting of trees on the point."[185]

The next year, the Wiltses wrote again to advise the DLF that Smoke Creek had been blocked with logs for six days and they had been marooned at their lease.[186]

In 1925, George Jamieson, one of the owners of Jamieson Brothers Lumber Company, built a sawmill on Joe Lake about half-mile east of the railway station on the north side of the track. It wasn't until the company had over 10,000 logs boomed in front of the mill one fall (with no intention of sawing them up until spring) and began talking about building a dam at the foot of Baby Joe Lake that realization hit that perhaps the DLF "would need to regulate the operations of the mill more closely."[187]

On Canoe Lake, lumbering had been revived in 1926 with the arrival of the Canoe Lake Lumber Company, which had taken over the Gilmour lumbering limits and built a sawmill at Potter Creek to try to make a go of cutting hardwood. Though there are some pictures of it, it is hard to fathom today that such a large building actually existed. The site is now covered with dense scrub pine trees that totally mask the two-story abandoned

---

184. Hamilton leasehold correspondence, 1938, Algonquin Park Museum Archives.
185. Wiltse leasehold correspondence, 1939, Algonquin Park Museum Archives.
186. Wiltse leasehold correspondence, 1940, Algonquin Park Museum Archives.
187. Joe Lake leasehold correspondence, 1925, Algonquin Park Museum Archives.

building from the shore. All that is visible near the shoreline is a giant concrete circle, which was the base of the sawdust burner. Loggers cut logs in Smoke Lake area all winter and in the spring towed the logs up from Smoke Lake to the sawmill in 36-foot-long cribs made of cedar logs. They used a 50-foot tugboat powered by a 40-horsepower single-cylinder steam engine that was fueled by slabs from the mill. The log booms were anchored from the Mowat Lodge waterfront all the way up to mill site on Potter Creek.[188]

These efforts weren't successful and the site was abandoned after a few years until 1939, when Joe Omanique bought the rights and assumed operations. Omanique built a road extension out to Highway 60 and a trestle bridge across Potter Creek. In spring, after the ice went out, the Omanique Lumber Company would release into Smoke and Tea Lakes logs that had been cut during the winter and piled down at the western end of South Tea Lake and on Smoke Lake. The loggers would run them down Smoke Creek, ferry them with barges across the end of South Tea Lake, up Bonita Narrows and Canoe Lake to the mill. The loggers' bunkhouse and cook shack were on a barge, and they used to tie it up to the low rock outcropping on Smoke Creek, just up stream from the bridge. There used to be incredible logjams, especially on the shore where the Tea Lake campgrounds are now.[189]

The Impact of Car Campers at Public Campgrounds on Multiple Use

Early on it became apparent that campgrounds and leaseholders were not a good mix, so efforts were made to locate Park campgrounds in areas where there weren't cottage leases or as was the case at Lake of Two Rivers and Rock Lake, acquire those that were in the immediate vicinity. On Rock Lake the Baulke cottages, on the south end of Rock Lake Campground No. 1, were repurchased by the DLF as part of the Barclay Estate buy-back, and taken down to accomodate what would become Rock Lake Campground No. 2 in the 1950s. All of the buildings on the Rock Lake Station site except for the Cottage known as "Old Shawna" on William McCourt's lease had been acquired from the Canadian National Railway, removed after the railway line was shut down and made way for Rock Lake Campground No. 1. On the north end of Rock Lake Campground No. 1, former Park Ranger Eady's cabin and the Stringer cabin down by the boat landing were repurchased and the land incorporated into the campground facilities. In 1987 after the lease expired, McCourt's "Old Shawna" cottage, the last remaining hold out of the former Rock Lake Station, was reacquired and removed. All that is left are the remains of Mrs. McCourt's rose and lilac bushes gone wild.

On Lake of Two Rivers in the 1960s a new amphitheatre and additional day use facilities were built to cope with tremendous increase in Park use during that time. There were a number of leases along the old cottage access road and north of the beach at the east end of the lake. As part of this development effort, a number of these leases were approved for purchase by the Ontario Parks Integration Board. As one leaseholder recalls:

> *"My mother recalled someone coming around to photograph the cottages at our end of the lake in the summer*

---

188. Gaye I. Clemson, ***Canoe Lake Chronicles,*** 2001, pg. 27.
189. Gaye I. Clemson, ***Gertrude Baskerville: The Lady of Algonquin Park,*** 2001, pg. 21.

of 1968. She said we were not interested in selling and would not let him photograph inside."[190]

Internal memorandums from the DLF, found in the Park museum archives decades later, discussed the situation:

> *"This property is one of those approved for purchase and was to be acquired along with other leases on Lake of Two Rivers to permit development of additional day use facilities. The leaseholder is very emphatic that he will not sell. The lease contains a 21-year renewal clause, which may complicate canceling same. This cottage is at the north end of the east shore of the lake and the shoreline there is quite rocky and unsuitable for bathing. I suggest we leave this cottage until the noise of nearby bathers drives him into our waiting arms."*[191]

Only two cottages were able to resist the waiting arms. The rest were repurchased by the Crown and removed by 1970.

The Impact of Day Visitors on Multiple Use

As early as 1939, the impact of campers, especially on interior campsites, was a concern to local residents, who began to play a stronger watchdog role in keeping an eye on what day visitors were doing. Over the years, both informally and formally (through the Canoe Lake and District Leaseholders Association, for example) they encouraged the Portage Store to install signs to show visitors how to sit and paddle properly in a canoe. They asked that canoe trippers be stopped from departing at late hours (after 4:30 p.m.) from the Portage Store. The unfortunate end result of late afternoon departures was, and still is today, that unskilled trippers who can't make the now mandatory two miles into the interior end up camping at portages, on abandoned lease or existing cottage sites. One year, to no avail, a suggestion was made that a large campsite be reserved up at Joe Lake Dam for campers who found themselves in this situation.[192]

This means that some leaseholders had and continue to have to deal from time to time with visits from a few who believe that cottage docks are great picnicking spots available for their use. A collection of empty beer cans and litter would betray these visits. On Canoe Lake it has over the years been an especially serious problem due to the behaviour of some of those renting canoes from the Portage Store for day visits. One year a leaseholder arrived on Canoe Lake and found a group using his shower. Another time, two women decided to stop and go topless sun bathing on the beach by the Camp Ahmek baseball diamond. They didn't notice that their prime sunning spot was in the middle of a boys' camp. Though less frequent now than in the past, every so often there was and is at least one group that decides that north-end leases, where leaseholders aren't home, are perfect camping spots. In the 1960s Popcorn Island on Canoe Lake (a frequent stopping point on the way up the lake) became known by many of the local kids as Pee Pot Island. Until a "Treasure Box" (a wooden outdoor open-air privy) was installed in 2003, the same problem would happen at the Tom Thomson Totem Pole and Cairn. Visitors would wander down to Hayhurst Point and use the Hayhurst family outhouse,

---

190. Lake of Two Rivers leasehold correspondence, 1968, Algonquin Park Museum Archives.
191. Ibid.
192. Canoe Lake and District Leaseholder Association minutes, 1960s.

thinking that it was a public facility. In the 1960s, vandalism increased to such a degree that leaseholders became very worried about key historic sites such as the Tom Thomsom Totem Pole and Cairn and the old Mowat Cemetery and undertook the regular maintenance of these sites.

Still today on Canoe Lake, those on the main route up the east side of the lake and at the entrance to Potter's Creek bear the brunt of the rescue work. All residents are well acquainted with basics of water canoe rescue techniques. In calm weather most visitors can eventually make their way up or down the lake given enough time. But when there is a strong north or west wind, or foul weather sets in, difficulties do occur. It's at times amusing to think of the number of wallets, cameras, car keys, house keys, and even diving equipment that now rests on the bottom of Canoe Lake. The Portage Store staff is also active in boating rescue and makes available canoe paddling instruction to the degree that they can.

Leaseholders' concern about the activities of naïve canoeists reflects not just knowledge of the potential dangers that can result from lack of proper canoeing, tripping and boating skills, but real concerns about visitor safety. Experiences on the lake have taught all leaseholders to be respectful of potential dangers. Dumping a canoe into cold water is no joke, especially in early spring or fall or in inclement weather. Getting lost on a trail or injured by wild animals due to food being left in inappropriate places (such as inside a tent) and accidents with axes or fire are frequent occurrences. Though wilderness rescue is much more easily accomplished today, the potential danger in the forest can't be minimized. Help could be hours or even days away, particularly if one was in the interior.[193] Most if not all leaseholders voluntarily (as would good citizens and community members anywhere) keep an eye out for the safety of the visitors around them. Algonquin Park is sometimes a novice's training ground. As the use of the Park increased after WWII, so did the frequency of these events. A few leaseholders have logged these rescue activities:

- Canoeists approached the Powells on Canoe Lake at dusk asking if their site was a campsite. It became apparent that they spoke limited English, had no car to return to, not much food and little camping skill. The Powells took them in for the night and sent them on their way in the morning.
- The MacKays once paddled out in their canoe on Lake of Two Rivers to rescue two young men whose canoe had capsized. They were able to pull the young men out and no doubt saved their lives. At least that was how one of the men described it years later when he met Mr. MacKay at a medical convention and informed him that it was his actions that had inspired him to become a physician himself.
- The Allins noticed a Portage Store canoe with two adults and one small child off the north end of Windy Isle on Canoe Lake on a day when there were very high winds and a great deal of rain and lightning. They were obviously struggling with the wind and were having trouble. The Allins coaxed them off the lake and saved them as lightning struck a few minutes later.
- The Thompsons found two young men camping overnight on the old Gale cottage site on Canoe Lake. Investigation the next day discovered that they had set a fire on top of an old pine root, which was still smoldering. Garbage had been left all around. They put out the fire and tidied up the site.

---

193. Even today it continues to be frightening to watch those who naively walk into dangerous situations without any idea of the risks they assume.

- The Campbells heard someone yelling late one night. They investigated and found a single canoeist trying to make his way up Canoe Lake towards Joe Lake. A strong wind was coming down from the north and he wasn't making much progress. They towed him up the bay and into Potter Creek. He was cold, frightened, and thankful.
- And the time a French couple stopped to ask the Nelsons near Whiskey Jack Creek on Canoe Lake for directions. All they had with them for several days in the woods was a baguette, a round of salami, and a bottle of wine. They were expecting to find boulangeries and hostels along the route, as was apparently the tradition in the south of France.

By 1947, the situation was so bad that J. R. Dymond, a resident of Smoke Lake and head of the Department of Zoology at the University of Toronto, and an initiator of the Park's first nature interpretive program was compelled to bring a number of key issues to the attention of his friend, Frank MacDougall, the then Deputy Minister of the Department of Lands and Forests (DLF).

First and foremost was Dymond's perception that visitors had little understanding of the "reasons for and functions of a provincial park." He suggested that the DLF should "publish a booklet on its provincial parks setting forth the functions of parks and describing the features of each." He also felt that the DLF needed a better way to inform the public as to appropriate behaviour in the Park. He suggested that display signs be posted throughout the Park informing campers that campsites needed to be kept tidy and sanitary, that cans and garbage needed to be buried, that rubbish shouldn't been thrown in the water, and how critical it was that campers be sure that their fires were out. He suggested that containers for waste paper and similar refuse be provided at parking places and public docks and that "steps should be taken to forestall possible dangerous sanitary conditions with the increased number of persons using the Park."[194] Though his concerns were acknowledged, solving these problems wasn't so easy and many options were tried including encouraging campers and cottagers to burn or bury their garbage and asking interior canoe trippers to haul their garbage out from the interior. However it wasn't until the mid-1970s after the first Algonquin Park Master Plan was approved that major progress was made. The total tin and bottle ban had a major impact, as did limits on the size of camping parties. Later a campsite reservation system reduced the congestion on many lakes.

Drownings on Algonquin Park lakes in the early years were rare, but they did happen. One unfortunate incident occurred on Rain Lake in 1939. Though the lake that day was perfectly calm, a group of fisherman dumped their canoe. Luckily, their guide, Delmore Hawke, was a quick thinker and "performed heroic and courageous service that was later brought to the attention of the Royal Life Saving Society."[195] At the Portage Store there were two near-drowning incidents in 1960 involving non-swimming trippers who were not wearing life preservers. Luckily for those involved, local leaseholders came to the rescue. To no avail, requests were made by the Canoe Lake and District Leaseholders Association to the Ministry and Portage Store Management asking that "non-swimmers be required to wear life preservers if venturing out in canoes."[196]

---

194. Letter to Frank McDougall from J. R. Dymond, 1947, Ontario Archives, Toronto.
195. MacCaulay leasehold correspondence, 1939, Algonquin Park Museum Archives.
196. Canoe Lake and District Leaseholders Association Minutes in 1960s.

Finally, in 1963, a visitor did drown, which jolted the Department into action. Two non-swimming young boys without life jackets overturned their canoe just off of the docks at the Portage Store on Canoe Lake. A leaseholder jumped in the water to save them. He was able to rescue one. The other he found in only 10 feet of water, but it was too late. The doctor from Taylor Statten Camp was summoned and worked on the boy for nearly an hour to no avail. After reviewing the accident, the DLF decided to appoint a Canoe Safety Officer "whose duty will be to check out each canoe going through this point for the various safety precautions good canoeists generally observe."[197] However, as the DLF went on to explain:

"It is not possible for us under present legislation to enforce the wearing of life jackets and the observance of other safety measures, so that our efforts for the time being will tend to be educational. In the final analysis this approach will probably prove the most fruitful in any case. This is the first time we have hired a Canoe Safety Officer and we look on this as an experiment for the balance of the summer that remains."[198]

The most recent drowning was on Lake Opeongo in the summer of 2004. Unfortunately, the victim met the general profile of those who drown in Ontario. Two young men in their early 20s, non-swimmers and not wearing life jackets, got into a canoe and it flipped not 20 feet away from the dock. Luckily, Kit Howe, an employee of Opeongo Outfitters and son of a Whitefish Lake leaseholder, kept his head and was able to rescue one of the canoe's occupants. Alas, the second one drowned.

With increased use of the Park, there was also an increase in the number of accidents on or about the lake. The leaseholders became water rescue personnel and the first line of defense for most emergency situations. The number of emergency rescues made to help those who dumped in bad weather, or because of their unfamiliarity with the proper loading and handling of canoes, is too numerous to count. Many leaseholders spend time providing directions to day paddlers and interior canoe trippers on how to paddle, sit in a canoe, and read a canoe-tripping map. Though every lake has its share of canoeists, the greatest number of problems are on Canoe Lake and Smoke Lake. This is due to the number of unskilled visitors and the size of the lake and strength and direction of the winds. As several residents reported:

"My father always befriended those confused-looking souls who turned up at the landing with the wrong or insufficient equipment. One of these was a family from Atlanta who appeared to have plenty of fishing gear but no blankets. Dad helped them to get packed in their boat, and offered to provide the missing items. They indeed turned up later as the evening chill descended, and a wonderful friendship started which included trips to Atlanta for all of us, and some 20 years later for my parents, a trip to East Berlin where the rescued camper had become an international opera star. Such are the lasting effects of Algonquin Park."[199]

As is still true today:

"We rescue at least two in a good year and in a bad year, dozens. In one season, there were so many [we would] get the boat out whenever we saw a canoe on the lake. One Labour Day Weekend in particular we

---

197. McMurtry leasehold correspondence, 1963, Algonquin Park Museum Archives.
198. Ibid.
199. Recollections from the Freeman family, 2003.

spent a whole day rescuing and transporting swamped canoeists until we ran out of gas."[200]

An incident on a May 24th Victoria Day weekend involved Duncan MacGregor, the father of writer and Globe and Mail columnist Roy MacGregor. The Beatons were outside working around their Rock Lake cabin when Helen looked onto the lake and saw a man in the water with his right arm slung over the side of the boat. Her husband Jack and son John dashed out in their boat, but they couldn't pull him out of the water. He had on a long down jacket and lumberjack boots. The water was frigid and he was so cold that he couldn't call for help. They pulled him alongside the boat to the shore and with one on each side of him, literally dragged him up to the cottage. Jack got him into dry clothes, gave him a shot of whisky and some soup and later delivered him back to the lumber camp all in one piece.[201]

But canoeing or boating accidents weren't the only kind of accidents. On Rock Lake one year, a floatplane took off from nearby Pen Lake and lost a propeller. The plane crashed into the lake and rolled over, but the three passengers, floating on seat cushions were rescued by local residents.[202] Another year, also on a May 24th weekend, leaseholders Joan and Lorne Somers pulled three people out of the lake who had dumped in their canoe. Unfortunately, one died, of hypothermia. Later the Somers were presented with OPP Commissioner Citations for their efforts.[203] Alas, not always were leaseholders or the Park Ranger able to get there in time. In one case, a canoe with a Boy Scout capsized when it got too close to a forestry plane that was taking off. One of the boys, unable to swim and not wearing a life jacket, instantly sank to the bottom of the lake.[204]

Another non-water incident involved a young Brad Steinberg and a friend. They had decided to go cross-country skiing along the Booth Rock Trail. Foolishly, they started out late in the day and when dusk started to fall, they decided to take a short cut back to the cottage. Alas they became disoriented and lost but luckily had matches as well as survival skills, and managed to build a fire. They made a bed of sorts under the roots of an upturned tree and spent a long, cold night huddled around their meager fire. In the morning, they made it back to the cottage and were able to thaw out. Aside from a little frostbite, both survived the ordeal unscathed and hopefully, wiser.[205]

---

200. Recollections from the Hutchins family.
201. Recollections from the Beaton family, 2003.
202. Recollections from the Eady family, 2004.
203. Recollections from the Beaton family, 2003.
204. Recollections from the Eady family, 2004.
205. Recollections from the Steinberg family, 2004.

Multiple-Use

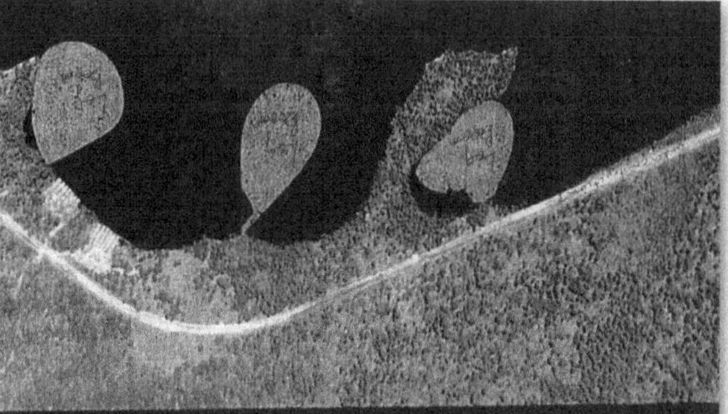

Aerial of Log Booms, Lake of Two Rivers MacKay Collection

MacRae Mill Log-Dump on the Ice at Lake of Two Rivers 1926
APMA #1295

Canoe Lake Log Boom 1942 APMA #1522

(left) McRae Sawmill on Lake of Two Rivers c1930s
APMA #238

Staniforth Sawmill on Kioshkokwi Lake c1960s Freedeen Collection

Rose Thomas Standing on the Log Chute Between Carl Wilson and Couchon Lakes 1932 APMA #14

Booth Depot Buildings at Kiosk 1923 APMA #34

Omanique Sawmill on Potter Creek APMA #1272

Staniforth Sawmill with Log Awaiting Sawing c1950s

Typical Log Chute APMA #234

All other photos MacKay Collection

Lake of Two Rivers East Beach 1967

Renting a Canoe and Going for a Paddle c1970s Clemson Collection

Winter Fun at the MacKay Cottage c1950s

Heading out on a Canoe Trip MacKay and Son Niall 1957

Two Rivers Beach 1967 Before Cottages Were Removed

Rory (L) and Niall MacKay (R) c1950s Snowshoeing

Chapter 5

Creating a Sense of Community

It's now been five years since I began this quest, and my pile of stories has grown to be nearly two feet thick. Though limited now to about 300 families, the size and depth of the extended families is amazing. Some families (like mine) are relatively small, with only about 10 family members using the cottage over a particular summer. For other families, there are more than four generations of users, with in some cases four or five siblings. On Rock, Cache, Canoe, and Smoke Lakes, family groups number more than 50 people who all share the same lease. Scheduling who gets which weekend must be a nightmare. Given my market research background, I decide to make a little spreadsheet model to see if I can estimate with a reasonable degree of statistical validity the potential size of the Algonquin Park leasehold community. I'm shocked to discover that even with very conservative assumptions, the model indicates that the community could well be the size of a small town, somewhere between 8,000 and 10,000 members. If each family member visits for even just one weekend a summer, the number of visitor-days of use is enormous. I start to wonder about the culture of this community, which of course leads me right to Cache Lake. As the former home of Algonquin Park Station, Park Headquarters, the Highland Inn the two still-active girls' camps, and Bartlett Lodge, Cache Lake has a long community history that I decide to explore.

Very few residents on Cache Lake have either electricity or telephones, so arranging to visit takes a bit of work. This usually involves phoning either Bartlett Lodge, which one can see across the lake from the boat landing, or someone who lives nearby. They in turn paddle or motor over to the cabin of the person one wants to visit and advise as to what time one is expected. The host then drives over to the boat landing, with the unspoken understanding that plus or minus 10 minutes on either side of the appointed hour is perfectly acceptable.

As I wander around the area I notice a parallel row of red pine trees to my right and left heading off in the distance for several hundred feet. Closer inspection indicates the edges of a massive foundation long buried in needles and leaves. I'm told later that this is the remains of a retaining wall near the site of the former Highland Inn, which overlooked the lake and the railway line that ran parallel to the water's edge. Built in 1908 by the Grand Trunk Railway, the Highland Inn was modeled after the upscale tourist hotels of the Adirondacks. It was an immediate success and was open until 1956, when it was condemned, torn down and pine trees planted on the site. In its heyday, it was the social and business centre of the lake, flanked by the train station (Algonquin Park Station), the Algonquin Park Headquarters building, and various outbuildings, including the staff and railway workers quarters.

The first Cache Laker I meet is Peter Burnett. He's the third generation to live in a little cabin on what they call "Porcupine Point," near the portage that goes into Head Lake. His great aunt, Irene Winans, was a great friend of Fanny Case, who founded Northway Lodge in 1908. Irene was both a camper and on staff at Northway Lodge in its early days. In 1914, she decided to take out a lease with her sister Helen after seeing ads in the local Rochester newspapers. For the first few years, the Winans sisters camped on the site each summer. Every morning they would rise with the sun and take a morning constitutional (i.e. walk) along the Head Lake portage. Upon their return, they'd paddle across the bay and set up a breakfast picnic, as their site had no sun until the afternoon.

The Burnett cabin is composed of one room with a screened-in verandah that has been turned into a quasi bedroom/dining room space. This is about as close as one can get to sleeping under the stars while still having a wooden roof. The gentle breeze off the lake keeps the bugs at bay. In the corner is a beautiful straight-back chair that still looks as lovely as the day it was hand-made by Irene and Helen. On the dining room table are several photo albums that contain the history and memories of their time on the lake. Continuing this tradition, Peter's wife Theresa shows me her lovely photo of Cache Lake at sunrise that won a prize for Best Photograph in Cottage Life magazine's 2004 photography contest.

We spend several hours reminiscing, with me scribbling notes furiously. At one point, I head up the hill outside of their back door to use the outhouse and discover a storage cupboard built into the side of the hill of a type I have never seen before. It has a heavy wooden door with metal fittings. Inside, it's as cool as a cucumber, and was used to store perishables before iceboxes became fashionable. It has probably been embedded in this hillside for over 80 years and yet has been preserved by the family as a tribute to the lives and difficulties of their forebears in coming to Algonquin Park.

After a lovely visit, Peter drops me off at the southern end of Wabuno Island where I meet Susan and George Rabick. Susan is from the King clan. Her grandparents, Harry and Jessie King, first came to Algonquin Park in 1934 after buying the lease from a fellow from British Columbia who had settled there in 1913. Their cabin also has a story to tell. The outside looks like wood siding, but in fact it is made of tin. Inside one wall there is this huge window covered with signatures and notes of all shapes and sizes. It reminds one of a college yearbook with its memories of bountiful and joyful visits by extended family and friends. Above my head is a beam on which is recorded the yearly mouse catch in their live mouse cage. The King and Rabicks have been counting mice since the 1940s. I note with interest that according to their count, the peak population year for mice was 1978. In the kitchen there is a huge wood stove, now used infrequently, that dominates the room. It reminds one of how central kitchens can be to family and community life. It also turns out that Peggy Cameron King, wife of Harry and Jessie's son Hal was a prolific writer. During the 1950s and 1960s she wrote hundreds articles for various magazines, a minor play, poetry and two humorous books. Some of her articles were informational (about for example, the opening of the new Park museum on Found Lake in 1952 and the Park sponsored wolf howls program). Other articles shared the various experiences of her family. Most were very humorous and tackled such subjects as figuring out how to conquer the Coleman lamps, learning how to single a canoe and screening visiting her daughter's boyfriends. They were published in smaller magazines and Sunday newspaper supplements and from time to time one would make it into one of the national magazines. In addition, they both were avid Cache Lake story collectors and in 1993 they won the first Cache Lake Leaseholders Citizen Award in recognition of their 30-year effort in capturing the history and "going-on" on Cache Lake. I settle in once more to hear another perspective of the Algonquin Park community spirit.

Community Connections

Just about everyone who has a lease in Algonquin Park has a strong connection to someone or something there. Usually, at least in the early days, the man of the family had fished or camped there for years and thought it would be an ideal place for his young families to summer. As a resident of Source Lake shared:

> *"My parents spent their honeymoon on Cedar Lake at Kish Kaduk Lodge in 1936, coming in by train from North Bay. They fished the Nippissing, Petawawa and other streams around Cedar Lake. Later, as the family grew, they spent many years camping at Lake of Two Rivers in the 1940s. At about that time, my dad became the accountant and financial director for Ms. Margaret Hamilton who ran Camp Tanamakoon. From there they heard about leases on Source Lake, acquired one in 1948 and I have been there every year since."*[206]

For others, the connection was attending one of the many children's camps. Dr. Charlotte Horner of Coburg, Ontario, for example, who was the Assistant Medical Officer of Health for the Northumberland Durham Health Unit, had attended Camp Tanamakoon and had been the youngest camper there. Her father was an architect and had designed the original buildings at Camp Tanamakoon. He also designed her Smoke Lake cottage, which she built with the gratuity she received from the Ministry of Health for her work in the Canadian Air Force during WWII. It was the first cottage in the area to have very large windows all the way around.[207]

Most of the south end of Canoe Lake and a number of leases on Smoke Lake are populated by people with connections to Taylor Statten Camps. Al Gordon, for example, was the nature instructor at Camp Ahmek in 1945/46. At Upper Canada College, Gordon had gotten very interested in raptors and hawks and even learned to fly falcons. Through a friend he learned about Taylor Statten Camps and followed the friend to Ahmek as a staff member, taking with him a kestrel and a sharp-shinned hawk. At Camp Ahmek he met and was very influenced by Mark Robinson, a former Park Ranger who was then 84 years old at the time. Robinson walked

206. Recollections from the Forrester family, 2004.
207. Recollections from Kay Graham, 2004.

with a cane and slight limp and would tell stories for hours, sharing lots of wisdom and insight. He also met John O'Henley, Arthur and Bob Ortiz, and Alex Millar, who all went on to be artists and later took out leases near each other on Smoke Lake. The group, plus other artists from Ontario College of Art, including now well known wildlife portraitist Robert Bateman, would frequent Kootchie Bay on Smoke Lake to paint. They'd arrive from the Madawaska River to fish, have a feast on shore and then paddle back to Cache Lake. Gordon's interest in forest birds continued. He went on to study forestry and eventually become a process (i.e. descriptive) scientist. He spent many years studying plots of trees at the Swan Lake Research Facility.[208]

Gordon Davies was an artist from Toronto who sent his son Douglas to Camp Ahmek beginning in 1936. Douglas's love of the Park led to a job at the Ontario Fisheries Research lab at Lake Opeongo. In 1948, the family decided to build their own cabin on one of the islands on Cedar Lake. Douglas spent many a summer canoe tripping from Tea Lake to Opeongo to Cedar, and all around the Kiosk area. Over the years, he fought fires, did fish creel census, and studied the black flies and deer flies of the area. He spent many a Saturday evening square dancing and round dancing at Whitney and at Rock Lake, where Sandy Haggart played a mean fiddle. One year he commandeered an open gas car on the old railway and escorted Marg McRae (whose father owned the sawmill on Lake of Two Rivers) home to Lake of Two Rivers from Rock Lake at 3 a.m. with the morning mist making the tracks hardly visible.[209]

On Source Lake, Joe Almendinger and Gil Yager were close friends from the time they were toddlers in Buffalo, New York, and they attended Camp Pathfinder together. Gil went there as a camper and later as a counselor, and even met his wife Marie there when she was the camp nurse. Joe first attended Camp Pathfinder in 1934, and later taught arts and crafts and did some canoe tripping. When leases became available on Source Lake, both jumped at the opportunity. The cabin on Source Lake was just about the most important thing in their lives, spending almost every summer, all summer, up there.

Michael Budman and Don Green, who went on to found leather goods and clothing manufacturer Roots Canada, as well as the Cooper, Goldman, and Tator families on Smoke Lake were all campers and staff at Camp Tamakwa on Tea Lake in the 1950s and 1960s. On Cache Lake, many of the connections were to Northway Lodge. As Jane Dise Bowles of Cache Lake explains:

> *"Fanny Case was friends with Jean Pattison, the daughter of Dr. T. H. Pattison, who was a professor at Rochester Theological Seminary. It was Miss Case who first brought Jean to Cache Lake around 1907/08. At Northway Jean Pattison met Maria Dowd when they both were counselors around 1908. They took out the lease together and had a cabin built in 1911. Maria went on to marry Jean's brother Frank in 1913. Jean went on to receive a medical degree from Cornell in 1919 and even managed to spend a few summers as camp doctor in the 1920s. She was a practicing pediatrician in New York City until 1953 when she retired but managed to come to Algonquin Park for at least a few weeks every summer. Our lease has always been in a woman's name and the male spouse has had to adapt to the Algonquin Park life. My mother brought my father in 1939. I brought my fiancée in 1967 after he passed the test. My sister brought her husband in*

208. Recollections from Al Gordon 2003.
209. Recollections from Douglas Davies in a 1975 submission to the Algonquin Park Master Plan, Algonquin Park Museum Archives.

1967. My two nieces have brought their husbands. My two sons have brought their girlfriends these past two summers and are the first male leaseholders in over 90 years."

Close friends, relatives, and neighbours introduced others to Algonquin Park. Some leaseholders have been coming for years, such as the Becketts on Smoke Lake, who have been enjoying the Park for five generations. The Beckett matriarch, Margaret, had brought her sons to go canoe tripping in the Park while she stayed at the Highland Inn soon after it opened and later leased property and built a cabin on Smoke Lake. Her sons went on to take leases on both Smoke and Canoe Lakes. Beginning in the 1950s, the Becketts would invite the family of a customer or supplier to visit their cottage each summer. In this way perhaps a score of families were introduced to the Park, its programmes and its environment. Some of these families returned in later years to camp in the Park or took out leases on their own.[210]

The Hillmers and the Campbells lived a block apart in Oakville. As the Campbells from Source Lake explained:

"Mrs. Hillmer loved to entertain at Source Lake in her one-piece strapless floral bathing suits.[211] *One year she invited the Campbells and the rest was history. Cameron Hillmer went to Queen's University and William Campbell went to the University of Toronto so there was a fun and great rivalry both in Oakville and at the cottage. In fact, according to daughter Laird, the Campbell's first outhouse was called the 'Queen's Hotel!' The Campbells went on to introduce Source Lake to the Chisholms. Anne Chisholm and her brother Lionel went to Camp Wapomeo and Camp Ahmek from the time they were eight years old. When they were teenagers, their father wanted a cottage. Through the Campbells they heard about Source Lake and so since both children had a passion for Algonquin they decided on Source Lake."*[212]

Jimmie Keens first came to Cache Lake with his friend Aylie Blackburn to visit Kay Brown and her brother Brock. On their way across the lake, they put out a fishing line in a hole off Hall's Point and caught a huge trout that Jimmie wanted to mount and take home. Instead, Aylie, who wanted to impress Kay, who was visiting with Liz and Helen Hall, suggested that they eat it for supper, to which Jimmie reluctantly agreed. By the end of the evening, Jimmie had fallen in love with Liz Hall. Eventually they married, as did Aylie Blackburn and Kay Brown.[213]

Some of the most creative connections involved the Davis family on Source Lake. They were visiting a friend on Cache Lake, Nick Zona, and went into Huntsville to do errands. Harry Davis decided that he needed a haircut and while doing so his wife Mary went for a walk down the main street. She passed a real estate office and saw a photo of an island on Source Lake. She was intrigued, walked in, asked the price and signed the purchase papers right then and there. She then went back to find her husband to tell him that they were now proud owners of an island and a cabin on Source Lake.[214] Mildred Turner was up visiting friends on Cache Lake and decided to swim over to say hello to others she knew across the lake. In the course of the conversation they

---

210. Recollections from John Beckett, 2004.
211. Recollections from Laird Sanderson, 2004.
212. Recollections from the Saunderson/Campbell families, 2003.
213. Richard Eldridge and Orville Osborne, ***Cache Lake Reflections,*** 1995, pg. 23.
214. Recollections from the Davis family, 2004.

told her that they were interested in selling. She swam back, told her husband, and they immediately made an offer. While staying at Killarney Lodge in the early 1970s, Beverley and Dr. Gordon Louden had decided to go out for a paddle when they were asked by Killarney Lodge owners Paul and Nancy Beggrow if they would check in on Len Slade at his cottage. The Beggrows had received a call from Len's wife Lorna that he might be having a heart attack. The Loudens found the Slade cabin, Dr. Louden examined Len and determined that he had a heart arrhythmia not a heart attack. From that day on the Slades and the Loudens became best friends. Later when the Slades decided to give up their lease, the Loudens took over from them.[215]

Leasehold Social Activities

The leaders and trendsetters in cottage social activity were then and still are today found on Cache Lake. The first residents' picnic was held on Sunset Point in 1921 and later that year the Highland Inn hosted the first canoeing and swimming regatta, which has been a tradition ever since. Sometimes tug-of-war, axemanship demonstrations, and even gunwale bobbing were added to the mix. In the 1930s, the association began to sponsor sailboat races with a course that ran all around the lake. By the 1950s, the races were so popular that there were a series of cups for different types of boats, the Evans Cup for sloops, the Bond Cup for Prams, the Wood Cup for Sunfish, the Treasure Island Cup for Lasers and the Fanny Case Cup for Albacores. And there were prizes for various races, including the Ken Unger Cup for best mixed canoe 40 years and older, the Northway Lodge Cup for best mother and child team, the Madden cup for best father and child team, and the Arthur Soles cup for best grandparent and grandchild team. The tripping guides from the Northway Lodge raced for the Turner Cup, which began as a canoe race from Park Headquarters, then went around past Northway Lodge to the first trestle. Participants would then carry the canoe across the old railroad bed, would then put the canoe back in the water and paddle back to Park Headquarters. The swimming races at the regattas also had cups including the Reeder Cup, for those over 40 years of age, the Pigeon Cup for boys ages 11-14, the Pierce Cup for Ladies, the Burrows Cup for girls ages 11-14, the Beauprie Cup for boys under 10 years of age, and the Bancroft-Rich Cup for boys and girls ages 10 and under.

Though there are no specific records, "Float Night" apparently began around 1925 when a few revelers at Highland Inn decided to decorate a boat and entertain the guests from the water. This quickly became an annual event on the second Saturday in August at dusk. Events got under way with a "Sail Past," first in front of the Highland Inn, later in front of the parking lot and even later in front of the Superintendent's house. Like the other activities, cups were awarded, including the Rigby Cup for the Most Artistic, the Jessie Logan Cup for the best single canoe, the Farmer Trophy for the most original, and the Reburn Cup for the most topical. After the "sail past," all would meet in the recreation hall to hand out trophies and ribbons and candy for all of the various festivities. In the 1940s, Mary Pigeon and Mrs. McLean organized square dances every Friday evening during July and August with the Pierce family donating the piano in memory of their son Tommy. They charged $.50 and the events drew large crowds. Junior dances were also held weekly for young people on the lake.

---

215. Recollections from Beverley Louden, 2003.

But Cache Lake wasn't the only lake with social activities. On Smoke Lake was the Smoke Lake Naturalist Club. In 1936, J. R. Dymond, a biology professor at the University of Toronto and Director of Zoology at the Royal Ontario Museum, had taken out a lease at the top end of Smoke Lake. Within a few years his reputation as a wildlife expert became well known and Jessie Northway from Nominigan asked him in 1942 if he'd be willing to conduct educational nature hikes for local residents. This he agreed to do and an institution was born. According to resident Nancy Martin, whose father James Savage was a good friend of Dymond's and had worked at the Harkness Lab on Lake Opeongo testing the effect of DDT on birds in Algonquin Park:

> *"They'd pick different spots each year and often the leaseholders meeting would be held before or after the hike. Two to three days before each event, they would blaze a trail and mark 20 or so specimens for identification. They would tie a string to the specimen and a number. The cottagers and kids would arrive for the nature hike and like a treasure hunt were each given a small pencil and paper with which to write down what they thought each specimen was (plants and trees etc.) that were marked on the trail. Everyone brought a picnic lunch and then we would have the plants identified and a prize awarded (usually a chocolate bar) for the best score for the kids. It was a wonderful social event for all of the children and adults on the lake who participated."*[216]

Another centre of social activity in the 1940s was Rock Lake. In 1940, Stewart Eady was appointed the local Park Ranger and moved his family into one of the houses formerly owned by a railway employee near Rock Lake Station. Their home quickly became the centre of the Rock Lake community. Cottagers would gather for the weekly arrival of the meat wagon from Whitney. Eady's wife Beulah loved music and would organize dances held every Wednesday and Saturday evening during the summers, often at the Barclay boathouse. She would hire bands and fiddle players from Whitney and she would sometimes do the calling. These dances were great fun and attended by most of the locals.

Other great sources of entertainment were Canoe Lake's Wam Stringer Memorial Square Dance Orchestra and the "Band de Soleil" named after the popular suntan lotion. With Hugh Gibson on banjo, Ralph Muller on trombone, and Dan Gibson on the doublebass sousaphone, the trio could often be heard playing on one of the member's docks around the cocktail hour. Wam Stringer, a local jack-of-all-trades, whose father had been a Park Ranger, played the fiddle, and had an amazing gift for music. Most instruments he could pick up and play instantly. Other members of the orchestra were Dan Gibson, who played the accordion and sometimes the piano; another friend Angelo, who played the guitar and was a great square dance caller; and Adèle Gibson or Barbara Redfern, who would occasionally fill in as guest pianists. The group would play at square dances arranged at Taylor Statten Camps, Camp Tamakwa, Camp Arowhon, and Arowhon Pines Resort or at the Hotel Algonquin. If needed they would drag a piano that they borrowed from the Hotel Algonquin to each dance location.[217] Gibson still has that well worn piano, which he uses to compose classical music and play the occasional ragtime tune.

---

216. Recollections from Nancy Martin, 2003.

217. Today that old piano resides at the Gibson cabin and still works after having been rescued from the Hotel Algonquin demolition team in the late 1950s. Gibson family interview, 2001.

There were also many others with musical talent who would share their skills with nature upon occasion. Frances Adaskin, a professional soloist and later in life a music professor, would practice her scales at the end of her dock and loved to serenade the north end of Canoe Lake. On Cache Lake, professional musicians Aldoph Kodofsky and his wife Gwen arranged for her piano to be hauled up to the cabin by a crane attached to the top of the cliff above their cabin site. The piano is still there to this day. Robert Hamilton's daughter used to play the harp on Cache Lake on moonlit nights, and Iain MacKay had a set of bagpipes, which he'd play standing on the end of his dock. As his son Rory MacKay recalled:

> *"While at university my father learned to speak Gaelic, learned to play the bagpipes and kept an extensive tartan collection. The windows of the cottage are draped to this day with MacKay tartan curtains made by my mother after instructions regarding how to line up the pattern of the tartan from my father. In the afternoon or evening my father would play the bagpipes. Sometimes campers from the other end of the lake would sit in canoes off shore from our cottage to listen to the music. It did not take a full moon, as suggested by Roy McGregor in his book* **A Life In The Bush***, to get my father to play. My father was not the only piper in the family, for he had my brother and me both take lessons, and we each had our own stand of pipes. I can recall times when all three of us would be playing in unison, marching up and down the cottage living room."*

Another player of bagpipes was Bill Rutherford on Cache Lake. A former brigadier-general, he'd stand on his point and play his heart out. He knew only two or three tunes, but according to resident folklore, his music "drenched the lake like a mist."[218] Canoe Lake was also the home of the South Shore Yacht and Country Club, whose inaugural meeting in 1953 was complete with logo and plans for T-shirts and uniforms. The club's objective was to be a non-profit organization devoted to cultural activities on Canoe Lake. Membership fees were set at $9 to be initiated, and $5 per year thereafter. Though meetings were only held during the first few years of the club's existence, it did establish several lake customs that have lived on ever since. These included a yearly contest called "Ice-Out," where contestants guess the day on which the ice will go out of the lake each spring, an annual sailing regatta, and an annual Commodore's Cocktail Party. The last formal meeting of the club took place in Toronto. No serious motions were proffered since it was apparent that members had some difficulty recognising each other in their city clothes.[219] In the late 1970s, many on the lake got enthused about sailing Lasers. Eventually the number of Laser sailboats on the lake grew to such a size that the annual sailing regatta became dedicated to Laser sailing. Held on the third weekend in August every summer, the event celebrated its 32nd anniversary in 2005. There are races for kids and adults, with trophies awarded for each class. The two main trophies, the "Tequila Sauza Trophy," (donated by Deacon Foster, who in the 1950s apparently held the Canadian distribution rights for Tequila Sauza) and the "Frid Cup," a hunk of driftwood with an attached laughing Copenhagen mermaid sitting on a seashell, are still awarded today.

---

218. Richard Eldridge and Orville Osborne, *Cache Lake Reflections*, pg. 35.
219. Gaye I. Clemson, *Algonquin Voices: Selected Stories of Canoe Lake Women*, pg. 153.

Fishing and Canoe Tripping

Since its inception, one of the key attractions of Algonquin Park for leaseholders as for so many other visitors has been the fishing and canoe tripping. The earliest recorded leaseholder fishing trip was in 1905 when Dr. Alexander Pirie and his close friend Dr. Thomas Bertram discovered and bought the Gilmour brothers' framed houses on an island in the middle of Canoe Lake. Another early visitor was Lyall G. Ireland, who first visited Cache Lake in 1913:

"On the day after my arrival [on the May 24th weekend 1913], we explored Cache Lake in the morning and in the afternoon went to Little Island Lake via Tanamakoon Lake, a trip involving two short portages, as I recall it. We trolled for an hour or two and caught a few lake trout. On the next day Bill [the local Park Ranger] hitched a team of horses to a "democrat" wagon and he and Mr. Bartlett and I drove over the bush road to Burnt Island Lake, on which Minnesing Lodge was then located. This road is in large part located on a beautiful open hardwood ridge, and it gave me a thrill to see several deer, the first I had ever seen free in their natural environment. We had a tea pail, beans and sandwich lunch on the shore of the lake and then went out and trolled for a while without any noteworthy results, to the chagrin of Bill, who had been sure we would connect with a big one. The fact that we didn't do much in the line of fish in the Burnt Island Lake didn't bother me much, as we had a wonderful day in the beautiful woods and on lovely waters. I fell head over heels in love with the Park, a love which persists to this day, and which led me back to it year after year for as long as physical limitations permitted."[220]

The next year, in the fall of 1914, Ireland became the first leaseholder to explore the northeast section of the Park. The CNR had just recently completed the railway line from Ottawa to North Bay that ran through the northeast corner of the Park. With a positive recommendation from Park Superintendent Bartlett, Ireland and several friends ventured forth from North Bay:

"In early September of that year we were on our way. [I] had written to Peter Ranger [the local Park Ranger] to tell him of the proposed time of our arrival. I say 'proposed time' with reason, as the timetable showed the time of departure from North Bay as after 9 p.m. in the evening. This turned out to be accurate, as it was four hours after 9 p.m. when the train, consisting of a combination freight and work train, on the tail of which was hitched a combination coach and a caboose, left North Bay. We rattled down the track, and finally, at about 2:30 a.m. the train stopped, and we were told we were at Coristine, and so alighted with our canoe, camp outfit and grub. At that time there was no Kiosk, and anyone bound for Kioshkokwi Lake had to disembark at Coristine, consisting solely of the section house, and find his way from there as best he could. The night being warm and clear, we decided to stay where we were until morning, and so spread our blankets on the sand between the main line and the siding, and slept there until day break, when, to our amazed pleasure, there came the lovely cacophony of a gasoline speeder, on which rode Peter. Peter and the speeder transported us and our plunder to the lake, where we unloaded at the spot where Kiosk station now stands. At that time there was no Kiosk, no lumbering operations, no people except Peter and his brother

220. Excerpted from a letter from Lyall G. Ireland to Bert Gillespie,1959.

Telesphore and a summer Fire Ranger; no buildings except Peter's shelter hut and the Fire Ranger shelter, an ancient one-room log shanty. We had no trouble in catching all the lake trout we wanted. We didn't get up to Manitou during that trip, but did thoroughly explore Kioshkokwi and the river as far down as the Pot Hole. After that I was an incurable addict."[221]

This love of, and sometimes obsession with, the exploration and monitoring of the Park interior by leaseholders continues to this day. In the early 1930s, Gerry Brown from Cache Lake often went on canoe trips with fellow leaseholders Henry Standerwick and Jim Bond. Their longest was 12 days in 1933, during which time they traveled 260 miles and visited 56 lakes, averaging 26 miles a day. On portages, they would change carrying canoes every 20 minutes or so. On one long portage Brown, who was carrying the pack, looked up and saw three bear cubs sitting beautifully near a white birch tree. He yelled to Standerwick "Bear to the left!" Standerwick yelled back, "No, you can't fool me, the trail goes straight ahead!" One other day, Brown accidentally dropped the canoe at the end of a portage on top of a spruce tree and a branch went right through the bottom. He repaired it with black marine glue and an old piece of canvas that he took along for just these sorts of emergencies.[222]

Ian McLeod from Smoke Lake recalls his first trip in the Park in 1949.

"I first visited the Park in 1943, when I was 10 years old, at the Dalglish cottage on Smoke Lake. A few years later, in 1949, when I was 16 years old, I worked as a Junior Ranger at Brent. George Phillips who was the Park Superintendent at the time was one of the last flying superintendents. We had a chance to fly with him several times, as it was a very dry summer and we were flown in to put out a number of fires on campsites that had not been properly extinguished. The Park was closed to travel in late August and another Junior Ranger and myself received special permission from George to paddle through the Park. I had arranged for my canoe to be sent up to Brent on the train and we paddled down the Big Trout route and down the Oxtongue to Lake of Bays, and then down the Muskoka River to Bracebridge where my brother picked us up. I acquired a real love for the Park that summer and continued to paddle and fish in the Park over the following years."

It was unusual for young women to go on canoe trips on their own in the 1930s, but quite a number of leaseholding women, including Esther Keyser, Kay Graham, and Charlotte Horner from Smoke Lake led the way. All had received a taste of canoe tripping while at local children's camps. In fact, as noted elsewhere, Esther Keyser went on to become the Park's first female canoe tripping guide.[223] As Kay Graham recalled over 60 years later:

"Charlotte Horner needed a fourth person and invited me along and we set off on a two-week canoe trip to Brent, Cedar Lake and back. It was the trip of a lifetime. We had food, maps and started off with rented canoes from Ed Colson at Joe Lake. We were not used to portaging two canoes and four packs so our first night on the Otterslides was the worst. At White Trout Lake, our axe handle broke. When we saw Mr. MacDougall, the Park Superintendent, flying over us, we signaled to him and he came down and gave us his axe. We did manage to get to Brent—rapids and all. That night Brent was having a square dance and we

221. Excerpted from a letter from Lyall G. Ireland to Bert Gillespie,1959.
222. Richard Eldridge and Orville Osborne, ***Cache Lake Reflections,*** 1995, pg. 39.
223. For details of Keyser's experiences, see ***Paddling My Own Canoe,*** 2004.

were invited to join them. It was a merry time and a great party. We spent the night in our sleeping bags on the floor over the local store."

For Judy Willson Bolt, the fever for canoe tripping in the Park was set for life at the age of 13. At camp she would go on as many canoe trips as they would allow. Where ever in the world she traveled and worked from then on she would always be homesick for the Park. As she recalled in 2003:

"One year instead of hammocks or apple pie-shaped ground sheets and pinned blankets, the camp had got a hold of some war surplus, individual screened tents. Each had a waterproof roof and ground sheet and were pegged into the ground and held up by four long poles with open screening all around the sides. My delight at sleeping in my own wild world with ground smells and shooting stars was pure magic."

As is also true today, canoe trips did involve some degree of danger. When the father of Source Lake resident Jim Forrester at the age of 16 took the first of many canoe trips, it didn't start out with much promise. He arrived by train at Canoe Lake Station with a friend for a two-week fishing holiday and headed for Big Trout Lake through the Otterslides. It was getting dark by the time they got to Big Trout Lake with a headwind and rain. As Jim Forrester recounted:

"Out in the middle of the lake, they began taking in water over the bow and slowly became swamped in the dark. They hung onto the canoe and drifted all the way back down the lake to a swampy, sandy area. In the process they lost their return rail tickets, a paddle, and most of their borrowed gear, then unsuccessfully tried to start a fire using a leather bootlace. My Dad carved a makeshift paddle out of shore driftwood to replace the lost one. Later in the morning they spotted a Camp Wapomeo trip and signaled to them. The trip paddled over and my dad explained their situation. The girls gave them breakfast and some food and they decided to return to Canoe Lake Station, hoping that the station agent would remember them and give them replacement train tickets. On the way south, they spotted a Park Ranger at a shelter hut at the south end of Burnt Island Lake near Minnesing Lodge and asked if they could stay. He agreed, so they then made a visit to Camp Minnesing and struck a deal with the kitchen. They would provide fresh lake trout daily in exchange for oatmeal, bacon, and various food staples. The lodge also loaned them blankets and pots and cooking pots. They spent the two weeks at the shelter hut, had a terrific vacation and became expert canoeists."[224]

Another dangerous fishing story involved Canoe Lake leaseholders Hugh Gibson and Ken Frid. At the beginning of their second year, studying at the University of Toronto, the two registered for school and then went off on a one-week fishing trip to Hogan Lake. As Hugh Gibson recalled in 2001:

"During the first day there was excellent fishing. Ken caught a five-pound lake trout and within a few minutes I landed a 16-pounder. Both fish were flopping all around on the bottom of the canoe and in trying to catch them, Ken put a knife not only through the fish but also through the bottom of the canoe. After a very rough canoe-patching job we decided to return to Canoe Lake and started out at about 11 a.m., when it began to snow. Rather than stop we kept on going, getting back to the Portage Store at 3 a.m. by moonlight. There was hoarfrost in the bulrushes and they nearly paddled into a moose in the Otterslides that was less than

224. Recollections from Jim Forrester, 2004.

20 feet away. To find their way across the portages we held flashlights in our mouths."

One of the leaseholder canoe tripping legends was established by the Laurier brothers of Canoe Lake in the 1940s, when they decided to attempt the now infamous "Brent Run." As was so eloquently stated by Chuck Beamish, who with Bob Anglin completed the run in 23 hours in 1990:

> *"The Brent Run is not done for mass public recognition. It's a race that you do for yourself. You only hear of a good time every eight or 10 years, so it's not the type of thing that everyone talks about. The rules of the race are all unofficial. There are people who keep time at Canoe Lake and you phone back or get verification once you arrive in Brent, but the rest is up to the paddlers. The people who paddle appreciate the rules that have been created, and they respect all the others who have attempted and completed the run."*[225]

It all began in 1934, when two Camp Ahmek staff members (Bill Stoqua and Bill Little) decided to see if they could paddle the 160-kilometer round trip from Canoe Lake to Brent and back in less than 24 hours.[226] They came close but got lost in the fog on Big Trout Lake and established the first record run of 32 hours. Until 1948 none came close to matching this record until brothers Carl and Hank Laurier decided to give it a try. With a miner's headlamp and a toothbrush for each of them, a huge lunch under their belt, some fruit juice and sandwiches packed they took off paddling north without a map. As camp counselors and guides they had gone back and forth to Brent frequently over the years and figured they knew the way pretty well. As Hank recalled in 2000 nearly half a century after the event:

> *"We made Canoe Lake to White Lake in four hours, using Carl's chestnut canoe. Though strong paddlers, both of us had arms that were trembling after hours of hard paddling. At Burnt Root, we met fellow Camp Ahmek staff member and later a Canoe Lake leaseholder, Don McCaskill, who was on a trip and landed at his campsite about 9 p.m. Don gave us a good meal so that we could continue all night. A little farther on, we hit a fork in the road and couldn't remember which way to go. Carl voted for going left and I voted for going right. We flipped a coin and went right, which luckily was the correct way. At 4 a.m. we met Porky Greenbaum on the second half of the Petawawa River who was guiding a trip out of Camp Tamakwa on South Tea Lake. One of their canoes had accidentally gone over the Petawawa Falls and split wide open like a melon. The trip was stuck by the side of the river. One camper was also missing. We pushed on and when we got to Brent, we called Jack Boyle the Park Ranger at Park Headquarters and told him that the Tamakwa trip needed rescuing. Jack replied that that was good to hear, since the missing camper had just been found and was saying that the rest of the trip had drowned."*

Unfortunately, the incorrect news of the alleged terrible drownings in Algonquin Park had already hit the CP newswire to great alarm by all. Hank and Carl then phoned into Camp Ahmek to register the fact that they had made it to Brent. This first leg was completed in 13 hours. On the return they hit headwinds on Big Trout Lake and lost an hour so it took 14 hours to get back to Canoe Lake. The previous record was broken.[227]

---

225. Liz Lundell, editor, ***Fires of Friendship: Eighty Years of the Taylor Statten Camps,*** pg. 201.
226. Bill Stoqua, an Algonquin native from the Golden Lake band was the first canoeing instructor at Camp Ahmek. During his tenure at camp he was considered one of the finest paddlers and teachers of paddling in the community.
227. The Laurier brothers' record held until 1990 when Ahmek staff members Chuck Beamish and Bob Anglin broke it by doing the run in 23 hours.

On canoe trips, novices have been known to bring just about everything but the kitchen sink, including row boats, lawn chairs, suitcases, and cases of beer. They would sit on their haunches and stare when leaseholder and camp trips would pull up to a portage with their skilled landings and departures. The person sitting in the bow of the canoe would jump out and sit on the bow to steady while the person in the centre tossed out the packs. They would then pick up their packs, grab the paddles and life jackets, and head off down the trail. The stern person would pull up the canoe, easily toss it onto his or her shoulders and off he or she would go. All of this taking place in only a few minutes. The best story of the effect of these moves on exhausted novice canoe trippers was from Canoe Lake's Dan Gibson. He and his brother Hugh had decided one summer to take a fishing trip into Red Pine Bay. Before they left, a friend who flew a Beaver aircraft, agreed to drop in, pick up their gear and return it to the Gibson cottage on Canoe Lake. As Dan recalled in 1998:

> *"About 9 a.m. on our last day out my friend arrived as expected. He left us with the canoe with a ¾-horsepower motor, two fishing rods and an empty brown bottle of Ballantine scotch that we intended to use to store drinking water at the first portage after Big Trout Lake. At the Burnt Island portage, Hugh was carrying the canoe, and I was carrying the pack and the motor. We met some visitors, complete with coolers, lawn chairs and suitcases, who had been out on trip for two days. They were going back for the rest of their mountain of gear and were shocked to see us with nothing but our canoe and fishing tackle. In response to their inquiries, I told them that they didn't need a tent, because they could sleep under the canoe; didn't need food because they could eat blueberries and catch fish. Then, just for effect, I then grabbed the scotch bottle and tossed it back. After a few gulps of what the visitors thought was pure scotch, I wiped my mouth off with the back of my hand and we both headed off paddling down the lake, trying not to break out in hysterical laughter. We could hear the visitors discussing that that was how they should trip the next time out."*[228]

Almost since its inception fishing has been a major social activity in Algonquin Park. As Lyall Ireland reported in 1914 upon his first trip to the Kiosk area:

> *"Almost every one of the five or six days of our stay in 1914 was fabulous. The speckled trout fishing was such as a sinful mortal has no right to expect—everywhere, at the Kioshkokwi dam and the rapids below, in Mink Creek, and at the head of Kioshkokwi. We called the latter spot the 'Chute' because of the then intact log chute (now completely gone), which we could, and did, walk all the way up to the pool below the Moosehorn portage. There was a dam at the outlet of this pool to hold the water for sluicing the logs down the chute."*[229]

In the early 1940s, Pete Purcell from Smoke Lake used to camp at Jack Hamilton's fishing camp on Ragged Lake or Jim Stringer's on Porcupine Lake, before those lakes were part of Algonquin Park. This was a time when one could reel in 20 three- to four-pound bass an hour.[230] Groups of anglers from all over Ontario and the United States northeast would, and still do, flock to the Park in the spring and fall for good trout fishing and in the summer for bass. As Robert Miller from Galeairy Lake recalls:

---

228. Note that the flying of personal aircraft into the Park was banned in the late 1970s.
229. Letter by Lyall G. Ireland to Bert Gillespie, 1959.
230. Recollections from Pete Purcell, 2003.

"Nothing can compare to the action experienced in playing a small mouth bass nor the subsequent mouth-watering meal. Of course, the big bass caught now are more apt to be 3-4 pounds rather than the 6-7 pounds of earlier years. A mounted 7-pound plus small mouth bass caught by my father graced our home for years. Likewise, my mother was a skilled fisherwoman and the Park booklet 'Fishing in Algonquin Provincial Park' still shows an unnamed photo of her holding an eel she caught in Galeairy Lake in the early 1930s."

In 1923, a resident fishing license cost $3 and was $5 for a non-resident. By 1942, a family fishing license had risen to $15 though it did cover parents and any children under 21. In those days, guides who allegedly knew the locations of all prized fishing holes worked for the major lodges. All summer they would take various parties on multi-week fishing trips through out the Park. There was also extensive airplane traffic as anglers would arrange to be flown in and out of distant lakes. As Gar Northway advised the Park Superintendent in 1932:

"My 'Irving Fishing Club' is going to Nominigan and as they are not 'fish-killers' you will be glad to have them in the Park. The guides have come to look upon their two weeks of work with us as perquisite and we are anxious to give them this work this spring. This year there will be 11 guides, three of whom will have regular park licenses. For the other eight the club will be paying for their licenses."[231]

As early as the 1930s, concerns were being raised about the decline of fish stocks. People who lived in various towns outside of the Park, east of Radiant Lake, would come in by rail, fish for a day or so, and then leave the next day. One Cache Lake resident, Alex DeHart Bruen, reported in 1935 that as far as he was concerned fishing had been terrible on Cache Lake since 1910:

"For the first couple of years after 1907, the lake was full of big bass and the trout fishing was fair. Since 1910 a good-sized bass has been a rare catch, so I assume that was about the time the supply of minnows gave out. Every bass I have caught in the last few years have been full of crawfish, showing no signs of lack of food of this type. I think that the lake would be a great deal more attractive if some type of minnow could be reintroduced, which would give the bass more food. The perch I have never found [to be] particularly good bait and as I remember the lake has always had a good many of them in it."[232]

In 1939, Mary Thomas from Kish Kaduk Lodge advised that:

"Fishing this season has been terrible with [many] visitors often not catching any at all. Our guests want to fish for bass."[233]

In 1939, Park Superintendent MacDougall sponsored the first fish creel census. All lodge owners had to issue and collect fish creel census cards to ascertain where fishing was good, where fish stocks had been depleted, and what fish were being captured. One end result was extensive fish planting and restocking in Algonquin Park lakes. Some of it was for experimental purposes to see what sorts of fish would survive in various lake

---

231. Northway leasehold correspondence, 1932, Algonquin Park Museum Archives.

232. DeBruen leasehold correspondence, 1935, Algonquin Park Museum Archives. Note that live-bait fishing was discontinued some time ago and a reminder posted by Algonquin Park Ecowatch exists today on Highway 60.

233. Thomas leasehold correspondence, 1939, Algonquin Park Museum Archives.

conditions. In the 1930s 10,000 black bass went into Rain Lake, 500 into Sawyer Lake, and as well there were speckled and lake trout plantings in Couchon and Mink Lakes. However, the job of stocking fish was not a fun job. As Jack Wilkinson, co-owner of Kish Kaduk Lodge on Cedar Lake recalled:

> *"In the 1930s, the fish would come up in cans from the hatchery in Pembroke, in those big old-fashioned cream cans with ice in them. We used to meet the train at 3 a.m. in the morning. We'd go down with our boats and take the fish off the train and we'd divide them up in these pack cans, you know the pump packs that you carry on your back for fire. We used to finally use those. We got sick of carrying these milk cans into the bush, so we found out that we could keep lots of ice in that pack can, and that we could put 50 or 60 trout in these pack cans and carry them that way. That's the way we used to pack the fish back to all these lakes."*[234]

It's impossible to be an Algonquin Park resident without at least one or two good fishing stories. Jake Pigeon, from Cache Lake, and a friend were boating across Cedar Lake after a relatively unsuccessful day:

> *"We passed two fishermen who stopped us at a distance and showed us that they had caught two nice sized lake trout. We didn't have quite the same luck but we had to show them what we had caught, so we pulled our one and only six-pound trout out of the holding tank and showed them, Then we dropped it back in and pulled the same fish out but held it differently. Then we pulled it out again, with two hands this time and repeated this same routine about five times. We then wished them good luck for the rest of the day. While we were pulling away, you could see these two guys looking at each other with long faces, not saying anything, but watching us putter away with big smiles on our faces."*[235]

Though not so common now, as "catch and release" is the norm, trophy fish were prizes to be kept and added to the cottage fishing folklore. Pete Purcell of Smoke Lake can regale every visitor with a detailed story about the events surrounding the catching of every single fish mounted on his cabin walls. Pete's father Jack Purcell was the undefeated Canadian badminton champion in the 1930s and 1940s. Not only was he inducted into Canada's Hall of Fame, he also was named Canada's Athlete of the Half Century in 1950 for non-body contact sports. Jack's badminton racket still hangs on the wall of the Purcell cabin, which he built on Smoke Lake in 1945. He married Helen Colson, daughter of George Colson (the brother of Ed Colson of Hotel Algonquin and the Portage Store fame). His reputation carries on today as a key inspiration and brand for Converse athletic shoes. The Purcell extended family is large with a number of members now with leases on Smoke Lake. According to Pete, the best taxidermist around in 1939 was Alfred Kay of Port Sydney, who charged $5 per fish and apparently did first class handiwork. The back of the Hubay/Helwick cottage and boathouse on Smoke Lake was decorated with wooden fish, each marked with the initials of the person who caught it, the weight and date.

W. Gibson Gray (known as Gib) and neighbour Ed Brook (who was a real outdoorsman), also from Smoke Lake, were loyal fishing buddies and spent lots of time in the 1960s fishing all over the Park. Gib Gray first came to Algonquin Park as a counselor at Camp Ahmek in 1936 and went on to settle on Smoke Lake in the

---

234. Interview with Thomas/Wilkinson by Rory MacKay, 1976, Algonquin Park Museum Archives.
235. Interview with Jake Pigeon by Don Standfield, 1991, Algonquin Park Museum Archives.

1940s. He practiced law in Toronto and in 1979, was appointed a Justice of the Supreme Court of Ontario (subsequently renamed the Ontario Court (General Division). He served as a Bencher for The Law Society of Upper Canada from 1964 through 1979 (Treasurer and CEO 1976-78) and became a Life Bencher in 1976. He retired from the Court in 1992. Every spring and fall there would be a "guys' fishing weekend." Gib's wife Nancy would pack and send up all of the food, complete with menus and in later years their daughter Katie would be sent along as the cook. Every night, all summer long, Tiny Norman would troll up and down the north end of Smoke Lake along a predetermined path that only he knew and never passed on. Even today, there are those that say that "Tiny's Trek" is the best-kept fishing secret on the lake.

Boating

Since most cottages were accessible only by water, boats and canoes had a special meaning and role in cottage life. Each cottager had his or her own style and preference. Some leaseholders preferred canoes, especially for morning or evening touring. An 18-foot Guide's Special chestnut canoe cost $79 in 1925 without paddles. A keel would be an extra $2, if put on during construction, and $3 if added afterwards. Sometimes even the best of plans went awry. Up on Radiant Lake, a new leaseholder named Roland Mudge had made arrangements for a canoe to be delivered to him at the Radiant train station. Alas, it arrived but then was returned to Bracebridge to await the payment of duty charges. Eventually, it was forwarded back to Radiant at great expense and frustration.

Some leaseholders liked 2- or 3-horsepower "putt-putt" motorboats, ideal for trolling for fish, whereas others liked large multi-engine inboards. A few owned mahogany or cedar-strip launches that were later replaced by much more durable, and long-lasting aluminum and fiberglass models. One of the most famous mahogany launches was a wooden Shepard boat owned by the Matthews family on Canoe Lake that they called the "West Wind". According to grandson Russ Matthews:

> *"It was a 6 cylinder, 112 horsepower inboard ski boat that was originally used at the annual Canadian National Exhibition water show to tow trick water skiers (6 skiing with another 6 standing on the shoulders of the first). When gaining speed the boat would creep out of the water into a natural plane. This meant that that there was virtually no ability for a skier to 'drag the boat', so if one wasn't careful when turning, one could go flying out over the boats wake."*

Another locally famous boat was the "Marmilwood" owned by the Taylor Statten Camps. About 30-feet long, built by Minette Shields in 1927 in Muskoka, it was originally owned by Lady Eaton (of the Eaton retailing family) at Lake Rosseau. Later it was purchased and restored by Stafford Smythe, the former owner of the Maple Leaf Gardens hockey arena in Toronto. Taylor Statten's wife Tonakela, also had a favourite boat that she called "Okeechobee" after a lake in Florida. It was a cumbersome boat and only she could drive and land it well. Still another was a 26-foot long Muskoka launch, weighing three tons called the "Wascana II", though Smoke Lake cottagers knew it as the "Queen Mary." Built in the 1920s, it was owned by the Ouchterlony family and cruised on Smoke Lake from 1955 until 1960. A special boathouse was designed, built and installed by Nominigan caretaker Jack Hamilton with a sling that would hold the boat out of the water. It is now on Lake Muskoka and has since won many prizes at the Port Carling Boat Show.[236] Another remarkable boat was the "Lady Nominigan", a 26-feet long, wooden inboard-outboard, with its engine mounted forward in the chassis. In the back it had white wicker chairs and red leather seats.[237] In emergencies or bad weather Gar Northway would set off in his launch from his cabin on Smoke Lake to pick people up from their cabins and take them to the Portage Store or to the Smoke Lake Landing. Smoke Lake resident Mary Cline, recounts a wonderful story about a neighbour's first visit to Algonquin Park in the 1940s:

> *"Lester Graf's wife had died tragically and my brother Manley thought that some time spent in the bush might be therapeutic. So Manley told him to bring up his hammer and put him to work. He arrived at the West Gate very late at night, having been delayed on his way up. The DLF officials at the gate suggested that he call Nominigan. Not realizing that it was a private lease, he ordered a boat and asked that they pick him up at the Smoke Lake Landing, which of course they did happily. Later of course when he found out that Nominigan wasn't the local taxi service, he was very embarrassed."*

Most people recognized each other by the look of their boat and could tell by the sound of the engine who was going by or who was coming to visit. On Canoe Lake the Gibsons' boat had a big bow and the driver sat atop an old egg crate. The Lauriers' "Silver Bullet" ran low to the water, and was incredibly fast. But the envy of some Canoe Lake residents was the "Queen of the Seas", a Z-77 racing boat with a souped up, 35-horsepower Evinrude racing engine, which ended up at the centre of some remarkable stories. The Z-77 had been built by St. Williams and came from Murdon Marine in Port Carling. Its racing career was short-lived, however, after it suffered some damage in a race, after which it was retired by its original owner to a garage, from which it was stolen.

Some time later, Dan Gibson bought for $50 from a maintenance man he knew what he thought was a broken old racing boat that had been damaged in a boating accident. Dan made the necessary repairs and used it for many years, until he sold it in the late 1950s to my father, Stan Clemson. Some 25 years later at a social gathering, a number of locals were trading boat stories. One lamented that his prized Z-77, with a 35-horsepower Evinrude engine that flew across the water, had been stolen back in the mid-1940s. After comparing, features and timeframes, the final conclusion was that my father had unwittingly bought a stolen boat!

I loved that boat as well and can remember as if it were yesterday, roaring down the lake at full throttle, with the wind in my hair and not a care in the world. The "Queen of the Seas," however, had one near-death experience in the mid-1960s. My brothers and I had come down with the flu and my mother misread the weather. She tied the boat to the dock facing in the wrong direction. A fierce north wind arose overnight and huge stormy waves washed over the transom, ultimately sending the boat to the bottom of the lake. Upon discovering the disaster the next morning, my mother called some neighbours who rushed over. They were able to obtain a winch and with some difficulty hauled the boat out of the water. One was a small engine expert, who proceeded to take apart the engine and spread the various parts out on the dock to dry. Miraculously, after he

236. Recollections from the Ouchterlony family, 2004.
237. Mary Northway, ***Nominigan: A Casual History***, 1960.

put it back together, it started after just one pull of the starter cord. The Queen's exciting life finally came to an unseemly end in the late 1970s when the boathouse roof collapsed and crushed her hull completely. Though completely inappropriate now, we towed the remains out into the middle of the lake and dedicated her to the deep. That marvelous Evinrude engine still lies in state under our cottage, though it may no longer be used on Canoe Lake anymore due to engine horsepower restrictions.

In the mid-1980s, boating regulations changed and all residents were required (on most lakes) to retire any engines greater than 20 horsepower. The only exceptions were camp boats and any visiting commercial boats. Later all water sports such as water skiing and wake and skim boarding were also subsequently banned. Though initially tough on the younger generations, after a few years, the resulting improvements in sound and water pollution made the loss of motorized water sports worthwhile.

Community Characters

Like any culturally rich community, Algonquin Park has its own set of unique characters. Some, such as the Stringer brothers and Winifred Trainor, have been written about extensively in other narratives. On Rock Lake there was George Elms, son of William McCourt's sister Eva, who was a retired air commodore group captain in the Royal Canadian Air Force. As previously mentioned, he owned a Seabee airplane and would fly up, land on Rock Lake and tie the plane up to a barrel just off of his dock.[238] One year he brought up from Ottawa a hydroplane to which he attached an 11-horsepower Fleetwin engine. With it he was able to roar across the lake at speeds of up to 35 mph. Later in the 1950s, when he heard that the DLF was tearing up the abandoned marine railway into Galeairy Lake, he bought the rails and built a small marine railway at his cottage in order to get his boat, "Eagle Beak," a red Mullins marine boat with an inboard motor, out of the water each fall.

On Source Lake in the 1960s, Betsy Stevenson, who loved to water ski (and continued to do so even after both knees were replaced) once skied topless around Camp Pathfinder Island on a dare. On Canoe Lake, although I can't imagine that it was possibly true, a friend of Mary Kendall Percival hitchhiked a half-a-mile ride on water skis from the Portage Store to the Percival's dock, wearing her clothes and suitcase in hand. On Whitefish Lake was Miss Wilma Rouse of Ohio, who arrived in 1939. She took over a cabin that had originally been built in 1922 by lumberman George Jamieson. Miss Rouse, as she was always called, had worked as the hostess at the Bigwin Inn near Huntsville. She was a single lady in the "Grande Dame" tradition. For years, she held tea parties and enthralled visitors with tales of her travels in Europe as a young lady. She had a big gong she would ring if she needed the help of neighbours.[239] On Smoke Lake there were a number of characters. One was Warner Troyer who had lost his leg in a car accident, but walked so well that few knew that he had been injured. He was a long-time CBC broadcaster, veteran of ***This Hour Has Seven Days, Public Eye***, and The ***Fifth Estate***, as well as the co-host of ***CTV's W5***. In his later years he was an investigative journalist and author of seven books, including ***Divorced Kids***, his realistic look at divorce and how best to cope; ***No Safe Place***, which profiled the case of mercury poisoning in the White Dog and Grassy Narrows native communities in

---

238. Note that flying into Park lakes was discontinued with the implementation of the 1974 Algonquin Park Master Plan.

239. Gaye I. Clemson, ***Rock Lake Station: Settlement Stories Since 1896***, pg. 35.

the vicinity of Kenora, Ontario; and ***Preserving Our World: A Consumer's Guide to the Brundtland Report***, a United Nations survey on such topics as population growth, food shortages, war, global warming, and endangered species. According to lake legend, at one lake party, one of the female guests offered to give each of the men a foot massage. When he saw her coming toward him he undid the buckle holding his leg in place. When she grabbed his foot, his entire leg came off in her hand. She fainted dead away.

On Cache Lake, Mosey Case, the sister of Fanny Case of Northway Lodge fame, loved to swim and would "skinny dip" off her dock every morning just about breakfast time. She also used to swim over to the post office to collect the mail every day, putting it underneath her bathing cap to keep it dry. Chuck Mason used to write messages on mushrooms and over time amassed a 40-piece collection. Iain MacKay loved flags. An early dock that survived many winters had a flagpole on each side. From these poles he would fly the Union Jack, or the Canadian Ensign, or the Flag of St. Andrew, or the Scottish Standard, or even his own MacKay banner. If the flags were up, Iain was in residence. Many years later, there was a movement to try to shut down the flying of flags in the Park. He fought the rule energetically, enjoyed being on the winning side, and then moved his flagpole up next to the cottage where it was not as visible, but he could still fly his flags.[240]

Barbara and Ross Rudolph once laid out a lawn bowling and croquet course amongst the trees—a prelude to the various Frisbee-golf courses that today dot the occasional leaseholder landscape. Once Spence Reeder brought his secretaries up from the city and set them up with typewriters on the dock. It didn't take long before all of the papers went flying in the water. Mac Hazlett used to borrow his grandmother's Clara's car to go into Huntsville. One time when he got back really late, he realized that he was nearly out of gas so he thought he'd borrow some from the Park Headquarters airplane gas tanks. Airplane fuel is not meant for automobile engines, of course, and Clara drove into Huntsville the next day blissfully unaware that a huge black cloud of smoke was trailing her down the highway. One resident used to go everyday to the parking lot and use the electricity outlet to shave. One day his son was fiddling in the car and the car rolled backwards into the lake. A neighbour was standing on the dock and saw it all happen. He dove into the water and saved the boy. It took a lot longer to get the car out and it took three days to dry it out and clean it up.[241]

On Canoe Lake, George Merrydew, owner of a tavern in Toronto, the Hotel Algonquin, and the old Mowat Lodge site, was a very large man and had a great sense of humour. All of the local kids soon learned that he loved to give them candy, which they weren't supposed to have. Bribing him with blueberries was a strategy that worked very well. They would hide the purloined candy in the forest to be consumed slowly and stealthily later. One of Merrydew's companions was a German lady who loved to ski behind his big wooden boat. While in it Merrydew refused to wear a life jacket although he couldn't swim. He would joke that if he ever fell or jumped in the lake it would likely raise the water level a good three feet. In the 1950s, Mrs. Manning, who lived nearby, decided that this situation needed to be remedied and so taught him how to swim, to the amusement of the children at the north end.[242] Skip Thompson got himself in big trouble by arguing with his future wife while they were out for an evening paddle. His fiancée, Pat, stopped the canoe by a stump and

---

240. Ibid.
241. Richard Eldridge and Orville Osborne, ***Cache Lake Reflections***, pg. 58.
242. Recollections from the Manning family, 1998.

told him to get out. He foolishly complied and she paddled off. It took some time, and a lot of yelling before a neighbour passing by rescued him. Deacon Foster, a Camp Ahmek alumnus, was married to a woman who was apparently very fearful of the Canoe Lake wilderness life, and was not impressed with the lack of proper bathing facilities. To solve the problem, Foster put a white bathtub on the end of the dock, so she could swim in it. It was a landmark for quite awhile, until he decided to construct a bathhouse. Unfortunately, the ¼-inch plywood that he used for the floor wasn't strong enough to support a bathtub full of water and the tub fell through, to rest for decades on the forest floor below.

Community Creators

In addition to a community of characters, Algonquin Park residents are also a community of contributors, many of whom have gone on to influence Canadian society in a wide variety of endeavours. Some are well known, and went on to receive the prestigious "Order of Canada," or its predecessor the "Order of the British Empire." Others not as well known but equally important are so many other civic-minded contributors to the Algonquin Park community. Among them are many business entrepreneurs, artists, scientists, university professors, school teachers, lawyers, government officials, doctors, photographers, carpenters and authors. It's actually quite impressive that such a small community should have produced so many contributors of consequence to the general Canadian good. Here are a few who have received national recognition.

Frances M. Adaskin – Canoe Lake

Awarded the "Order of Canada" in 1977 in recognition of a life devoted to music, Frances Adaskin was a soloist and accompanist of international repute. She was beloved of her colleagues and pupils at the University of British Columbia, where she founded the Music Department.[243] As a young woman she was a singer under contract with Canadian National Railway, and sang at all of its hotels across Canada. She often serenaded members of the Canoe Lake community when she practiced her scales and performances from the end of her dock.

Murray Adaskin – Canoe Lake

Awarded the "Order of Canada" in 1981 for his work as a leading violinist and composer, Adaskin's works have been widely performed throughout Canada and abroad. He devoted 23 years to the teaching of music at the University of Saskatchewan at Saskatoon and added immeasurably to the cultural life of that province and city.[244] In the 1950s, he decided to build a studio-cabin on Canoe Lake and transported the piano across Canoe Lake on the Ahmek barge. When in residence, he was often invited to Camp Ahmek and Wapomeo to play or visit with musically inclined campers. He later composed the Algonquin Symphony and also the music for the evening grace, which is sung at Camp Ahmek to this day.

243. Excerpted from www.gg.ca/honours/
244. Excerpted from www.gg.ca/honours/

Ralph Bice – Rain Lake

Awarded the "Order of Canada" in 1985 for his work as a trapper, hunting guide, outdoorsman, municipal politician, school trustee, writer, and raconteur extraordinaire, Ralph symbolized the pioneering spirit of the North. For over 70 years, the "Old Man of the Woods" made outstanding contributions both to the trapping industry and to his community of Kearney, Ontario.[245] Ralph Bice took his first canoe trip in the Park in 1912 with his father who was an Algonquin Park Ranger. In 1917 he started working as a fishing guide out of Highland Inn and later developed his own guiding business, called Poplar Point Camps, based first out of Eagle Lake (later called Rain Lake and now Ralph Bice Lake) and later in Kearney. Bice was also a prolific writer and over the years wrote marvelously witty and humorous articles for the Almaguin and Huntsville Forester newspapers. Later in life he became an ardent conservationist and in 1985 received a Directors Award from the Friends of Algonquin Park.

J. R. Dymond – Smoke Lake

One of Canada's best known zoologists in the 1950s and 1960s and a key figure in the conservation movement in Canada, J. R. Dymond was for many years a Professor Emeritus at the University of Toronto, the Director of the Royal Ontario Museum of Zoology, and one of the founding members of the Federation of Ontario Naturalists. He was awarded the "Order of the British Empire" for his role in "making Canadians aware of the need to conserve their natural resources, not just the wildlife alone but the whole ecosystem of life, soil and water."[246]

Dr. George D. Garland – Smoke Lake

Awarded the "Order of Canada" in 1984, George Garland, retired Professor of Physics at the University of Toronto, has made major contributions to Canada's knowledge of the earth's crust and upper mantle, and of its gravitational fields. He has also rendered notable service to the Royal Society of Canada and international scientific bodies.[247] In addition, he was a well known rescuer of canoeists in trouble on Smoke Lake, a founding father of The Friends of Algonquin Park, and author of a Friends bookstore bestseller called Glimpses of Algonquin Park that commemorated the first 100 years of the Park.

Daniel A. Gibson – Canoe Lake

Awarded the "Order of Canada" in 1994, not only was Gibson an outstanding nature photographer, he also was a pioneer in recording techniques for capturing natural wildlife sounds and has created unique audio and video productions by marrying nature to music. These collaborations have been popular as a way of experiencing nature, but equally important has been his role in creating public awareness of the importance of conservation, wildlife, and the natural heritage.[248]

---

245. Ibid.
246. Dymond obituary in the ***Canadian Field Naturalist,*** October/December edition, 1965.
247. Ibid.
248. Excerpted from www.gg.ca/honours/

Roy MacGregor – Lake of Two Rivers and Cache Lake

One of Canada's most gifted storytellers, Roy MacGregor was awarded the "Order of Canada" in 2005. Though not technically a leaseholder, his roots in Algonquin Park go very deep and his feelings for the Park are strong. His grandfather was a key member of the Algonquin Park Ranger staff at Lake of Two Rivers for decades, and a cousin still retains a lease on Cache Lake. His skill in articulating the powerful influence of cottaging and camping on the Canadian identity is renowned.[249]

Charles A.G. Matthews – Canoe Lake

Chuck Matthews was awarded the "Order of Canada" in 1974 for his leadership in the field of printing and lithography and his initiative in applying the silk screen process to the reproduction of the works of Canadian artists.[250] His firm, Sampson and Matthews, used this technique to make good reproductions of Group of Seven paintings, which were supplied to every WWII Canadian military post.

Dr. Taylor Statten II – Canoe Lake

Awarded the "Order of Canada" in 1987, "Dr. Tay" is a well known child psychiatrist and second-generation president of the Taylor Statten Camps. His father had been involved in YMCA's "Boys' Work" since he was a young man. In 1921 Taylor Statten established Camp Ahmek for Boys on the northeast shore of Canoe Lake, and with his wife Ethel, Camp Wapomeo for Girls in 1924. The Stattens first came to the Park and became leaseholders in 1913 and went on to spend over 30 years providing summer camping experiences for children. Well loved by all, Statten was a natural born leader whose focus was always on leadership training and character development.[251] Dr. Tay continues this tradition of providing an environment where children from all walks of life and from all countries can come together in outdoor activity. In his professional capacity, he assisted troubled students and taught at the University of Toronto.[252]

C. Richard Sharpe – Cache Lake

Awarded the "Order of Canada" in 1998, Sharpe has distinguished himself as the head of one of Canada's largest retail chains. His advice and expertise were often sought during his business career by organizations like the Board of Trade of Metropolitan Toronto and the Business Council on National Issues. He was also Chair of the Retail Council of Canada and Junior Achievement of Canada. In retirement, he has volunteered for many civic ventures and fund-raising activities, giving his time to the Wellesley Hospital, the Boys and Girls Clubs of Canada, and the Sir Edmund Hillary Foundation, among several other professional and charitable organizations.[253]

---

249. Excerpted from www.gg.ca/honours/
250. Ibid.
251. Liz Lundell, editor, ***Fires of Friendship: Eighty Years of the Taylor Statten Camps***, pg. 18.
252. Excerpted from www.gg.ca/honours/
253. Ibid.

Sydney Staniforth – Kioshkokwi Lake

Sydney Staniforth was awarded the "Order of the British Empire" for his work in Ottawa during WWI as a $1-a-day man running the Veneer Log Supply Crown Corporation. The firm supplied veneer logs for the war effort that were used to build the mosquito bomber.[254] He later went on to found the Staniforth Lumber Company that operated in Kiosk until it burned down in 1973.

Dr. Robert Volpé – Cache Lake

Awarded the "Order of Canada" in 2003, Volpé was an internationally renowned endocrinologist, researcher, and Professor Emeritus at the University of Toronto. He was the first to highlight the role of specialized cells of the immune system in thyroid disease. As a former director of the Endocrine Research Laboratory at Wellesley Hospital, he has been a mentor to many young scientists and physicians from around the world. The recipient of numerous awards, he has held leadership roles in many medical associations. A dedicated volunteer and medical advisor to the Thyroid Foundation of Canada, he is known for his exemplary commitment to patient care.[255]

---

254. Doug Mackey, ***The Fossmill Story: Life in a Railway Lumbering Village on the Edge of Algonquin Park,*** pg. 188.
255. Excerpted from www.gg.ca/honours/

Community

Log Sawing Contest at Regatta Day c1940s APMA #757

Annette Dods Stoddard on Float Night, Cachce Lake (date unknown) APMA #2064

(right) Cache Lake Float Day 1933 APMA #6460

Cache Lake Regatta 1958 APMA #6267

Cache Lake Regatta 1927 APMA #6205

Highland Inn Regatta 1920 APMA #325

Canoe Lake Swimming Regatta Events 2000 Clemson Collection

Source Lake Kayak Race Start 2005 Dernoga Collection

Source Lake Regatta Preparation
Dernoga Collection

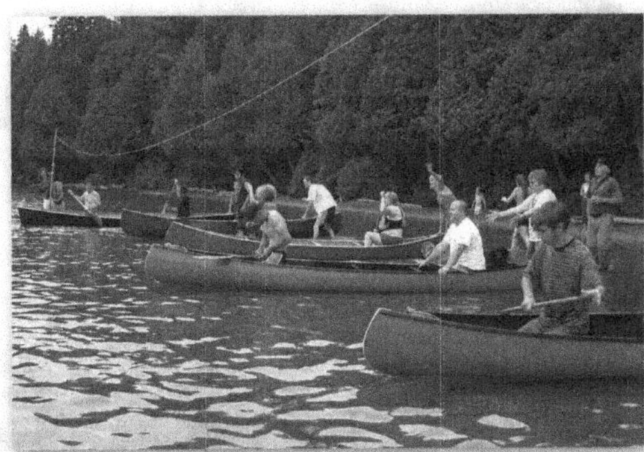
Preparing the Doubles Canoe Race Source Lake 2005
Dernoga Collection

Kayak Expedition 2005 Source Lake Parents Dernoga Collection

Canoe Lake Canoeing Regatta War Canoe Race Finish 2000 Clemson Collection

McCourt Family Summer Gathering outside Old Shawna c1940s
R. Taylor Collection

Rock Lake's Russell Family (date unknown)
Greer Collection

Rock Lake Get Together (date unknown) Greer Collection

Rock Lake's Pepler Family Gathering 2003 Sharpe Collection

Louden Family 1985 Lake of Two Rivers Louden Collection

Galeairy Lake Miller Family Get Together 1934 Miller Collection

Gar Northway of Smoke Lake on the dock with guests c1937 APMA #490

Northway Launch c1940s APMA #486

Cache Lake Rec Hall Dance c1940s APMA #512

Jessie Northway in the Garden c1937 APMA #487

Oucterloney's of Smoke Lake in Launch 1955 APMA #4056

Jack Hamilton Smoke Lake 'Jack of all Trades' APMA #4051

Thanksgiving Celebration on Source Lake 2004 Anne Chisolm (L), Jim Forester, Brian Maltman Dernoga Collection

Thom and Tere Dernoga Winter Camping Dernoga Collection

(left) Oops Wrong Season Thom Dernoga Going for a Paddle Dernoga Collection

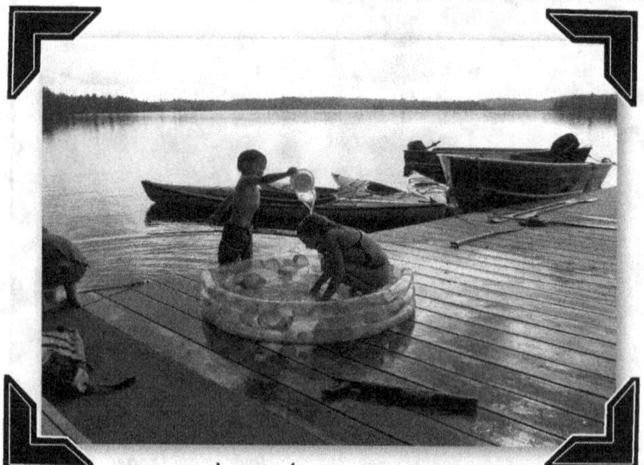

Source Lake Socializing 2005 Saunderson Collection

Kayak Kids Source Lake 2005 Saunderson Collection

Dr. Iain MacKay and Wife Elizabeth
c1970s MacKay Collection

MacKay Parents in Front of Wood Pile
MacKay Collection

Peggy Turner From Cache Lake Heading out on a Canoe Trip While at Northway 1919 APMA #6096

Judge Gib Gray on Cottage Deck c1990s Wahl Collection

Hiking Along the Tracks Near Cache Lake c1920s
Burnett Collection

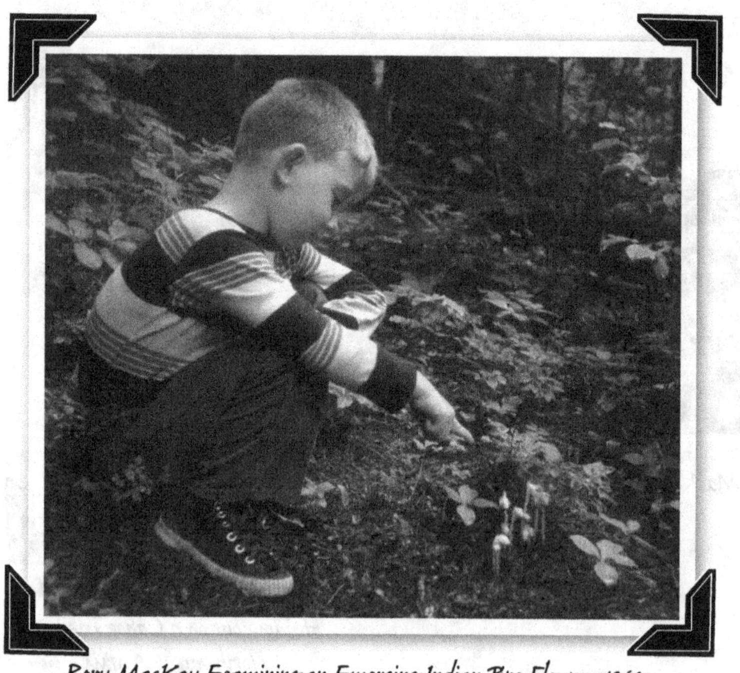

Rory MacKay Eeamining an Emerging Indian Pipe Flower c1960s

All photos this page MacKay Collection

Ester Keyser 2005

(right)
Three Wild Bagpipers c1960s
(L to R Rory, Niall and Dr. Iain MacKay)

Chief Ranger Tom McCormick c1940s MacKay Collection

Spring Fishing Trip in the North
Alger Collection

Andy Grant showing off his prize fish on Little Couchon Lake
Alger Collection

Fishing at the Couchon Falls c1950s

Frank Braucht Standing Outside his Canoe Lake Cabin
Casa Mia McFarlane Collection

The White Throat

Silvery notes in the silent night,
Five in number, clear and bright,
Poured from the throat of a sleeping bird.
You and I have heard.
Why does he utter that liquid song
When all the world is still?
Is his midnight spirit born along
By the lilt of his daytime trill?
Perchance his little feathered breast
Holds dearly the secret in ours.
That life is here abundantly deep,
That he nestles close and breathes in his sleep
"Ah Sweet Canada, Canada, Canada"

A Poem by Irene D. Winans

Chapter 6

Championing the Park Environment

I have always been conscious of role that I play in protecting Algonquin Park. I don't recall any formal coaching from my parents, but there must have been or I learned it all by osmosis. Perhaps being a neighbour to Dan Gibson, a well-known nature photographer, nature sound recording genius and founder of the Solitudes record brand, also enhanced my education in environmental concerns. Dan Gibson introduced my father Stan to Algonquin Park, and one of Dan's daughters was one of my closest friends when we were children growing up on Canoe Lake in the 1960s. Dan and my father had originally met when both were working for Ashley and Crippen photography and spent time together doing a film for the Ontario Government Department of Travel and Publicity. Dan invited my father up for a fishing weekend, and he immediately fell in love, as so many do, with the wildness of Algonquin Park. Dragging my somewhat reluctant mother along, my father chose one of the last available sites on the lake, located on a high ridge at the south end. The bay to the south was full of stumps and deadheads left over from the logging days and the raising of the water level by several feet in the late 1890s. Every weekend my parents would drive four or five hours to Canoe Lake, and spend all day clearing the site and building a cabin made of lumber that they were able to obtain from a second-hand lumber store. Dan would loan them his boat and motor and all of the lumber would be painstakingly hauled across the lake and up the steep hill to the cottage site. In hindsight it makes one wonder why on earth they would go to all that trouble when cottage lots were available in cottage country much closer to Toronto. As with so many others, Algonquin Park had woven its magic.

Dan is a giant bear of a man with a presence that fills and dominates every room he enters. It's impossible not to love him, as he has a wild sense of humour and is a storyteller extraordinaire. He first came to Canoe Lake in 1937 as a camper at Taylor Statten's Camp Ahmek. Summer camp planted the seeds of a lifelong love of nature and its symphony of sound. His interest in photography led to an interest in filmmaking. In 1946, he put the two together, founded his own company, Dan Gibson Productions Ltd., and began his career in the production of nature films. However, as Dan explained:

"In those days, there weren't any stock libraries from which to source background nature sounds, so I was left with the task of capturing nature's sounds myself. My work in synchronizing sounds with visual content, which later turned out to be groundbreaking, succeeded in transporting audiences into the wilderness in a way that had never been done before. In every season and in every type of weather, I would listen to and record nature's voices, from moonlit Canadian northern forests to sun-baked deserts in the American southwest, from crashing Pacific waves to snake–infested swamps in Florida, broadening and enriching my library of recordings. I then would sculpt geographically accurate listening experiences that represented a dynamic journey, which caught listeners' imaginations."[256]

I can remember seeing Gibson often, with one or more of his sons, at all hours of the day and night, in all sorts of locations, with his newly invented sound parabola, photographing and recording every aspect of nature, both living and not. For example, my sons and I ran into him on Bonita Narrows in the summer of 2004. He and his son Danny were filming the water as it rippled in soft waves against the rocky face along the shore. I'd seen that image and heard that sound hundreds of times in my life, but watching him film it made me see it with new eyes and pay attention to it again in a much fuller way.

One of Gibson's first feature films, "Wings in the Wilderness," (for which he won a Canadian Film Award) was shot predominantly on Canoe Lake. Gibson had acquired a number of goslings from the Guelph Waterfowl Research Centre. He set up a feeding station in the little bay near his cottage and watched them grow. The geese imprinted on him in a major way. They would come when he called them and loved to untie his shoes and pull his hair. As they grew older, the geese got adventuresome and would visit the girls sunbathing at the nearby Senior Wapomeo swimming dock. He taught them to fly by racing down the lake in his boat yelling, "Here geese! Here geese! Come on geese!" Eventually they did learn to fly—but at a high cost to Gibson. He got the idea of filming the instruction flights, and rigged up $5,000 worth of camera equipment to a remote-controlled airplane that he could maneuver while his boat was traversing Canoe Lake. Alas, something went wrong and the airplane and camera equipment spiraled into the water. Divers were hired to try to find it, but to no avail. Eventually Gibson had to find a new home for the geese and they were moved to the Boyne River National Science School, run by the Toronto Board of Education. Getting them there was a challenge. More than once they took flight when they were let out of their cages for a food break. Once they landed by his car just as the Ontario Provincial Police came along. Upon being told that it was illegal to own migratory birds, Gibson showed the OPP officer government documentation authorizing his ownership and transit of the geese. At that point the OPP officer drove off, muttering under his breath "Boy do you have a problem!"

It's been a long time since I've been inside the Gibson's cabin, yet little has changed. A few more ribbons on the wall and a renovated kitchen are the only major differences. The tall bar stools by the counter, the long, broad wooden picnic table that serves as the dining room table, the screened-in porch to the south from which one can see the multiple feeders for birds, squirrels, and chipmunks are an integral part of his environment. As children, we'd spend hours sitting motionless on his front stoop, waiting to feed the chipmunks peanuts out of our hands. If we were lucky they'd climb on to our shoulders for a visit and snack. With no biological facts at my disposal, I've decided that each generation of bird and chipmunk

256. Solitudes Web site www.solitudes.com

must pass on in their DNA instructions as to how to get to the Gibsons. So that no matter where, or under what circumstances they are born, they know where to go to spend their summers.

In the living room is a huge stone fireplace built in the 1950s by local handyman Felix Lucasavitch (whose father also helped build the huge central fireplace at the nearby resort Arowhon Pines on Joe Lake). His somewhat cryptic response to Gibson's request that he build something rough to suit the décor of the cabin was that that was the only kind of fireplace that he knew how to build. Dan welcomes me with open arms and as we settle in during a rainy afternoon begins to tell me about the leaseholder role in treasuring the Park environment.

Long History of Caring

One of the core values binding Algonquin Park leaseholders together is their abiding desire to protect the Park from harm in whatever way possible. This includes its forests, its waterways, its wildlife, and the quality of the air and water. In 1938 the Canoe Lake and District Leaseholders Association was founded to not only promote a community spirit amongst the leaseholders of the Canoe Lake District, but also to cooperate with the authorities in maintaining laws and regulations governing the administration of the Park, the protection of animal life, and the preservation of natural beauty.[257] In 1957, long before organizations such as Algonquin Park Ecowatch came into existence, this same group adopted the "Conservation Pledge" from the Toronto Anglers and Hunters Association:

> *"I give my pledge, as a Canadian, to save and faithfully to defend from waste, the natural resources of my Country, its soil and minerals, its waters, forests and wildlife."*[258]

Since their beginnings, all of the leaseholder associations have been and continue to be active and opinionated organizations. They debate and discuss a wide range of environmental issues and are often the first to bring them to the attention to Park officials. More often than not it has been the associations that over the last 75 years have kept an eye on nearby logging operations, lake water levels, the status of fish stocks, and the impact of campers on campsites, trails, and leaseholder sites.[259] As indicated previously, it was the Cache Lake Leaseholders Association that launched the first public protest in the Toronto press in 1929 against the granting of timber rights to the McRae Lumber Company to log in Canisbay Township, which includes Cache Lake. To diffuse the issue, the Department of Lands and Forests Minister, Finlayson, established a 30.5-meter "no cut zone" around the shoreline of Cache Lake.[260] This encouraged Frank MacDougall to extend the

---

257. Canoe Lake and District Leaseholders Association minutes, 1938.
258. Canoe Lake and District Leaseholders Association correspondence, 1957.
259. Part of the Canoe Lake and District until 1960, when Smoke Lake leaseholders established their own association. Those living in the Rock Whitefish area formed the Rock Lake/Whitefish Lake Leaseholders Association in 1998. Those living in the north of the Park established their own working group and held their first meeting in the summer of 2004.
260. Gerald Killan, ***Protected Places: A History of Ontario's Provincial Parks System,*** 1993 pg. 60.

regulation in 1939 to encompass all lakes in the Park.

In the postwar years, it was painful for leaseholders to watch the environment around them degenerate due to the pressures of overuse. In 1950, over 1,000 floatplanes flew 1,137 anglers into isolated parts of the Park interior. The number of cars entering Algonquin Park grew from 28,662 in 1950 to 47,200 in 1953. The Lake of Two Rivers campground was suffering from overuse. One comment made was that the campsites were so close together that you could reach the salt and pepper shaker on the next person's table.[261] The once-pristine water in Cache Lake was polluted and unfit for drinking.[262] Though leaseholders played only a small and quite insignificant part in the resulting degradation of the Park's ecosystem, the recreational, occupational and political pressure from conservationists resulted in a desire to "restore Algonquin Park to a more natural state."[263]

In 1954, Frank MacDougall, who was now the Deputy Minister of Lands and Forests, issued the infamous Lands and Recreational Areas Circular #24 to all division chiefs and field offices. For years he had been a dear friend to a number of leaseholders. But for him, one can only assume that something changed as those relationships were broken and impact of these policy changes would affect the lives of leaseholders for decades. With no public hearings nor consultation of any sort, a new government policy was confirmed to over 100 people at the Canoe Lake and District Leaseholders Association annual meeting on Sunday, August 1, 1954. The first leases to expire were to be in 1976, with the last ones expiring in 1996. Not surprisingly, the Algonquin Park resident community was devastated. After over 40 years of encouragement and support, leaseholders of all sorts, including those who had started children's camps, and commercial lodges and built cabins, were now considered unwelcome. The very idea that leasees were perceived as the cause of Algonquin Park's problems had many scratching their heads.

After getting over the initial shock, most of the leaseholder associations—though generally supportive of the idea of returning the Park to its natural state—felt that such a goal was impossible without controlling its use by visitors. According to discussions captured in the minutes of various association meetings, it was felt that the Department needed to ensure that Park visitors understood the park regulations, and that the DLF needed to employ an adequate number of staffers to enforce the regulations. Without this understanding, it was rightly feared that "the destruction of the natural attractiveness of the Park would be hastened under the new policy as compared with the previous."[264] Attempts by the leaseholders to raise issues concerning the impact of the inexperienced campers seemed to go unheeded. Visitors' apparent disregard for the maintenance of the Park's natural beauty, including the leaving of smoldering fires, untidy campsites, and destruction of trees, was of significant concern. The Department made an effort to produce and distribute educational literature at the Park gates, only to find it thrown away and not read by visitors. Ultimately, it was the leaseholders who took care of campsites and unskilled campers on leasehold-occupied lakes, especially as park management budgets grew smaller and smaller.

---

261. Recollections from Rory MacKay, 2005

262. Gerald Killan, ***Protected Places: A History of Ontario's Provincial Parks System,*** 1993, pg. 77.

263. Ibid, pg. 88.

264. Canoe Lake and District Leaseholders Association minutes, 1954.

In the late 1960s, things began to come to a head. There was a "growing public fear that pollution was having an enormous deleterious impact on natural environments and that this posed a threat to individual health and well being."[265] In 1968, members of the various lake leaseholder associations came together to establish the Algonquin Park Residents Association (APRA) in response to the newly announced Ontario park classification system and the issuing of a first attempt at an Algonquin Park Master Plan.[266] As outlined in a letter to the Park officials, the mission of the new organization was to:

1. Act united in all matters concerning the common rights and interests of leaseholders.
2. Encourage the establishment of a long-sighted and firm policy for the protection of animal life, the preservation of the natural beauty of the entire Park, and particularly the Algonquin heartland.
3. The provision and maintenance of recreational areas for the enjoyment of all persons without discrimination as to income, age, vitality and health, and to actively support such policy.[267]

APRA's first initiative, led by President Don MacMurchy of Canoe Lake, was to sponsor a wide-ranging study of the Park issues from the leaseholder perspective. In December 1969, representing over 1,000 person-years of "association with and knowledge of the Park," APRA submitted probably one of the defining documents of its history.[268] Running to over 40 pages, the study, "***Algonquin Park: A Park for People,***" included not only a detailed analysis of the Park's existing features and issues and their relationships to one another, but also detailed criteria against which any Park planning needed to be measured and a specific set of goals for Park utilitization. According to the report, the Algonquin Park Master Plan should express the following goals:

1. To preserve and enhance the unique character of the Park, particularly the Algonquin Heartland
2. To provide an environment for optimum visitor use of the Park
3. To provide a wide variety of recreational opportunities in and near the Park
4. To assign maximum visitor capacities to all zones within the Park that are based on natural regenerative capacities of the land
5. To recognize the role of the automobile as the principal mode of access to the Park
6. To provide legislation and control mechanisms needed to implement the plan[269]

The study's conclusions are as true today as they were when first presented in 1969. After considerable additional public discourse (over 100 briefs were received), the final Algonquin Park Master Plan was issued in 1974 with many of the leaseholder recommendations included in the plan. Of key importance was the idea of enabling perimeter access points to take some of the usage pressure off of the Highway 60 corridor.

---

265. Gerald Killan, ***Protected Places: A History of Ontario's Provincial Parks System,*** 1993, pg. 160.
266. Ibid, pg. 166, for details as to the 1967 proposed classification system and its impact on Algonquin Park.
267. Algonquin Park Residents Association organizational announcement letter, 1968.
268. Algonquin Park Residents Association report, "Algonquin Park: A Park for People," 1969.
269. Ibid.

Summary of 1969 APRA Report Conclusions

1. **A Place for People**
The natural recreation areas of the province are measurable and expendable resources. The demand for outdoor recreation space in Ontario grows at a rate far greater than our population increase. We must wisely plan all our provincial parks to ensure that future generations of Ontario residents can know fresh air, clean water and unspoiled natural beauty. Algonquin Park Leaseholders rank amongst the foremost of citizen groups who respect the value of Algonquin Park, as a place for people and contribute (greatly) to its conservation.

2. **Immeasurable Value of the Heartlands**
The heartlands of Algonquin provide an unsurpassed environment for the young and the seasonal outdoorsman. No other part of Ontario provides a better natural classroom for teaching of self-reliance, for illustrating to children the wonders of nature, the importance of discipline and leadership, and to each child, something about him or herself. We believe that the heartlands must be preserved for the enjoyment and education of future visitors.

3. **The Leaseholder as a Responsible Participant**
The leaseholders in Algonquin have played a vital part in making the Park a better place for all to visit. Rescue work and clean up are considered by cottage owners to be substantial but non-specified responsibilities that run with each lease. The leaseholder is prepared to contribute towards the operation of the Park, to make their involvement with Park self-sustaining and at no burden to the general taxpayer. Comprehensive Park planning must include a positive role for leaseholders in stabilizing and preserving the natural environment of the Park. Not only is there a definite need for leaseholders (proven true many times each season), this need increases proportionately to the number of additional new trippers, campers and day visitors.

4. **Ecology – The Basis of the Plan**
The Park affords many kinds of recreational environments, each with varying use capacities. The Association staunchly holds that many more people could enjoy these resources provided that logical land use patterns are planned and densities of use are kept within ecological limits. Developed recreational facilities that attract large numbers of visitors should be placed in a high capacity circulation corridor located at the outer edges of the Park. Concentric bands of decreasing use activities should shade off into the wilderness heartlands preserved for the visiting naturalist and canoe tripper.

5. **Access as a Basic Planning Tool**
Access is the key to the proper distribution of Park activities and density control. APRA strongly recommends the development of a ring road system located near the boundaries of the Park. All intensive recreation areas such as auto and trailer camping grounds should be well spaced in the first tier or activity zone adjacent to the ring road. Outfitting stores and tourist resorts should be selectively located in this tier. Interpretive features such as nature schools, nature trails, museums and historic sites, along with children's camps and low-density summer cottage development, should be sited in the second tier. The third tier of development would include lakes that are within five to seven miles of canoe start-off spots where the largest concentration of canoe campsites would be required. All land beyond the third tier would be considered wilderness heartlands where no specific facilities would be required or developed.

Champions for and Treasuring the Forests

Up on the top of the cliffs, above Skymount Bay's sandy beach, was a fire tower that was part of a tower network built after WWI throughout the Park. The Fire Rangers who manned it earned 15 cents an hour and lived in a one-room Park Ranger cabin by the beach. Another tower overlooked the west shore of Smoke Lake. Built in 1925, this one was very unique because it was mounted eight feet above the top most branches of a 102-foot tall white pine tree. It came complete with platform, railing, and a room that could hold three men. Built of spruce poles that had been hauled up to the pine top by rope and then cut there with axes, the frame was fastened into place with angle braces. When John Standerwick Jr. of Smoke Lake was a teenager, he and two friends climbed it and said that they could see five lakes from the spot. It swayed in even the slightest breeze. This treetop tower was not used for fire detection after the 1930s, but did stand for a full 50 years until, according to local residents John Standerwick Jr. and George Garland the top of the ancient tree was knocked off in a summer storm in 1975. Though no longer visible from the lake, the remainder of the tree with the ladder still attached was still standing in 2000.

As use of the Park increased, so did the number of fires. Fires at campsites became more common with leaseholders playing a major role in putting them out. As was a common report to the DLF in the 1940s and 1950s:

> *"This it to let you know of another fire which I and my friend discovered yesterday in the yard of Skymount cabin. This now makes two within nine days there. Like the first, it was still a ground fire by the time we found it but unlike the first we know this time who left it. It was a larger fire than the other one and was perfectly placed for becoming a fire of major proportions both below and above ground. What bothers me is not the trivial effort of occasionally extinguishing a potential threat to my and other people's property, but the knowledge that without augmented vigilance on this lake, I or others may not be lucky enough to discover the next or succeeding fires until it is too late to do much about it."*[270]

In one summer, for example, the Camp Tamakwa staff extinguished a fire on a campsite on Tea Lake, and George Hayhurst did the same at the Tom Thomson Cairn on Canoe Lake. On another occasion, in 1936, there was a fire at the south end of Smoke Lake. Gar Northway from Nominigan used his large launch to quickly ferry men and equipment to the scene. They were able to put it out before it became a fire of huge proportions. On most lakes informal fire brigades were formed and still operate today. All leaseholders are knowledgeable as to who on their lake have fire pumps and what to do if a fire is discovered. In the summer of 2004, the Smoke Lake brigade was called into action. A lightning-induced fire was spotted on the hill above West Bay. While one leaseholder boated up to the Smoke Lake Hangar to advise Park officials, other cottagers came to the rescue and were mainly responsible for extinguishing the fire.[271] Though no cottages have ever been destroyed by forest fire, over the years lightning has destroyed its fair share. On Canoe Lake, lightning strikes in the 1960s destroyed the Davidson and Braucht/McFarlane cabins. On Smoke Lake, in 1987, lightning struck the Lawford cabin and destroyed a major portion of the main building. Every wood-

---

270. Cache Lake leasehold correspondence, 1947, Algonquin Park Museum Archives.
271. Recollections from the Lawford family, 2003.

to-metal surface, such as hinges and doorknobs, was scorched. The Lawfords' daughter Janine was paralyzed for a while as she had bare feet resting on the floor when the lightning hit.

Champions for and Treasuring the Wildlife

The observation of wildlife is a constant part of the Algonquin experience and every leaseholder has lots of stories about their experiences with wildlife. As Robert Beesley on Smoke Lake shared:

> *"When we were very young, in the 1950s, deer would come right up to our cottage and eat out of our hands, and with four children our bread supply rapidly disappeared. We had the occasional visit from a bear or moose and also all manner of smaller animals, including a fox, just last summer. We have also had the dubious pleasure of hosting the not-so-welcome species—the very moment our boathouse roof was reshingled several years ago, every seagull in the Park decided to call it home. They now have expanded to the dock and raft as well. We have also a 'year of the mouse' every so often. One year, there was such a steady stream of them, who scampered across the main beam of the cabin rafters that my brother dubbed their route* The 401.*"*

In the 1940s, deer were plentiful and moose were scarce and rarely seen. Some deer even became quite friendly. Ed and Molly Colson who ran the Hotel Algonquin had a number that would hang out, waiting for handouts. Each was given a name to fit its personality. In winter, Ed Colson would head into the bush on his sleigh and cut tender cedar branches for them. One special favourite, named Billy, used to roam quite extensively and also became a friend of Gertrude Baskerville on Tea Lake.[272] Even the Park Superintendent reported in 1945 that:

> *"The deer are coming up to the back door for a handout every afternoon. There were eight there feeding out of the barrels one at a time. A buck with a decent spread took a dislike to a doe and hit her a swat with his horns side wise and darned if he didn't knock one side off."*

In the last 20 years, the most common visitors have been moose. At the Hutchins cabin on Smoke Lake they often pass right by and stare in the front windows for several minutes.[273] Laird Saunderson on Source Lake told of how a moose he had named George would come down and hang his chin on the clothesline.[274] Brad Steinberg from Rock Lake and a friend had an unfortunate experience with a moose one winter. They had snowshoed down the plowed Rock Lake Road into the cottage with their golden retriever and a toboggan with supplies for the trip. The boys saw a large bull moose in the woods that, upon seeing them, charged across the road. Brad and friend dove into the bushes, but Timber was badly trampled. Brad managed to stuff his scarf and glove into the gaping wound in her chest and carry the dog back out to the vehicle and on to a vet. Timber had surgery, a bad infection and a lengthy recovery, but her ribs were wired back together. Luckily the moose's hooves had missed her vital organs.[275] On a brighter note, another remarkable wildlife story involved

---

272. For details of Gertrude Baskerville's experiences with Algonquin Park wildlife, ***Gertrude Baskerville: The Lady of Algonquin Park,*** 2001.
273. Recollections from the Hutchins family, 2004.
274. Recollections from the Saunderson family, 2003.
275. Recollections from Helen Steinberg, 2004.

a Canadian ruffed grouse that Robert Miller met at his lease on Galeairy Lake.

"Upon arriving in early August to open up the cottage, I came around one corner and a Ruffed Grouse with two peeps met me head on. The grouse immediately was protective of the peeps, swelling up like a balloon as she confronted me. A simple 'coo-coo' voiced by me convinced her that she had nothing to fear, for she immediately deflated and we were on a friendly basis for the rest of the summer. There was nothing tentative about my acceptance, for mother grouse would bring the peeps by every two or three days. On one occasion while we were having a cookout in front of the cottage, mother grouse dusted herself on the path while the peeps were busy picking and eating from shrubs and bushes here and there. Most remarkable was the bond established with me. On hearing their faint sounds, even in the distant wood, I would 'coo' and immediately hear the distinctive sound of beating grouse wings and mother grouse flew in to greet me. My closest encounter was experienced at our outhouse. I 'cooed' and in she flew, landing on the peak of the 'biffy' and then came down to the edge of the roof where, literally, eyeball to eyeball, we briefly 'cooed' to each other before she flew back to the peeps. We never attempted to touch nor did we ever feed the grouse."

Yet another amazing wildlife experience took place in the water just off the Miller dock.

"With my profession as a sailor and submariner, I had developed a great love of the sea and all that is within it. Galeairy Lake became the benefactor of this love, and I still am often seen with my mask, snorkel and fins swimming the lake to discover its underwater delights. Fish in Galeairy Lake normally move quickly away when confronted. They are curious about this human swimmer, but observe from a distance that often precludes me from seeing them in the limited-visibility water. This norm was changed one summer when, much to my amazement, I came upon a snapping turtle and a bass swimming together, there normally not being any harmony between the two. (How many fishermen have pulled up their stringers to find only fish heads left after a turtle feasted on the rest). I examined the big turtle, about 25 pounds, while the bass watched from a position close by. Upon concluding, I swam away and the 1½-pound bass followed, thus the beginning of another summer friendship.

I swim most days whether the weather is hot, cold, calm or stormy. My bass friend, although not waiting at the water's edge, most often would join up with me as the daily swim progressed and followed me very closely whether I was diving to investigate the bottom or swimming on the surface. I would occasionally put on a burst of speed with my fins, which would cause the bass to race past me until I slowed, at which point the bass would come back, look in my face mask, as if to say, 'You can't beat me! Why try?' When I would stop and rest with my feet on the bottom, the bass took up position between the calves of my legs and wouldn't move until I was ready to swim again. Friend bass was not above harmlessly nipping me on the body, it not being clear whether it wanted to get on with the swim or whether there was indecision as to my tastiness and edibility. I started to carry a few kernels of dried corn, which it would eat out of my hand. My final day of vacation, I swam one last time with the bass. It was not there the following summer. Not having had this experience repeated over the years, I am not sure whether this bass was 'crazy' or perhaps 'extra smart.' I like to think it was the latter which made our time together so very special."

Until the 1950s, wolves in Algonquin Park were considered a menace. The DLF would set snares and poison traps and rangers killed wolves at every opportunity. As was reported in 1935, "we get the thriftiest and strongest wolves in snares and not in traps. We very rarely get old and decrepit wolves."[276] Leaseholders always found wolves willing for the most part to share the forest with human visitors. Arthur Kenny on Cache Lake once met a wolf on the railroad bed that trotted off when he told it to leave. At the Keens' cabin on Cache Lake, what seemed like a half-tame wolf that was often seen near the old museum stayed around for days and would look in the windows of their cabin.[277] At the Henrys' cabin on Smoke Lake, a wolf trotted across the back of the cottage about 20 feet from their back door.[278] In 1939, J. R. Dymond tried to convince the DLF that their obsessive pursuit of wolves was unnecessary. He sent to MacDougall a report by a colleague named Dunne, who had spent a winter tracking wolves in the Park. The report included observations about wolf habitat, such as the difference between day and night travel routes, hunting methods and size of packs, and the inability of wolves to always secure deer. This began the change in thinking that perhaps wolves were a species to be protected, not destroyed. Today, the popularity of the Park-sponsored summer "wolf howl" shows how far attitudes have changed.

One of the roles that leaseholders have taken on in the last few decades has been to help with the protection of loons. In 1988, a group of leaseholders on Canoe Lake noticed that Whiskey Jack Creek had become a popular loon-nesting site. However, fluctuations in water levels in the spring would frequently wash out the nests. Sometimes visitors would get too close to the nesting mother and she would get frightened off of her nest. This would leave the eggs open to predation. In the old days, when the late Canoe Lake Postmaster Everett Farley tended to the dams, his careful watch kept things close to a natural state and the problem was minimal. After much discussion and experimenting, a project was initiated to build a floating raft that could be disguised as a loon's nest. The first experimental floating nest was a six-foot by eight-foot raft, with accompanying natural vegetation, built by leaseholders John and Jeff Ridpath, Dan and Danny Gibson, Don Lloyd, and Chuck Gray. A nesting pair found it and successfully hatched a baby loon. Since then, a pair of loons has nested there every year, though not always successfully. A few years later, another successful raft was launched on Bonita Lake and later one up Potter Creek and another one down in the southernmost bay of Canoe Lake.

Champions for and Treasuring the Water

In addition to worrying about the wildlife and the quality of the fishing, leaseholders also had tremendous concerns about water quality. Records show that the first leaseholder-identified problems with water quality were noted in 1933. Louisa Blecher, a leaseholder on the long-abandoned Mowat Town site, wrote the DLF to request an investigation into the 'deplorable condition of a garbage dump maintained by the camps on the east shore [of the entrance to Whiskey Jack Creek]'.[279] Two rangers, Kennedy and McCormick, came out to investigate but no report of any consequence was forthcoming. By 1935 Blecher was angry and undertook to have a water analysis done. She was advised by the Ontario Department of Health that all of the water around

276. DLF correspondence, 1935, Algonquin Park Museum Archives.
277. Richard Eldridge and Orville Osborne, ***Cache Lake Reflections,*** 1995, pg. 40.
278. Recollections from the Henry family, 2004.
279. Blecher lease correspondence Algonquin Park Museum Archives 1933 and excerpted from Gaye I. Clemson's, Algonquin Voices; Selected Stories of Canoe Lake Women 2002.

the entry to the creek was very much contaminated. In 1936 Louisa again wrote to advise that another dump had been started just south of the one that was already there. This time it was in the form of a floating raft with the contents partly in the water. This raft was destroyed by fire but another was then started 400 feet south of the remains of the original floating raft. As Louisa so eloquently stated herself,

> *"One cannot believe that civilized people can be so filthy as to permit the condition to exist which I observed this morning. Directly on the shoreline was a large pile of excrement and toilet paper dumped there from toilet cans along with garbage, tin cans, mattresses etc. There is seepage from the litter into the water even with the water level being low – some 3 feet below normal. I cannot be assured of health with such filthy conditions existing so close to my home."*[280]

That same year Gillender and Krantz, also neighbours to the dump, echoed Louisa's concerns about the handling of garbage at the dumpsite. As they wrote so poignantly, "not only is the smell of garbage and disinfectant distressing, but the fact that wash water is going straight into the lake is a menace to health."[281]

In 1956, cottagers and campers in the Park were advised to boil or chlorinate all drinking water whether tested for purity or not.[282] A couple of years later, Chuck Gray had the water in front of his Canoe Lake cabin tested by the Department of Health. The test results showed bacterial counts that made it still unfit for drinking without chlorinating or boiling. No one knew why. There was some speculation that it was a result of Hurricane Audrey, which struck the U.S. Gulf Coast on June 27, 1957, and landed in Canada on Canada Day, July 1. As was recalled by Don Lloyd of Canoe Lake and others:

> *"So much water fell that it overwhelmed many of the beaver dams. The ones holding back March Hare Lake east of the Camp Ahmek waterfront broke, which sent a huge wall of water down the rocky gorge, which lead to Hickey Creek (now called Wigwam Bay). That plus overflow at Joe Lake Dam made the water level in Canoe Lake go up over three feet."*[283]

At the south end of Canoe Lake, the water level rose almost to the front steps of the Portage Store. The Thompsons' fireplace was completely underwater, as was the whole of their north point. They were even able to paddle the canoe under the front porch to inspect the footings beneath the house. The flood put a foot of mud on the Stringer cabin floor on Potter Creek. Pappy Stringer refused to leave the house, so his son Wam had to paddle in the front door to rescue him out of the kitchen. At Janie Roberts' place, the storm brought down 17 trees and Janie had to paddle out and erect a flag to mark the end of the dock. At the Grays', Dorothy got up to feed the baby in the middle of the night and had to run out in the wind and rain to pull the canoe halfway up the hill so that it would be above the high-water mark. Those on Smoke Lake had to paddle to the parking lot at the Smoke Lake Landing and move their cars so that they wouldn't float away. Trails were flooded, trees came down everywhere, and on Smoke Lake the water piled up and overflowed the bridge at Highway 60, which was the only exit for all the leaseholders on the east side of the lake.

---

280. Blecher correspondence in the MNR lease archives
281. Gillender and Krantz correspondence in the MNR lease archives
282. Canoe Lake and District Leaseholders Association minutes and correspondence, 1956.
283. Liz Lundell, editor, ***Fires of Friendship: Eighty Years of the Taylor Statten Camps***, pg. 130.

By 1968, it was apparent to some leaseholders, especially those on Lake of Two Rivers that something was seriously wrong with the water quality on many of the Highway 60 corridor lakes. That summer it was estimated that over 2,000 visitors had camped at the Lake of Two Rivers campground, a site that could support half that number.[284] Mary Macaulay, daughter of the Honorable Leopold Macaulay and a Lake of Two Rivers leaseholder had for years, been sending samples of the lake water on Lake of Two Rivers for testing several times each summer. In July of 1968, the results from a water sample from near her cottage came back unsatisfactory. She took her concerns to Park officials and was told that cottagers were causing the high degree of pollution due to their inadequate sewage disposal methods. Surprised at this response, she took her concerns to the Algonquin Park Residents Association (APRA). As recalled by Dr. Iain MacKay, the then Vice-President of APRA:

"[We] immediately decided to do a survey. Consequently, in August 1968, water testing kits were obtained from the Public Health Laboratory Service of the Ontario Department of Health and following their techniques and using sterile precautions, water from several locations in each of the [16] inhabited lakes along the Highway 60 corridor was tested and reports were received on each sample. This report was discussed with Park officials in early 1969, presented in detail at the APRA summer annual meeting and to the Minister of Lands and Forests in December. I was later criticized by some departmental personnel for doing this survey. I was told not to use the Public Health Laboratory Service of the Province of Ontario for any further survey. The Laboratory Director was informed of this reprimand also."[285]

Of the 62 samples drawn from 16 lakes and rivers, 48% showed that fecal coliform organisms were present, and an additional 30% had other coliform organisms present to such a degree that additional testing was recommended before the water could be considered safe for drinking. Only 22% of all of the samples drawn had no fecal or other coliform organisms present.[286] Needless to say, the majority of the heavily polluted areas were the densely populated areas around campgrounds, children's camps, the Portage Store. The worst situation was at Pog Lake and Lake of Two Rivers. In August 1969, the DLF posted signs closing all Lake of Two Rivers beaches that remained for the rest of the season and began to initiate regular water testing. Later, according to the recollections of Dr. MacKay:

"The earth pit toilets used at the Lake of Two Rivers campground were removed, sewage holding tanks were installed and a sewage collection service was initiated. In addition, proper washing and laundry facilities were established, the overflow area at the former Relief Camp was closed and the campground capacity was reduced."[287]

On Canoe Lake, one of the perceived major contributors to the extensive outboard motor-oil scum and destruction of shorelines was the "Miss Algonquin Park." Established in the early 1960s by the concessionaire of the Portage Store, the "Tom Thomson Memorial Boat Tour" was a major draw to the lake. Originally a wooden cruiser, the boat would take tourists on an hour-long, 16-mile trip tour. It would cruise north up the

---

284. Algonquin Park Residents Association report, "Algonquin Park: A Park for People," 1969, pg. 42.
285. Recollections from Dr. Iain MacKay some years after the event.
286. Algonquin Park Residents Association report, "Algonquin Park: A Park for People," 1969, pgs. 45-50.
287. Written recollections from Dr. Iain MacKay some years after the event.

lake past the Tom Thomson Totem Pole and Cairn, then down the west side of the lake and through the Bonita Narrows to South Tea Lake and back. This tour was so successful that a few years later, the "Miss Algonquin Park," a glass-topped, 100-passenger, all-weather steel vessel was imported from service at the Toronto Islands in Lake Ontario. In 1969, it carried close to 24,000 people, each paying $1.50 a person. Though a great generator of tourist dollars, it had significant environmental impact as it ran on diesel fuel and generated a very large wake. Over the years, the wake did a fair bit of damage to leaseholder docks, retaining walls, and sections of shoreline all along its route. Eventually, one presumes that leaseholder complaints and new regulations intending to return the Park to a more natural state contributed to its 1973 demise.[288]

Champions for and Treasuring Algonquin Park's Heritage

In 1930, Taylor Statten, known as "The Chief," spearheaded the creation of a commemorative totem pole that was erected next to the Tom Thomson Cairn that had been placed there by artist friends of Tom Thomson in 1917.[289] Though not native to the area, the totem pole became a landmark and an immediate tourist attraction on the lake. The best description of its origins can be found in the "***Fires of Friendship***" history of Taylor Statten Camps and is repeated here.[290]

> *"One July day in 1930, Miss Blodwin Davies of Toronto arrived in camp in search of information concerning Tom Thomson. Small groups met to talk about the artist and to discuss plans for a celebration in his honour. Larger groups became interested and soon the whole camp was infected. As a result of this enthusiasm, it was decided to erect a totem pole near the cairn, which would preserve in symbolic form the spirit and the achievement of the artist. The pole was designed by Hal Haydon and Gordon Webber. It was carved by Jack Ridpath (owner of the Toronto firm Ridpath's Ltd., a maker of fine furniture), but was painted in camp. Frank Braucht, a Canoe Lake resident, orchestrated the 25-foot pole's erection, which was difficult due to the fact that it needed to stand 'four-square' to all the winds that blow across Canoe Lake. On August 16, just as the sun was setting, crafts of every description silently slipped away from Big Wapomeo, Little Wapomeo and the Ahmek shore to gather near Hayhurst Point. While the boats were taking up their positions, 'The Chief,' Mark Robinson, a retired Park Ranger and Thomson friend, and others climbed up to the cairn. Mark Robinson dedicated the totem pole and added a few words of tribute to the artist. A birch-bark canoe filled with wild flowers was paddled silently down an aisle of boats to a landing at the foot of the hill, where a guard of honour was waiting to carry it to the top. The canoe was placed at the foot of the totem pole, the paddles of the canoes below flashed in a salute, and simple emblems, wreaths of evergreen and wild flowers, were cast on the water. As the sunset began to fade and twilight stole softly in, the boats slipped quietly away and the majestic totem was left in the northern peace and quiet, a picturesque symbol of a great artist and his deep love of the trails and waters of the north."*

Decades later, in 1959, with the support of the Canoe Lake and District Leaseholders Association, nearby

---

288. Gaye I. Clemson, ***Canoe Lake Chronicles,*** 2001, pg. 114.
289. For details into the mysterious disappearance and death of Tom Thomson see ***Canoe Lake, Algonquin Park: Tom Thomson and Other Mysteries.***
290. Liz Lundell, editor, ***Fires of Friendship: Eighty Years of the Taylor Statten Camps,*** 2000, pg. 66.

resident George Hayhurst rebuilt the Tom Thomson stone cairn. Frank Braucht added the commemorative poem describing the totem's figures and their meaning, which was then framed and attached to the totem pole. A rededication ceremony was held that August. Today, the Tom Thomson Totem Pole and Cairn is a major attraction to the Canoe Lake area and is maintained by the cooperative efforts of the Canoe Lake and District Leaseholders Association, local neighbours and Park officials, but spearheaded by Canoe Lake residents John and Jeff Ridpath, the son and grandson of Jack Ridpath.

In addition, three other major historic sites are protected and preserved by leaseholders of Canoe Lake. First is the Mowat Cemetery, where Thomson was buried for a short time after his untimely death.[291] Located on a hill above what was at the turn of the 20th century the bustling lumber town of Mowat, this historic site contains two occupants who rest inside a gray picket fence. One is a lumber mill hand named James Watson, who died in a mill accident in 1897. The second is leaseholderThomas Hayhurst's son Alexander, who died at age 8 in a 1915 diphtheria outbreak. There are those of us who believe that Thomson's spirit if not his bones still reside there, although officially he his buried at Leith near Owen Sound, Ontario. A second site at the north end of Canoe Lake includes the remains of the Canoe Lake Mills, the chip yard, and the town of Mowat. The Mowat town site has been reclaimed by forest and water. On a calm, sunny day, if one looks down into the water, one can see that the lake bottom is covered with large slabs of wood, which is all that remains of the chip yard that once blanketed the land. To the south, a few short steps into the forest reveals the footings of the sawmill that once dominated the shoreline. The third historic site is the remains of a sawmill, that may be found about a half-mile away up Potter Creek. This one was built and operated in the 1930s and 1940s by two different lumber companies and, except for the circular cement base of the sawdust burner, is completely hidden from shore by the spruce trees that have grown up around the site.

On Rock Lake are two other historic sites that are unofficially kept an eye on by the members of the Rock Lake/Whitefish Lake Leaseholders Association. First is the Barclay Estate, which is located on the west side of the lake and includes the cement pillars that supported the three-slip boathouse that had served as a social centre and dance hall for the lake for many years. Also evident (at least to the knowledgeable observer) are the remains of the estate's house and tennis courts and the nearby Men-Wah-Tay Station. Across the lake are the possible remains of a collection of Indian ceremonial pits and rock cairns tucked away in the forest, used perhaps for visions quests by Indian bands in the area centuries ago.[292] On Cache Lake, is the Recreation Hall, built as part of the Highland Inn as a storage facility in 1932 as well as the sites of both the former Highland Inn and Algonquin Park Station and related trestle bridges, which were the lifeline of the community for the first 50 years or so of the 20th century.[293]

Including the author, a number of community members have over the last century been contributors to the human heritage of the Park. Lake of Two Rivers' Roderick MacKay, a high school teacher, historian and a part time archeologist has written an important book about Algonquin and another about the Bonnechère area.

---

291. For details of this incident see ***Canoe Lake, Algonquin Park: Tom Thomson and Other Mysteries,*** by S. Bernard Shaw.

292. For details of this find, see ***Rock Lake Station: Settlement Stories Since 1896*** by Gaye I. Clemson, pg. 33.

293. Unfortunately in March 2006, the roof of the Cache Lake Rec Hall collapsed due to the weight of the winter's snow. It is unclear as of this writing if it will be rebuilt.

He is also the original writer and maintainer of the official chronology of Algonquin Park. As mentioned previously, also from Lake of Two Rivers, his brother Niall researched and wrote the history of the Ottawa, Arnprior and Parry Sound Railway. Don Lloyd, from Canoe Lake has written a detailed guide of canoe trip routes to aid those canoe tripping into the interior. Helen Mooney Wright has written both a book about her childhood near Joe Lake Station, and another about key Park Superintendents who influenced the Park's growth and development. Mary McCormick Pigeon from Cache Lake has written two booklets about her life both on Brule and Cache lakes. George Garland from Smoke Lake edited a compilation of stories that was used to celebrate the 100-year anniversary of the Park in 1993. Ester Keyser, with her the help of her son John, wrote a book on her experiences as the Park's first female canoe tripping guide. Joanne Kates, a well-known Toronto food critic and Joe Lake leaseholder, wrote a handy guide that has been updated several times to exploring Algonquin for first time visitors. Dr. Edmund Kase chronicled the life of Park Ranger Jack Gervais. Of course the now nationally known Roy MacGregor often refers in his writing, to his many childhood summers spent on Lake of Two Rivers at his grandfather Tom McCormick's cottage.

Environment

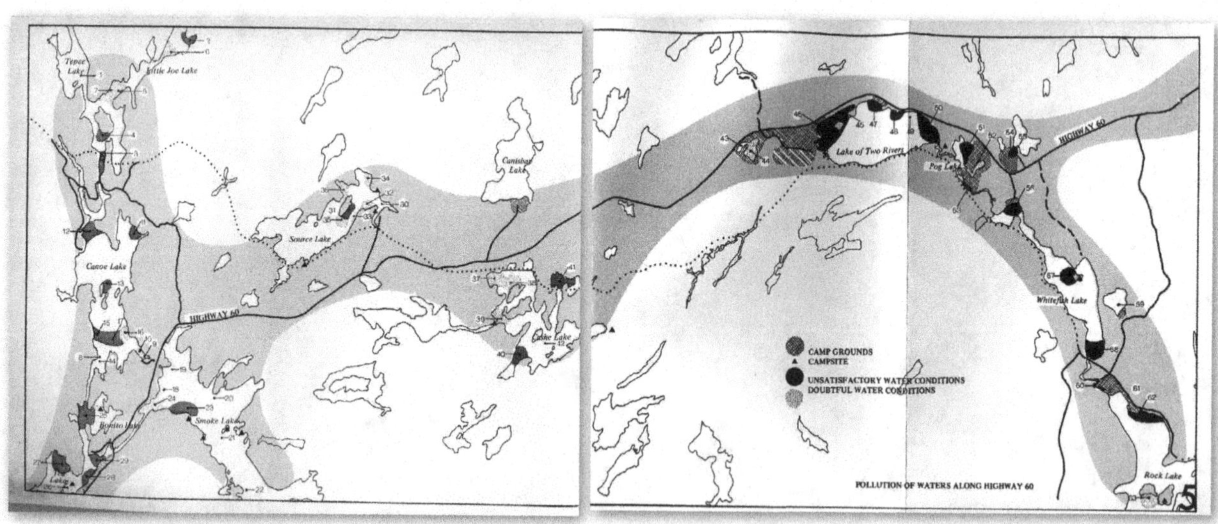

Map Illustrating Areas of Water Quality Concern 1969

Nature Photos by Thom Dernoga of Source Lake 2005

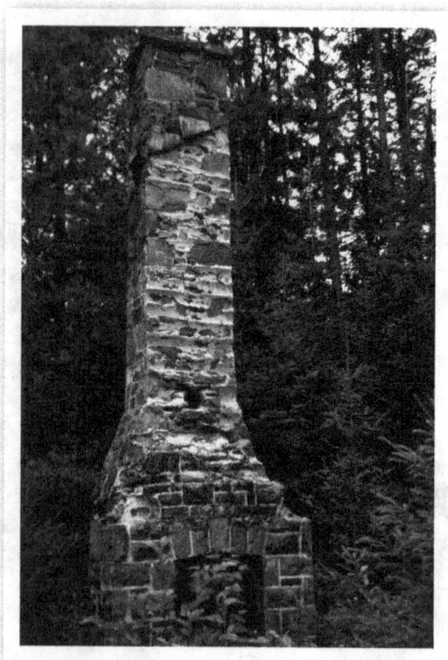

Farley Chimney 1998 Remains on Potters Creek
Clemson Collection

Minnesing Fireplace 1978 APMA #4472

Closing Lake of Two Rivers Beach MacKay Collection

Houston Chimney Remains on Canoe Lake
Clemson Collection

Chuck Gray Inspecting Canoe Lake Loon Raft
Gray Collection

MacKay Cottage View From Lake MacKay Collection

Cache Lake Leaseholds Beaupré Collection

Barely Visible From the Water Beaupré Collection

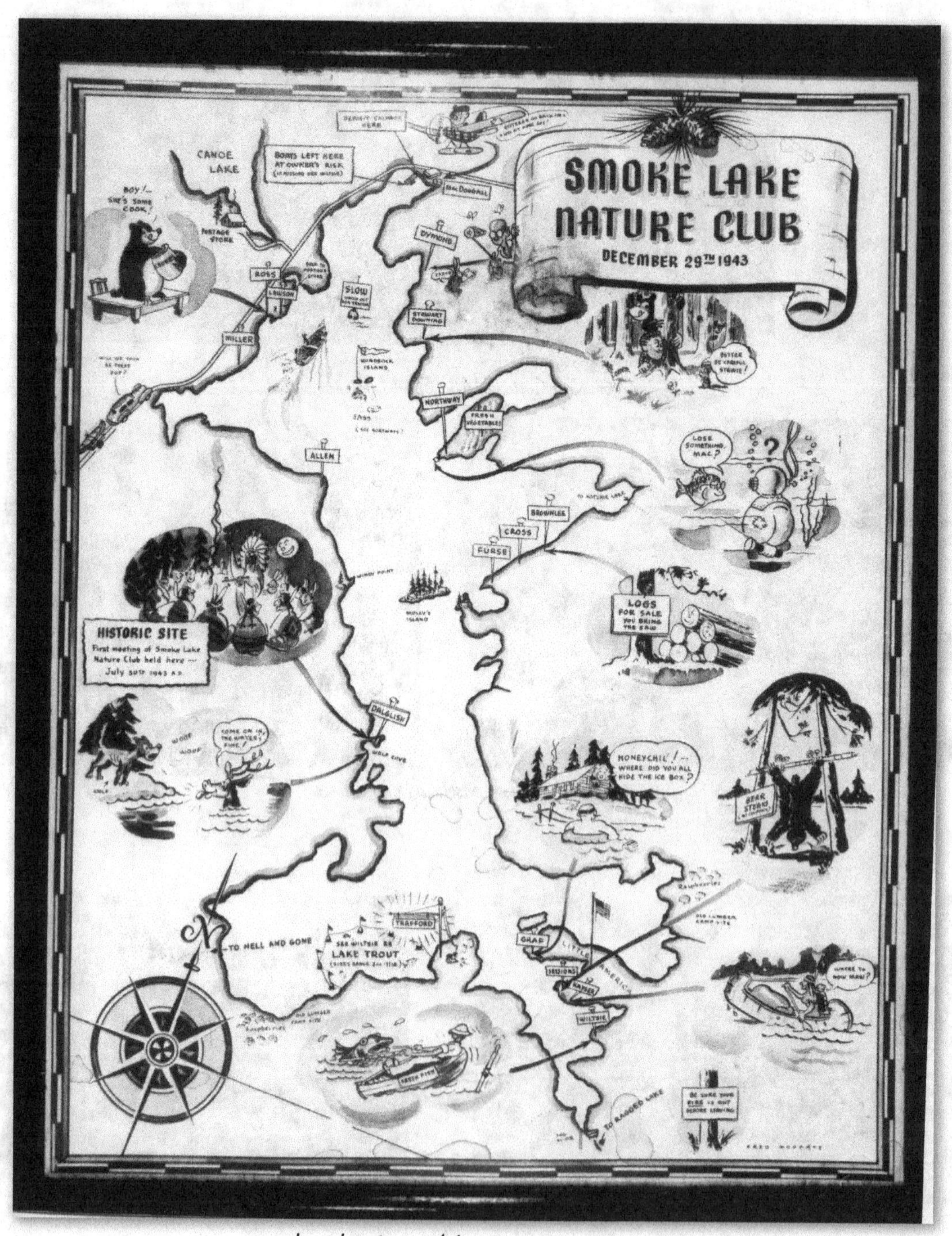

Smoke Lake Nature Club Map 1943 APMA #2396

Chapter 7

Contributions to Quality Park Experiences

This project has now become an obsession and nearly eight years of story-collecting have passed since I first ventured down this trail. In the course of my research, I've also discovered that leaseholders have been engaged in a wide range of activities in the Park designed to contribute to quality experiences by all who visit. I am curious to find out if there is anyone who might have some insight into the character of some of these people, as most if not all of them are long gone. I'm told that George Garland on Smoke Lake is the person to see. I call him on the phone and he invites me down to visit him at his cottage on the south end of Smoke Lake. George first came to Algonquin Park, as a child in the 1930s. His recollection of the train ride in from Scotia Junction is a fascinating story. A geophysics professor by trade, he has played an active role in many aspects of Algonquin Park life. As an Algonquin Park historian, he compiled and edited a book published to coincide with the 100th anniversary of the Park in 1993. Called **Glimpses of Algonquin Park**, *it is a collection of historical documents from the early Algonquin Park explorers to Esther Keyser's narrative of watching a loon being born in her tiny bay on Smoke Lake.*

In addition to being a longtime Director and Founding Father of the Friends of Algonquin Park, George is well known as a frequent rescuer and shelterer of canoe trippers. His cottage is located on the far south end of Smoke Lake, about a quarter of a mile north of the Ragged Lake portage. Smoke Lake is one of the largest and deepest lakes in the Park and can generate fierce headwinds for canoe trippers paddling both north and south. Unfortunately, the topography of the lake is such that the full extent of the wind from the north is often not evident until one is just about parallel to George's dock. Over the years, his dock and often his living room have been places of respite for many a tripper unable to make it up the lake. One of his funniest stories was reported recently in Cottage Life magazine. One day as he sat on his dock enjoying the afternoon sun, he saw a woman in the bow of a canoe several hundred meters off shore sitting in a way that was totally unsafe, given the size of the waves and the strength of the headwind. He yelled out to her: "On your knees! On your knees!" She looked at him and yelled back, "I certainly will once I get out of this canoe and off this godforsaken lake!"[294] *On another occasion, a letter to the editor was published in the Toronto Star reporting that over the course of Canada Day in 2001, 15 strangers of all shapes and sizes, unable to battle the whitecaps, ended up on George's dock. As Ryan and Colleen Robinson from Georgetown, Ontario, wrote about this saviour of Park visitors:*

> *"George welcomed each and every one with open arms. He proceeded to take us into his warm cottage where he lit a fire and served everyone a welcome cup of hot chocolate or tea. By nightfall, it was evident that the lake was still unsafe to paddle. Without hesitation, George invited us all to stay the night. Some of us ended up sleeping on his living room floor, while others occupied his porch, his bunkee and his boathouse. Needless to say, we were all ever so grateful for these accommodations. [George] did an amazing job of making 15 strangers feel welcome and at home. We truly enjoyed his company and will always remember him as our Smoke Lake Saviour."*[295]

One of George's other hobbies has been to track down the location of specific painting sites in Algonquin Park of famous Canadian artist Tom Thomson. One site that he and others had been unable to identify was that of "Northern River," one of Thomson's most celebrated works and one that he allegedly called his "Swamp Picture." In 2001, George's curiosity got the best of him. He had studied the Mark Robinson, the Park Ranger when Thomson painted "Northern River" in 1914-1915. With Canoe Lake resident John Ridpath, who knew the area well, George headed east from Canoe Lake off into the bush. About halfway along the Drummer Lake portage, they bushwhacked north and eventually found a donut-shaped swamp, which they guessed was likely the swamp of Thomson's "Swamp Picture." Even though nearly 90 years had passed, it looked, according to George, substantially the same as it did when Thomson painted it.[296]

To get to his cottage from mine on Canoe Lake, I head south through Bonita Lake Narrows, turn east at the Tea Lake Campground, and pass under the Smoke Creek Bridge. The bridge was replaced in 1999 after a horrific lumber truck crash and fire that destroyed the original wooden, creosote-soaked structure. I miss the smell of creosote and the barn swallows that used to summer there every year. Originally a small narrow waterway with barely a trickle in summer, Smoke Creek is now reasonably deep, unless one strays too far from the middle of the waterway. I take it slow so as to not hit any rocks or deadheads from the logging days. I recall a funny story told to me by the relatives of Kay Beckett, a longtime Canoe Lake resident whose brother Reg had a lease on Smoke Lake.

> *"Frequently the two families, one on Smoke Lake and the other on Canoe Lake, would get together for meals and a bit of socializing. Kay Beckett had a high degree of self-confidence in his ability to navigate Smoke Creek and always came through it at full throttle. Both Kay and Reg shared a love of the finer things in life, including an excellent Scotch named Islay Mist. One Saturday evening, after having a late dinner at Smoke Lake, Kay set off for Canoe Lake at his usual full throttle. Perhaps Kay was a bit tired, or perhaps there was a scotch-induced mist on Smoke Creek, but he hit a rock*

---

294. ***Cottage Life*** magazine, May/June edition, 2005.
295. ***Toronto Star***, letter to the editor, July 2001.
296. Though called "Northern River" by the National Gallery, which bought the painting in 1916, it was allegedly known to Thomson as his "Swamp" picture.

near the bridge and the boat sank. It was later salvaged and used for many years as the Portage Store Taxi."[297]

Once out of the creek, I head south past Sandy Beach or what some call "Rangers Point," which was for me a favorite childhood picnicking spot with a wonderful stretch of shallow water with a sand bottom. Nearby in a meadow and the forest once stood a local Park Ranger cabin and the tree-built fire tower. After a few minutes I pass on the east shore Nominigan Point and then Molly's Island. Eventually the long east and west arms of the lake stretch out on either side into the distance, and George's flagpole comes into view. Even with a 9-horsepower engine, it takes a good 30 minutes to traverse the length of Smoke Lake. George is happy to see me and welcomes me with lunch. We settle down on his porch and he shares his tales of Park leasehold ventures.

Contributors to the Park Interpretive Programs

In addition to their current role as protectors of some of Algonquin Park's heritage sites, Algonquin Park's leaseholders have also made major contributions to ensuring that those who visit have a quality experience. Many of those contributions have been in the form of commercial tourist ventures. But one that has perhaps been the most lasting contribution has been the role played in the establishment of interpretive programs by J. R. Dymond, a Smoke Lake resident and leading Canadian naturalist.

At the behest of fellow Smoke Lake resident Jessie Northway, J. R. Dymond and fellow naturalist James Savage had been leading nature hikes around Smoke Lake for a number of years. The success of these hikes led to the formation of the "Smoke Lake Naturalist Club." Frank MacDougall, who became the DLF Deputy Minister in 1941 and was a good friend of Dymond's, heard of these activities. He was also familiar with Dymond's knowledge, experience and professional life at the Department of Zoology with the University of Toronto, so in 1944 asked Dymond if he would consider developing a similar framework for a public program. Dymond agreed, and in the summer of 1944 conducted a series of nature hikes and talks at the local youth camps and lodges. By 1946 the program had become a three-pronged effort that included conducted nature hikes, public lectures, and a wildlife exhibit tent. The exhibit tent was set up at Cache Lake near the Park Headquarters. It included a few mounted specimens of birds and mammals that had been donated from the Royal Ontario Museum. Later, in 1947, living amphibians and reptiles, plants, and geological models were added. The program was a success and that first summer over 3,400 people signed the guest register, jumping to nearly 6,000 in 1947.

According to Allan Helmsley, who helped Dymond set up the program, the first conducted nature hikes were pretty basic. Using a mile-long existing portage and railway tracks, the hike started at the Highland Inn on

297. Recollections from the Beckett family, 2004.

Cache Lake. It ran eastward along the old railway bed over one or two of the abandoned railway trestles and then immediately turned south. It then climbed to the top of Skymount ridge, and provided a fabulous lookout over the whole of Cache Lake.[298] Later they also used a trail at Canisbay and established the Deer Lake Nature Trail that led to a bay on Smoke Lake. Hand-printed labels containing the names and brief characteristics of trees, ferns, and common wildflowers were attached to the plants. Initial advertising was a bulletin put up at the Lake of Two Rivers campgrounds and at the various lodges in the Park. Dymond was a unique hike leader because he liked to lead hikes that resulted in meaningful discourse and questions. He loved to share his ideas about ecology and the complexities of the environment. His objective was "to stimulate interest, not give all the answers but create mystery and provoke thought."[299] For the first few years, hike leaders would distribute a mimeographed list of common plants and animals. When Dymond led them, he'd start at 9:30 a.m. or 10 a.m. and always included lunch. To him, lunch was an important part of the whole hike, because he got to know the people a little better. He had found over the years that people were more relaxed and open for conversation while sitting down having a sandwich. It gave him time to talk to people and gave them time to ask questions.[300]

During the program's first year, in 1946, there were 22 hikes with 366 participants, as well as nine evening lectures at the Highland Inn. The early success of the program encouraged Dymond to propose that a certificate be provided for those who had obtained a certain knowledge of nature with four grades of naturalist: Beginning, Junior, Intermediate, and Senior Naturalist. Within each grade, there was a target number of trees, birds, and other forms of plant and animal life with which naturalists should be familiar. Dymond also felt strongly that participants also needed to grasp what he called "certain principles of behaviour in the forest." These included such things such as not killing any plants or animals without good cause, and not destroying the beauty of trails and roads by defacing trees or uprooting plants or throwing paper and other litter about.[301] The success of these various programs convinced Dymond that professional-looking, illustrated booklets that visitors could obtain for a small charge needed to be prepared, so that the participant could become familiar with some of the commoner plants and animals.[302] He also felt that a permanent Park naturalist staff and a proper museum building were needed. He lobbied Deputy Minister MacDougall extensively, and in 1952 the Algonquin Park Museum opened at Found Lake. Its first year of operation with completed exhibits was in 1953, during which time attendance reached 52,000 visitors According to Allan Helmsley:

> *"The first lecture in the lecture hall that could contain 100 people was standing-room only. We then added an outdoor program at the Cache Lake Rec Hall that took place in July and August. There was no set agenda and the naturalists would talk about whatever interested them. Lodge owners in the area welcomed the program and would turn over their dining rooms every other week and all the guests would come to the 'nature' talk."*[303]

---

298. Today this original trail forms part of what is now called the Track and Tower Trail located off of Highway 60 at km 25.
299. Interview with Allan Helmsley by Ron Pittaway, 1976.
300. Interview with Allan Helmsley by Ron Pittaaway, 1976, and the Dymond Interpretive Program Report to Dr. William J. K. Harkness head of the Fish and Wildlife Division of the DLF in 1947, 1947.
301. Dymond Interpretive Program Report to Dr. William J. K. Harkness head of the Fish and Wildlife Division of the DLF in 1947.
302. Ibid.
303. Article by Ron Tozer, "50 Years of Interpretation in Algonquin Park," published in ***Interpscan, 1994.***

These initial efforts spawned a comprehensive program that is now an integral part of the Algonquin Park experience. The centrepiece is the Algonquin Park Visitor Centre, which opened in 1993, just in time to celebrate the Park's 100th anniversary. Dymond's idea for a few Park-related booklets about the natural world in Algonquin Park is now a huge collection of booklets about all aspects of the Park's ecosystem, including trees, plants, birds, insects, butterflies, mammals, mushrooms, reptiles, and wildflowers, as well as over a dozen technical bulletins managed by the Friends of Algonquin Park about various aspects of Algonquin Park life. His ideas about how to conduct hikes have led to the production of 17 trail guides that introduce hikers to a different theme about Algonquin's human or natural history. Each guide contains a map of the walking trail, and the text is keyed to numbered posts along the trail.[304] During the summer months there are a wide variety of guided hikes, canoe outings, and a special daily program for kids at the Visitor Centre—all of which are extensions of J. R. Dymond from Smoke Lake's efforts to provide and encourage interpretation of the natural world in Algonquin Park.

Contributions to the well being and management of the Park have been a part of the Algonquin Park leasehold experience since its early days. As mentioned previously, it was the residents of Cache Lake in 1929 who raised the first public firestorm in the Toronto press that ensured that Cache Lake shorelines were protected from logging. It also led to the precedent-setting Park policy that no timber could be cut within 300 feet of any lake or highway or within 150 feet of any river or portage. In 1938 the Canoe Lake and District Leaseholders Association (CLDLA) was founded to cooperate with the authorities in maintaining laws and regulations governing the administration of the Park, the protection of animal life, and the preservation of natural beauty.

With these goals in mind, many leaseholders and youth camp staff members lent a hand in maintaining portages when the DLF was short staffed during WWI. Today, some lend a hand by supporting the Adopt-a-Trail program on Highway 60.[305] It was the 1969 APRA Report that proposed the idea of a ring of access points so that recreational facilities could be spread less densely over a greater area and reduce the concentration on the Highway 60 corridor. This report was also one of the first—if not the first—to recognize, validate, and bring to public focus the water pollution problems in Park lakes in the late 1960s.[306] In this same report, leaseholders suggested that their rental fees be raised so that their involvement with the Park would be self-sustaining and not a burden to the general taxpayer. It was also Cache Lake residents who proposed, motorboat size restrictions and at one point even suggested a complete ban of motorboats on all Park lakes.

Leaseholders have also made an important contribution to and role in the development and growth of The Friends of Algonquin Park. Established in 1983, The Friends of Algonquin Park, a non-profit charitable organization, is dedicated to furthering the educational and interpretive programs in Algonquin Park. Operating under five-year agreements with the Ontario Parks, The Friends is responsible for:

"Developing and reprinting Park-related publications and funding Park projects through the proceeds from

---

304. www.algonquinpark.on.ca

305. For example: Dr. Robert Clappison and Jan Richmond from Canoe Lake monitor the Hardwood Lookout Trail and the Peck Lake Trail respectively.

306. Algonquin Park Residents Association Report, "Algonquin Park: A Park for People," pg. 2.

> *sales at The Friends' two bookstores in the Park, private donations, and various fundraising efforts. The activities of The Friends of Algonquin are coordinated by a volunteer Board of Directors who reside in different parts of Ontario. Since its establishment, The Friends has grown to a membership of over 3,000 people, and continues to attract support from around the world as the organization becomes better known.*[307]

On the Board of Directors over the years have been a number of leaseholders, including Brian Maltman of Source Lake, the late Dan Gibson of Canoe Lake, George Garland of Smoke Lake, and Don Lloyd of Canoe Lake. Over the years, a number of leaseholders have been recognized by The Friends for their significant contribution to the Park, including Ralph Bice from Rain Lake in 1986 for his contribution to the well being of the Park and eloquent writing skills; Edmund Kase from Brulé Lake in 1987 for his outstanding work in making Algonquin known to young men and women; Omer Stringer in 1988 for his contribution to canoeing and water safety; Adele Ebbs from Canoe Lake in 1989 for her contribution to youth camping in Ontario; Mary McCormick Pigeon, Mary Colson Clare, and Esther Sessions Keyser for their roles as "Pioneer Ladies of Algonquin Park;" Dr. Al Gordon from Smoke Lake in 2004 for his forestry research on spruce budworm, spruce genetics and nutrient cycling in Ontario's boreal forests; George Garland in 2005 for his long standing service for the Friends; and in 2006 to both Dan Gibson for his contribution to filming and recording the natural world; Taylor Statten I (The Chief) for his contribution to youth camping in Ontario. In addition, Algonquin Park leaseholders have been both large and small financial supporters of the organization both as individuals and as lake organizations. Many of the names on the benefactor plaques in the entryway and several of the exhibits at the Algonquin Park Visitor's Centre are there because of contributions by leaseholders and their families.

Founders of Youth and Adult Summer Camps

Another important aspect of helping ensure a quality experience for visitors to Algonquin Park has been the provision of services to both day visitors and overnight guests uninterested in either interior canoe tripping or car camping. Though commercial ventures were encouraged in the early years, they faced increasing restrictions as time passed. Commercial ventures were limited to one per lake and though allowed to occupy larger sized parcels of land, they were also subject to higher rental fees. Ideas for commercial ventures came in all shapes and sizes. The first to be introduced to the area were the children's camps, including seven that still exist today:[308]

- Northway Lodge – Cache Lake, 1908
- Camp Ahmek – Canoe Lake, 1921
- Camp Pathfinder – Source Lake, 1914
- Camp Wapomeo – Canoe Lake, 1924
- Camp Tanamakoon – Tanamakoon Lake, 1925

307. www.algonquinpark.on.ca/friends.html
308. For those interested in the history of these camps, see ***Summer Camp: Great Camps of Algonquin Park***, by Liz Lundell and Beverley Bailey.

- Camp Arowhon – TeePee Lake, 1934
- Camp Tamakwa – Tea Lake, 1936

Though commercially unsuccessful, two other boys' camps were also established in the Park in the mid-1910s. The first was Field's Camp, located on two acres on Little Joe Lake about three miles north of Joe Lake Station. It was established in 1916 by Albert Field of Ohio, who built a cabin with an attached kitchen and a verandah along the front with the intent to use the property as a boys' camp. For a number of summers, 12 boys came to learn camping and wilderness skills. In 1920, Field submitted a formal application to expand his use to five acres. He wanted to establish what he called a "school camp" and gave it the name "Ahmeek." The location was ideal in every respect, according to the then-Deputy Minister:

> *"It is set on a peninsula in a fine grove of white birch, a few pine, spruce and balsam trees, with an excellent sand beach in front. The point is surrounded on three sides by water, approx. 300 feet wide, gradually increasing in width as you leave the lakeshore. The cleared area is negligible but the bush is thinned out so that the point for some distance in the rear of the building resembles a park. The property includes three canoes and a rowboat. The building is of clapboard construction well built, and in an excellent state of preservation. The house is stained green and has a good roof. At the rear and close to the kitchen is a good well with iron pump. Rustic cedar logs support the roofed verandah and porch. The fireplace situated on the back wall of the living room is of stone and massive. There is a good trail leading from the rear to Big Joe Island Lake and Simms Pit on the railroad."*[309]

However, Field's Camp lasted just 11 years before Field abandoned the lease, and in 1929 the lease was canceled by the Crown. Though left empty for a time, it was eventually sold to the Kates family, who owned nearby Arowhon Pines Lodge.

Another short-lived boys camp was Camp Waubuno that was established on Waubuno Island on Cache Lake in 1918 by George Brower. He was a teacher at Blair Academy, a private secondary boarding school located in northwest New Jersey and had taken out a two-acre lease in 1912. He brought a group of 10 boys from the academy to the Park for eight weeks of camping and fishing and learning outdoor skills. Though making ends meet was a challenge, in 1919 he decided to give it another try and this time brought up 16 boys for the summer. As he later wrote to the Park Superintendent:

> *"I felt encouraged, and should have taken out a larger lease but I didn't feel sure and deferred, thinking that I would see what the prospect would be for this coming summer. In January 1920 came a body blow to my plans and myself. Rheumatism gripped my feet and legs and has kept me in its clutches for three months, disabling me at times, and confining me to my room. Under this adverse condition, I was hoping to have younger and physically abler men come up to Camp with me, take over the care of it, take out a larger lease and build up a larger camp and ultimately relieve me of all responsibility."*[310]

---

309. Fields leasehold correspondence, 1929, Algonquin Park Museum Archives.
310. Brower leasehold correspondence, 1920, Algonquin Park Museum Archives.

Alas, Brower's illness continued and soon after he sold the property to Henry Standerwick, a fellow teacher at Blair Academy. Standerwick had never seen the camp until he took it over. In 1924, Standerwick and his partner, L. W. Perrin, brought up 20 boys for a six-week season. Their slogan read, "***Real Camping for Real Boys in Real Woods: Six Weeks of Virile Outdoor Living. It Can't Be Beat.***"[311] The camp included a 60-foot boathouse that was used to store the dozen canoes in the winter. A trail led straight up behind it to a two-story main lodge with a sliding glass door, a kitchen, and an icehouse. On the left side of the main lodge was a large tent where Standerwick stayed and on the right side were 12 to 18 tents that housed the boys, two to a tent. The camp lasted only until 1927, when Standerwick converted it back to a private lease. As previously mentioned, a third camp, Camp Minnewawa, operated by Professor W. Wise was in existence on Lake of Two Rivers from 1911 until 1930 but little correspondence about the operations of this camp have been uncovered.

Another camping venture, this time for girls, that didn't get off the ground was one launched by two lively friends Hannah Gillender and Annie Krantz, who were both schoolteachers. In 1923, Krantz who was from Philadelphia and Gillender who was from England arrived from the United States for a vacation at Nominigan Camp on Smoke Lake. Their intent was to start a camp catering to Canadian girls that would be 'in harmony with the spirit that decided to set aside Algonquin Park as a national playground.'[312] They had a wonderful visit, selected some choice land on a picturesque point and in December of that year wrote a note to the Department of Lands and Forests requesting leases for nine parcels. Unfortunately they were unaware of the Park policy at the time of issuing only one lease per person. Why they didn't request a 'license of occupation' as was the custom for activities of a commercial nature is not known. For some reason the DLF seemed to view this application as potentially a scheme to avoid paying the $75 commercial lease fee and was not supportive of their efforts. For many months the ladies corresponded with the DLF trying to get their application in a form that would gain approval. Eventually in the spring of 1924, such approval was granted, but by then their vision had faded, perhaps due to the launching of Camp Wapomeo on nearby Canoe Lake and they lost interest in the Smoke Lake property. In 1925, the two decided to obtain a private lease on Canoe Lake, which they kept until the mid 1970s.

In the early 1930s, there were also two attempts to create camping environments where adults could learn about the outdoors, though neither achieved any commercial success. As previously mentioned, the first was a camp established in 1925 on Kioshkokwi Lake by a P. T. Hill from New York State. The second was located on what is now known as TeePee Lake, then known as Buck Lake, about two miles north of Joe Lake Station, The Red Gods Inc. obtained a lease in 1929 for a 20-acre parcel. The land, on the west shore of the lake, was subdivided into one-acre lots. The promoter's plan was to build "Camp of the Red Gods" for adults, with accommodations for up to 200 people. They commenced building and by the end of 1932 the site contained 20 single cabins, eight family cabins, two larger cabins with verandahs, a large main lodge, a bunk house, ice house, stable, and eight outhouses. In addition, there was a large dock and boathouse as well as a shallow

---

311. Richard Eldridge and Orville Osborne, ***Cache Lake Reflections,*** 1995, pg. 75.
312. Gillender and Krantz leasehold Correspondence 1923 Algonquin Park Archives.

protected bathing pool for children.[313] The property reverted to the Crown in 1932 due to non-payment of rental fees but was operated during 1933 by Norman Crewson from Cache Lake on behalf of the creditors. Crewson later went on to manage Whitefish Lodge on Whitefish Lake for a number of years. At one point there was a suggestion by the Park Superintendent that "maybe the CNR or retailers Simpsons or Eatons could be encouraged to take over the property as a summer camp for employees."[314] This idea wasn't pursued, and in 1935 the property was leased to Lillian Kates, who soon after established Camp Arowhon on the site.

Until the 1950s, Park officials seemed to be concerned that leaseholders might turn their leases into commercial ventures. They were constantly vigilant about whether or not leaseholders were taking in legitimate guests or operating small tourist businesses on the side. For example, in 1936, one Cache Lake resident requested in his wife's name a second lease, located some distance from his existing lease. In a report to the Deputy Minister, the Park Superintendent reported:

> *"I asked him what he intended to do with his present parcel and he said rent it or he would sell it. In view of the fact that there is becoming a tendency of different persons to secure several leases or to erect several cottages and rent one or more, the [department] should scrutinize all applications to see if speculation is the major consideration. As this parcel is remote from his present one, he cannot readily use both for his living quarters. Before a lease is issued to him, it will be necessary for him to notify us in writing, that it is not his intention to use this parcel for speculative purposes in any form, nor is it the intention to rent or sublet the building, which he must erect thereon."*[315]

Later that same summer, a resident of Smoke Lake wrote to ask why the Park Superintendent had sent Park Ranger Mooney over to ask them if they were keeping tourists. As she stated:

> *"We do have friends with us, on and off during the summer as most people do at cottages, but we were very much surprised at Mr. Mooney's call and should appreciate having an explanation as to the reason for it."*[316]

The DLF replied that:

> *"Ranger Mooney's inquiry was part of his routine duties, and is an inquiry made of cottagers in the Park. It is made because leases have in the past gradually changed character from leases taken out as private ones to commercial ones, and the Department wishes to know this. As there were several leases in this category during the past year, it was felt better to ask leaseholders outright about the matter especially as in the case of new leaseholders where the owners may not be familiar with the regulations."*[317]

Esther Keyser got into some trouble in 1938, when she naively sent in a sample of her ***Wilderness Canoe Trips*** brochure to the DLF. Park officials immediately assumed that she was running a commercial guiding operation and were very concerned. She was quick to explain that:

---

313. Report from Ranger Mark Robinson 1932; 1934 advertisement flyer written by Deputy Minister Cain.
314. Kates leasehold correspondence, 1932, Algonquin Park Museum Archives.
315. Cache Lake lease correspondence, 1936, Algonquin Park Museum Archives.
316. Smoke Lake leasehold correspondence, 1936, Algonquin Park Museum Archives.
317. Smoke Lake lease leasehold correspondence, 1936, Algonquin Park Museum Archives.

"Several friends have asked me to plan trips for them in the Park. This is not intended in any way to be a business or profit-making proposition. I simply get canoes and food and guides together for them, meet them at Canoe Lake and start off with them. By arrangement with Mr. Musclow our groups start from his camp and return to that point. Parents or campers arriving in advance stay there. Canoes and equipment are kept at his lodge if we have more than one trip and are stored in my cottage the rest of the time. He gets a certain amount of business in this way both for meals and overnights."[318]

Park officials were convinced but with some reservations:

"We have such trips coming in from outside the Park. This case seems one of a leaseholder capable of conducting trips, taking them out in the same manner as a Park Guide takes out parties. Providing she uses her lease as a private one only and lets her trips stay at regular tourist places I would suggest that she be treated much as any Park guide who organizes and takes out similar trips. In the meantime kindly have one of your Park rangers make a close supervision of the operations of [Mrs. Keyser] as from the printed literature supplied it would appear that there is considerable possibility that the operations of her husband and herself in catering to the general public might easily be placed in the class of commercialism."[319]

By the late 1940s, anything that hinted of commercialism was strictly against Park regulations. In 1948 Mrs. Davies, from Smoke Lake, wrote to ask if it was possible for her son's Boy Scout troop to run canoe trips through Algonquin Park using her lease as a base from where to start and finish the trips. Though the Park Superintendent had no objection to canoe trips being run through Algonquin Park from any leaseholder property as the starting and finishing point providing they were not operating a commercial lease, Deputy Minister MacDougall did and advised Mrs. Davies that:

"The policy of the Dept in regard to private leases is that they are for the private use of the leasee. While allowing the boys to use your point as a summer camping ground is not a commercial venture in any way, it is felt that in the best interests of all leaseholders the practice must be discontinued."[320]

Long Gone Commercial Lodges

Nevertheless, leaseholders played a part in a number of successful and not so successful lodges and other commercial ventures of one sort or another. The most historic of all, which are long gone were Mowat Lodge on Canoe Lake, the Hotel Algonquin on Joe Lake, the Highland Inn on Cache Lake, Nominigan Camp on Smoke Lake, Camp Minnesing on Burnt Island Lake, Kish Kaduk Lodge on Cedar Lake, Opeongo Lodge on Opeongo Lake, Glen Donald Lodge on Source Lake and Whitefish Lodge on Whitefish Lake.

Mowat Lodge[321]

In 1907 Shannon and Annie Fraser moved to the small town of Mowat that existed on the northwest shores of

---

318. Keyser leasehold correspondence, 1939, Algonquin Park Museum Archives.
319. Ibid.
320. DLF correspondence, 1948, Algonquin Park Museum Archives.
321. Excerpted from ***Algonquin Voices, Selected Stories of Canoe Lake Women*** by Gaye I. Clemson 2002

Canoe Lake. Shannon Fraser had been appointed to supervise the settling and dismantling of the then bankrupt Canoe Lake Mills.[322] The Frasers spent their first six years at Mowat leasing the old Mowat hospital up on a hill above the old mill site. In 1913 they decided that the tourist trade had some promise and acquired a lease that included the old mill hand kitchen and boarding house. This they turned into Camp Mowat. A Mr. R. P. Little claimed to have been the first guest in the fall of 1913. The camp, later renamed Mowat Lodge was,

> *"An unprepossessing two story, white-washed, wooden structure with a veranda across the front. Set on rising ground some distance from the water it faced the old mill yard, a "treeless, desolate area of thirty acres or more covered with pine slabs and sawdust. Some abandoned buildings from former days were still standing (a horse barn, a storehouse etc.) and by the lakeshore were the ruins of the old mill."*[323]

Annie Fraser kept her own cows and chickens, which supplied the hotel with fresh milk and eggs. At first the Frasers catered to campers visiting Canoe Lake and advertised their ability to provide meals, supplies and mail for those who wished to camp at one of the lake's many campsites. Later they started supplying boxed lunches and would deliver them around the lake to those folks camping or picnicking at various spots.[324] They also advertised the medicinal value of fresh air and a wilderness environment, which attracted people recovering from lung related illnesses. Mowat Lodge was an immediate financial success though considered third place in quality after the Highland Inn and the Hotel Algonquin. This was no doubt due to its reasonable rates, very rustic and casual atmosphere and excellent cooking. Fraser bought a horse-drawn coach, later called 'The Hearse', from an undertaker, which he would use to meet the train each day to escort guests to the lodge.

Though nothing is known today as to the cause, the original Mowat Lodge was destroyed by fire in November of 1920. There is some speculation by current locals, that the probable cause was likely a knocked over coal oil lantern or sparks from the fireplace. The Frasers abandoned the site but soon after took out a lease for the property next to the old mill foundation and had Mowat Lodge re-built. The new Mowat Lodge was again an immediate success and survived until 1930 when once again it burned to the ground. This time the Frasers gave up, moved to Kearney and then later to Huntsville. In 1931 the charred ruins reverted to the crown.

Hotel Algonquin

In 1908 Lawrence Merrill from Rochester, New York established the Hotel Algonquin on a hill, southwest of Joe Lake Station. The Hotel Algonquin was considered by most to be a bit more rustic than the Highland Inn. The outside was made of custom cut wood slabs, and so attracted patrons who enjoyed "roughing it" at least a little bit. Guests would usually come for a month and spend time picnicking, hiking, swimming or fishing on the lake or in the local area. Over time it became a favourite place to launch fishing trips into the interior of the Park. Often the women would gather on the veranda to talk, crochet, knit, play cards or go for walks around the property, while the men went on fishing expeditions. There were always a few women who would join their husbands on these trips. But most liked the hotel and its environment and were especially happy when their husbands went off for a few days and left them to themselves.

---

322. See Gary Long's ***When Giants Fall*** for details on the Gilmour logging venture on Canoe Lake
323. Ottelyn Addison, ***Tom Thomson - The Algonquin Years*** pg. 13
324. Ottelyn Addison, ***Early Years in Algonquin Park*** pg. 80

In 1917 Ed and Molly Colson, who had been managing the Highland Inn decided to buy the Hotel Algonquin and soon after moved to Joe Lake. According to Ed Colson's niece, Mary Colson Clare, the hotel had about 20 rooms, two big screened-in porches and three bathrooms shared by all the guests.[325] There were various wood stoves that would be lit when it got a little cool in early spring or late fall. Each bedroom was equipped with a nice washstand with pitcher, oil lamps for late night reading, iron or wooden beds and nice wooden dressers. In the kitchen was a big wood burning range that was unbearable to cook on in the summer but a great generator of heat in the spring and fall when it was cold. The hotel charged $18-$22 a week for the most expensive rooms including all of the meals. One person's job for the whole season was the washing and ironing of all of the hotel linens using a propane washing machine and a great big electric ironing machine. After a long stint at the Highland Inn, Lizzie Dennison, granddaughter of Captain Dennison from Lake Opeongo, was the main cook. She would also help in the spring getting the hotel ready for the summer guests. In winter she would cook at a nearby lumber camp. All of the dishes were heavy china and the dining room would fit 50 or 60 people sitting on pressed back chairs at 8 wooden tables covered with fresh linen tablecloths. During the years that the hotel was occupied during the winter, the dining room became a walk-in freezer for the supplies that were brought in every two weeks.

Next to the hotel the Colsons established the Joe Lake Outfitting Store (known as the Colson Store by the locals) to offer canoe tripping guides and outfitting. At the time, Algonquin Park was a favourite spot for those interested in camping and fishing. But no one would have dared go out on a fishing trip in those days if they couldn't paddle and manage a canoe. If they weren't knowledgeable about survival in the woods they took a guide. The guides all came from the surrounding area. Many would log or trap all winter and guide for the hotel all summer. According to Ralph Bice, in it's heyday, the Colson Store was the best outfitting store in the Park. Ed brought in his sister Annie Colson, known as Aunt Annie by everyone, to run it. Though somewhat severe looking, Annie Colson was well loved by all. She had had a difficult childhood as her mother had died when she was a teenager and it had become her responsibility to raise the family. She lived with her brother and Molly most of her life and had previously been in charge of the outfitting store at Highland Inn. Annie could,

> *"Set up a list of supplies as well as most guides. People would call or write in their tripping orders before they came up. She would pack all their flour, rice and whatever else they wanted in cotton bags. The eggs were packed into pails and along with tents and blankets were packed into big packsacks. No one had sleeping bags in those days."*[326]

The hotel was open from early May until the end of September. This all meant that Colson Outfitting Store was a busy and popular meeting place for all sorts including guests, guides, leaseholders and staff from the children camps. There was always some reason to stop by. Most wanted to get supplies at the Colson Store, talk to the guides or to Ed Colson or just generally hang around. In 1920 the Colsons decided that they needed a break from Canoe Lake. They moved to Renfrew to run Renfrew House, a Temperance house built

---

325. Ed Colson's brother George's daughter
326. ***Along the Trail in Algonquin Park*** by Ralph Bice, pg. 54

by a mining magnate by the name of O'Brien. Annie Colson went off to Alberta to run an orphanage and Ed's brother George and his wife Mary took over the day-to-day running of the hotel. This worked well until 1927 when, at the age of 51, George died suddenly. Ed and Molly then returned to Algonquin Park and resumed the management of the hotel.

After Highway 60 opened in 1936, fewer and fewer people took the train. It wasn't very convenient to come by boat, so more and more visitors were launching their canoe trips to the interior from Portage Bay. To meet this need, the Colsons opened The Portage Store and hired Joe Cousineau and his daughter Lucille from Brulé Lake to run the day-to-day operations. By 1943 the Colsons decided that running both the Portage Store and the Hotel Algonquin was getting to be too much to manage. They sold the hotel to George Merrydew owner of a tavern in Toronto and retired to an empty Omanique Lumber Company office near the northwest side of the trestle bridge at Potter Creek Bridge. Annie Colson left Algonquin Park and returned to her roots in Guelph where she later died. In 1945, Molly took ill in 1945 and died peacefully later that year. As a tribute to her, the Canoe Lake and District Leaseholders Association placed a memorial brass plaque on the big island in Smoke Lake, which was her favourite picnicking and camping spot. From then on it became known as Molly's Island. Over 100 people came to pay their respects in July 1946 at the unveiling. Molly had been a major anchor of the local Algonquin Park community for nearly 50 years. The plaque contained the following inscription:

> ***"Her spirit was one with the lakes and forests she loved – her heart and hands, ever at the service of those who called to her. Canoe Lake resident 1900 – 1945."***

Highland Inn – Cache Lake

For most if its existence, the Highland Inn was a major centre of activity for Algonquin Park residents. Allegedly designed by the architect who designed the Wawa Hotel on Lake of Bays, construction began by the Grand Trunk Railway in 1906. As indicated previously, it opened in 1908 with Molly Cox and J. Edwin Colson as its first proprietors. At first it was a small inn with eight rooms and a dining room with a verandah. Over the years it grew to have two wings and could accommodate 200 people. In 1914 accommodation rates were $2.50 to $3 a day and $16 to $18 a week. In the 1920s, it would cost $30 a week for a room with a detached bath or $7.50 more for a private bath. By 1925 rates had risen to $45 per month when depression wages were $10 per month.[327] It was clearly a vacation resort for the upper class. According to Cache Lake lore:

> *"During the winter a big toboggan slide was built at the end of the tennis court and an expanse of water in front of the Inn was kept clear of snow so as to keep the temperature down and make the ice hard enough. A local resident, Bill Yaskovitch, was in charge of cutting the ice. When ready he'd score a patch of clear ice criss-crossed and he'd saw out a block. The pressure would cause the block to pop up higher than the ice around it. He'd pull out the block (most were around 200 pounds) with the help of a horse and drag it on runners over to the icehouse. The icehouse would store 200 blocks that was sold to residents in the summer for one penny a pound in 50-pound blocks. In most years 1,000 blocks were needed to keep items cool at Nominigan and*

---

327. Barney Moorhouse, ***Centennial Series 1993,*** pg. 34.

Minnesing and the Highland Inn would need over 3,000 blocks. A great summer job was to be the local ice boy who'd deliver ice to each of the cottages and the camps."[328]

By the late 1930s, the CNR, which had taken over the rail line from the Grand Trunk Railway, was finding the Highland Inn to be unprofitable so they sold it in 1938/39 to Charles Paget of Huntsville, who was given a commercial lease by the DLF. With his two sons, Edward and Norm, Paget reopened in 1940 with hundreds of people coming to the gala opening. However, tragedy struck in December of 1943 when a fire destroyed the huge wooden water tower. Standing 80 feet high, it contained thousands of gallons of water. The fire apparently broke out in the heating equipment, which is used to prevent the pipes from freezing during the winter. It swept through the understructure and so weakened it that finally the big tank slowly collapsed.[329] By 1955, this type of resort was less popular and probably unprofitable. It was acquired by the Crown and torn down two years later.

Nominigan – Smoke Lake

As mentioned previously, Nominigan was built by the Grand Trunk Railway and opened for business in the spring of 1913. The buildings were patterned along the lines of those common to the Adirondack Forest in the northeastern United States.[330] As described by Mary Northway in her booklets recording the history of Nominigan:

"Its main lodge was built of cedar logs with walls chinked with moss and cement, and a shingled roof. The main entrance led into a rotunda, which was a large room with fireplace that opened both into the dining room and the rotunda and was the sole source of heat. Even with several Quebec heaters when a cold west wind blew in the spring and fall it could at times be frightfully cold. The rotunda contained a piano, a desk, a number of rustic chairs, a table, water cooler and clock and a set of stairs that led to the second floor. In the northwest corner was a registration desk at which postcards and candy bars could be purchased. On the ground floor was an office, then a passageway off which there was a bathroom and three bedrooms. Under the stairs there was a cupboard for storing wood for the fire.

Leading off from the rotunda was a dining room with tables and chairs to accommodate approximately 50 people. The dining room was always set with white tablecloths and linen napkins and wild flower bouquets set on each table. In the high season four sittings were required for dinner. The china was heavy white with green Grand Trunk Railway writing. Leading from the dining room was a small pantry for dishes, equipped with a sink with hot and cold water. The kitchen adjoined the pantry and contained a huge wood burning range and two cupboards for crockery and pans. The stairway to the six staff bedrooms and two bathrooms led from the kitchen. Over the dining room and rotunda were the 10 guest bedrooms and two bathrooms. All of the bedrooms contained beds, bureaus and chairs as well as beautiful buttercup yellow porcelain wash bowls and pitchers. All the windows were fitted with screens and the general exposure was to the south. There was a large verandah overlooking the lake, a delightful outlook and the entire building was only about 30 feet

---

328. Richard Eldridge and Orville Osborne, ***Cache Lake Reflections,*** 1995, pg. 99 & pgs. 105-108.
329. Newspaper article of Dec. 7, 1943, reprinted in ***Cache Lake Reflections*** by Richard Eldridge and Orville Osborne, pg. 28.
330. Audrey Saunders, ***The Algonquin Story,*** pg. 77.

from the water's edge. The capacity was 60-70 guests with 20-30 staff.

Located adjacent to the kitchen was a staff dining room and storeroom that consisted of a large dining room, a storeroom and a washroom that was used as a laundry. Close to the kitchen was an icehouse that held 400-500 blocks of ice and was built with two storerooms at the main entrance. These are small but housed all of the perishable supplies such as meat, vegetables and milk, which were brought in by stage along the tote road from the Highland Inn or by paddle and portage from Highland Inn or from Canoe Lake by portage to Smoke. Later one of the Park Rangers, George May, tore down the dam in Smoke Creek and they could get launches through to Joe Lake Station and avoid the Canoe to Smoke Lake portage. Also on the property was a log guide house that contained a large assembly room with fireplace, a bunkroom and a verandah. According to Aubrey Dunne, who was a Fire Ranger stationed at Smoke Lake from 1924-1927, there were square dances in the guide house nearly every night. A hundred yards away from the main lodge was a stable that accommodated two cows at one end and a team of horses in the centre with a recess for a stage. Over the stable was a loft for hay and oats. Nearby was pump house with a water pump connected to a huge water tank that enabled indoor plumbing in all of the bedrooms and the kitchen."

On a ridge to the east of the main lodge was a row of cabins. Each could accommodate eight to 10 people with a ground-floor living room, stone verandah, and massive stone fireplace. On the second floor was a spiral stairway to a balcony off of which were two bedrooms and a three-piece bathroom. The whole establishment was lit by acetylene piped in from a storage tank located near the guide house. In the bay to the east was a boathouse that held canoes and rowboats and a streamlined launch. Laundry was done by the Chateau Laurier Hotel in Ottawa and sent there by train twice a week. At capacity it looked after nearly 100 people: 60 to 70 guests, a manageress, a chief mechanic, six cabin girls, a cook, a porter, four dining room girls, assistants, a teamster and the guides.[331]

In the spring of 1928, a fire destroyed the six cabins due to a suspected blockage in the acetylene system. The cabins were not rebuilt and the hotel was shut down. It remained empty until 1931, when Gar Northway from Toronto bought the buildings and assumed the lease for the 10-acre parcel from the CNR.[332]

Camp Minnesing – Burnt Island Lake

In the early 1940s, Manley Sessions, brother of Esther Keyser and resident of Smoke Lake, wanted to find a way to live with his family full-time in Algonquin Park. His strong friendship with the various Park Superintendents over the years gave him the inside scoop, so when he heard in the summer of 1946 that Camp Minnesing on Burnt Island Lake had become available, he jumped at the chance. At the time, it was owned by a Dr. Henry Sharman, a retired California scientist who had used the property as a Christian school. Sharman, according to Audrey Saunders, "was a very religious man who bought Minnesing Camp in 1923 to hold seminars to study the life of Jesus."[333] As George Garland, a Smoke Lake resident who canoe tripped extensively with

331. This detailed description comes from both a detailed report by the CNR in 1930 and descriptions in Mary Northway's ***Nominigan: The Early Years,*** pgs. 1-5.

332. Ibid pgs. 20-26.

333. Audrey Saunders, ***The Algonquin Story,*** pg. 77.

Camp Ahmek in the 1930s, remembered:

> *"Often we would run into groups from this camp out on some of the campsites where they would be singing hymns or sitting in a circle reading their scriptures. We used to look at them with some mild amusement. They seemed to mix their experience with paddling and fishing and sailing with quite a serious study of religious matters."*[334]

Camp Minnesing's roots in Algonquin Park went way back, having been built in 1913 as a sister lodge to Nominigan Camp on Smoke Lake by the Grand Trunk Railway, which also had built the Highland Inn on Cache Lake. Like its twin, it was remote, accessible either by a "democrat," or by "11 miles over a very rough road, or by canoe from Joe Lake station, which required hiring a guide and renting a canoe."[335] It was also a popular spot for launching fishing expeditions into the interior. However, its economic viability as a resort was in question and in 1923 the CNR sold it to Sharman. Sessions was so enthusiastic that he immediately jumped at the opportunity and in the fall of 1946 drove to California to meet with Sharman at his home in Carmel, California. He brought along references and letters to illustrate his "good character" and eventually convinced Sharman that he would manage the resort on Christian principles. In January of 1947, the transfer of the property and lease to Manley Sessions was approved by the DLF.

Sessions couldn't wait to inspect his new acquisition and so skied in along the access road in the early spring of 1947. Like Nominigan, Minnesing Lodge had a main lodge as well as several cabins. According to Manley's daughter Mary Sessions Cline, each cabin had a porch that ran three quarters of the way around the front, a large fireplace, two bedrooms on each side of the fireplace, and another bedroom upstairs. The staff quarters and guide shack were located at the back of the lodge. Sessions soon hired Si Cline, a graduate of Colorado's School of Mines, who had seen an ad Sessions had placed in a Buffalo paper looking for help to manage and run what was now called Minnesing Lodge. Manley quickly produced a marketing brochure that he sent out to people in the Buffalo area and hired two workers to help with the heavy work and the guiding for canoe trips. His plan for the 1947 season was for Minnesing Lodge to be available for spring fishing for a restricted clientele and open in the summer for selected individuals and families as well as groups."[336]

Soon after the snow melted, it became very clear to Cline and Sessions that there were serious problems with the access road from Highway 60. A lumber company that had timber limits in the area had nearly ruined the first three or four miles of the road. They evidently used it to haul logs out, scraping away all of the gravel, bunching the dirt up like dikes along the sides, and making it a muddy mess. Sessions wanted to protect it from general travel during the wet season as one or two unnecessary trips at that time would do more damage than a regular daily trip during July and August. He asked to erect a prominent sign indicating that it was unsafe for any vehicles over 3,000 pounds at any time and impassible except for vehicles of high clearance. Persons using this road would do so at their own risk and were warned not to attempt to travel the road during

---

334. Interview of George Garland by Rory MacKay, 1976.
335. Audrey Saunders, ***The Algonquin Story,*** pg. 77.
336. Sessions leasehold correspondence, 1947, Algonquin Park Museum Archives

the wet season in spring or fall (May, June, September, and October).[337] Supplies and sometimes guests were brought up from Joe Lake Station by boat or canoe and the portaged the half a mile to Burnt Island Lake. As Esther Keyser wrote in her book, Paddling My Own Canoe, getting in and out that first year was not a pleasant experience:

> *"Each week someone would have to trek to the Highland Inn to get fresh supplies. That first year they used a weapons carrier vehicle, which got stuck all the time on boulders and in the mud. The wheels would spin and trees would fall. Initially all of the guests would arrive at Joe Lake Station and were ferried in by canoe over several portages."*

In the summer of 1947, it was clear that Sessions' daughter, Mary, had fallen in love with Si Cline. The two were married that fall and decided to spend the first winter of their married life together at Minnesing Lodge. A hole dug in the ground became the "fridge," and a battery-powered radio provided their only source of entertainment, often broadcasts of hockey games. Fishing for food, cross-country skiing, clearing the ice out front for skating, and the occasional trek to Smoke Lake kept them busy during the long winter. In the late fall, Cline and Sessions went hunting, outside the Park, and each got two deer and two bear that they hung in the icehouse, which supplied them with meat for the winter. When Mary got pregnant, they used a local Whitney doctor who gave Si a book on obstetrics just in case there was an emergency and they couldn't get to town. In the spring of 1948, Mary went home to her mother to give birth, and soon returned with her three-week-old baby in a canoe.

Guests would generally come for a week, with many spending their time fishing and enjoying recreation activities on Burnt Island Lake. Sessions owned and operated Minnesing Lodge for six years, until 1952. But as Mary Sessions Cline shared:

> *'There was never enough manpower and money. Si worked at the time for $1 a day and I was responsible for doing all of the laundry. Sheets had to be ironed using an old hand roller. I also waited on tables in the dining room if needed though my sisters were in charge of the dining room. My mother Jean home-schooled us and via this method we did pass our high school exams.'*

For some unknown reason, the DLF wouldn't renew the lease, so Sessions had no choice but to sell the property back to the Crown in 1956. It was dismantled soon after. The Minnesing Road was abandoned until the 1990s, when parts of it were reopened as a biking trail.

Kish Kaduk Lodge – Cedar Lake

Another lodge that was for a time very popular in the north was Kish Kaduk Lodge on Cedar Lake. As mentioned previously, Edwin Thomas had been a section foreman for CNR and spent many years in the Canoe Lake area. In 1927 he applied for a lease for a two-acre parcel on north end of Cedar Lake. He wanted to start a lumber supply camp and stopping place for tourists. The lodge that he built had a big living room and dining room with remote cabins able to accommodate 30 to 35 guests. Getting there was a challenge.

---

337. Ibid.

Visitors would take a train to Brent, then travel by boat to the lodge. At one point, they had 15 to 20 guides who would take tourists on fishing trips in the area. Mrs. Thomas herself did all of the cooking and obtained permission to keep several cows in a nearby pasture so that the lodge would have fresh milk and butter.

Spring, when the trout fishing opened, was their main season. Within a couple of years it was clear that their summer resort was a success. In 1934 the Thomas's decided to put in a phone line, with which there were a number of technical difficulties that caused interference on the CNR section manager's phone line. Though eventually resolved, the problem arose again in 1937 and soured relationships with the CNR. Things didn't improve when the Thomases discovered that the CNR was dumping old track ties into the lake. Not only did they clutter up the shoreline in front of the lodge, but also were dangerous obstacles to canoes and boats, as they weren't easily seen when there were whitecaps, as was often the case on Cedar Lake.

In 1942, as the tourist pressure started to increase, the carelessness of campers with their campfires became a significant concern. As Edwin Thomas wrote in July of that year:

> *"We always do our best to impress upon people leaving here on canoe trips and also on day trips the danger of making their cooking fires in bad places and also the importance of seeing that they are properly put out. We find that the worst offenders are the ones that throw away their cigarette butts and our guides are constantly warning the guests of that habit. I would like to have some signs that warn people of the fire danger of carelessly throwing their cigarette butts."*[338]

In 1948 the lease was renewed, and in 1966 it was transferred to Edwin's daughter Rose and his nephew, Jack Wilkinson. Rose had been helping her parents run the lodge since childhood. But the nature of the business had changed. By 1968, guests weren't very interested in staying in the lodge and wanted their own housekeeping cottages so as to make their own meals themselves. In response to this Rose and Jack received permission to convert some of the small cabins to housekeeping cottages. The lease was renewed again in 1974 but by 1975 life in the bush was becoming difficult for Rose and Jack, who by then were in their late 60s. They sold the lodge that fall under the proviso that they be retained for life to supervise the demolition of certain improvements and maintenance of the remaining buildings in return for free rent.[339] Jack Wilkinson spent much of the next few years taking down various cabins and cleaning up the site. A couple of years later they bought a house in Deep River, and retired after nearly 50 years on Cedar Lake.

After Rose and Jack left the area, the MNR decided to allow the lodge to die a natural death. However, by 1983 it had been vandalized a number of times and reached "a very deteriorated state and serious hazard due to broken glass, nails and the weakened condition of the buildings. Vandals had even gone so far as to cut some of the main beams in the lodge."[340] Later that year, the buildings were removed and the site rehabilitated.

---

338. Thomas leasehold correspondence, 1942, Algonquin Park Museum Archives.
339. Ibid, 1975.
340. Ibid, 1983.

Opeongo Lodge – Lake Opeongo[341]

Opeongo Lodge was originally a single log cabin built in 1902, likely by the St. Anthony Lumber Company to feed the Whitney sawmill at Sproule Bay, the terminus of a small logging railway. In 1925, Sandy Haggart established a small tourist business and asked for a "Letter of Occupation" for the cabin so that he could use it to store canoes and boats and canoe tripping gear that he would rent out. Eventually the railroad was shut down and the rails were removed, so Haggart bought a car, which he used to transport passengers along the railroad right of way. In 1930, he dismantled a nearby bunkhouse, built and used for some years by the St. Anthony Lumber in Whitney, and used the material to build two additional cabins at his lodge. He also took over an old government boathouse, built in 1923, in exchange for materials to construct a replacement. This set the stage for a long love-hate relationship between DLF and Haggart. He was often late with his rental payments and resisted efforts to have him improve the appearance of his unpainted buildings. In 1936, he sold the lodge and the outfitting business to Joe Avery. By the 1940s, Avery had 20 men whom he hired out as guides, charging $35 a week per person. In 1946, he got permission to install a gas pump, but was not allowed to advertise that fact on his Highway 60 sign. Avery died in 1955 and his son Ken took over the business in 1958, but wasn't allowed to lodge guests. In 1968, the old Opeongo Lodge building burned down and was replaced by the present store. Its name was also changed to Opeongo Outfitters to better reflect its role as a provisioner of canoes, supplies and guides. In 1977, the Averys lost the concession bidding competition and moved their business to Highway 60 just outside of Whitney. They were able to keep their water taxi service at Opeongo. Wendy and Bill Swift took over the concession in 1990 and renamed it Opeongo Algonquin under the corporate umbrella of their Algonquin Outfitters operation near Dwight.[342]

Whitefish Lodge – Whitefish Lake[343]

With Whitefish Lake more easily accessible due to a spur cut from Highway 60 in 1937, Charles Young, a professor at Cornell University in Ithaca, New York, expressed interest in 1938 in building a general tourist business similar to some of the other successful lodges in the park, such as Bartlett Lodge and Killarney Lodge. He wanted to secure a lease covering a five-acre parcel at the north end of the lake with the intent to build a central hall and individual cabins. In addition to renting overnight cabins, Young wanted to rent canoes and sell supplies. He engaged Norman Crewson (the former caretaker from Camp of the Red Gods on Teepee Lake) to build a house for himself on this property and generally look after his interests.[344] The Deputy Minister was concerned that such an enterprise within the Park boundary:

> *"Does not compare equally with a boys' or girls' camp where the tenancy is supervised to the extent of maintaining control over the occupants of the various cabins on the property. I would very much appreciate your careful consideration as to the advisability of permitting a camp of this nature to be established. It may be perfectly satisfactory but the season these cabins will be occupied will undoubtedly be considerably longer than the*

341. For other details concerning Lake Opeongo, see ***Opeongo,*** by S. Bernard Shaw.
342. S. Bernard Shaw, ***Opeongo.***
343. Excerpted from ***Rock Lake Station,*** by Gaye I. Clemson.
344. Whitefish Lodge leasehold correspondence, 1938, Algonquin Park Museum Archives.

average boys' or girls' camp and if they are to be only overnight guests, the occupants will be in a considerably different class than those occupying cabins or tents under a supervised tourist camp where the management of the camp is responsible for the decorum and the names of the occupants may be obtained at any time."[345]

Frank McDougall, the Park Superintendent at the time, reassured him that:

"The trend of the tourist business seems to be to this type of lodge and while as you say it will cater to a different type of transient business, the transients will be coming through the Park anyway and while they are at a tourist camp they are under better supervision than if such a camp is not available. We have not had trouble with the other camps of similar nature and the experience has been that many who come to stay overnight often prolong their stay if the surroundings are nice. I believe the development will be in the interest of the Department and it will provide at the head of Whitefish Lake a location where boats may be rented and people accommodated. There will be a man, Crewson, in charge of the place on whom responsibility can be placed and our Park Rangers are in that vicinity to check when necessary."[346]

Unfortunately, Young's timing was terrible, as soon after the lodge was built, WWII broke out and the tourist business in Ontario dropped off dramatically. By 1943, Young advised the Park Superintendent that he was not at all satisfied and felt that Crewson was failing to live up to the terms of the 10-year contract. He didn't open the lodge for the 1944 season and in 1945 sold it to John T. Connolly of Buffalo, New York. Connolly originally intended to fix it up for private use, but changed his mind. In 1946, he opened Whitefish Lodge again for business. During Connolly's first couple of seasons of operation, some visitors sent complaints over the quality of accommodations and services to Park officials. Though Park officials' inspection indicated that some of the complaints may well have been vindictive, there was little that the DLF could do and the lodge's reputation suffered as a result. However, business must have been satisfactory as in 1950, Connolly requested additional land parcels upon which he erected a garage and recreation hall.[347]

Four other lodges and fishing camps of a commercial and non-commercial sort that existed for a time in Algonquin Park were Glen Donald Lodge on Source Lake, Musclow Lodge on South Tea Lake, and the Turtle Fishing Club on Lake Traverse and Poplar Point Camps.

Glen Donald Lodge – Source Lake

In December 1949, William and Gertrude MacDonald obtained a commercial lease for 7.2 acres on the northeast shore of Source Lake. On the parcel the MacDonalds had built a main lodge with kitchen and dining hall, a staff house, a pump house and boiler room, 11 cabins, three storage sheds, and an icehouse. The lodge was designed to accommodate 30 guests in both the cabins and the main lodge. Its recreation facilities included four boats, four canoes, and two motors. Their first season, in 1950, was very successful with more than 450 guests registered. The lodge was so successful that in 1951, it was listed in Mayfair, one of Canada's

345. Whitefish Lodge leasehold correspondence, 1938, Algonquin Park Museum Archives.

346. Ibid.

347. After the 1954 policy change, Connolly was interested in "exchanging" his property for some he had found outside of the Park. The DLF refused, so Connolly kept Whitefish Lodge until his death in 1965. It was then acquired by the Crown from his estate.

society magazines at the time, with the following recommendation:

> *"GLEN DONALD LODGE—This is downright luxurious for a camp so far north. New and still growing, the lodge is located on Source Lake in Algonquin Park. It consists of a main building and several unusually large and well built bungalows with picture windows and all conveniences. Comfortable rustic furniture blends well with knotty pine walls and stone fireplaces. The variety and quality of the meals are good."*[348]

Unfortunately, accessibility was a problem. Guests would arrive at the Source Lake Landing and honk their car horns. The MacDonalds would then send a boat over to pick them up. Though some guests had heard of the lodge and would make advance reservations, many more would see the signs on Highway 60 and drive in. By 1950, the proliferation of signs on Highway 60 had become such that the DLF instituted a new set of regulations. All signs on Highway 60 could be erected no closer than 50 feet from the centreline of the highway. Only one sign would be permitted for each lodge and it had to meet a standard set of specifications set down by the department. For MacDonald, this was a significant problem. As he wrote at the time:

> *"Standard signs will convey nothing as to the character of the place to the traveling public. In addition they are not readily seen and consequently many guests have gone miles out of their way and created a highway hazard due to the necessity of sudden stops and U-turns."*[349]

After much correspondence the department relented, and allowed MacDonald to add a phrase to his sign: "Following the Pattern of the Old English Posting Inns."[350] Though summer business in 1951 was within 8 percent to-10 percent of expectations, their spring and fall business was exceedingly low.[351] In 1953, MacDonald cut his season to 2½ months, but still found it difficult to get people to cross the lake in the early and late part of the season. He asked if it was feasible to have a road put in to his site or a light on his Highway 60 sign and at the Source Lake dock. These requests were refused and within a couple of years he closed down. The lodge and its contents were sold back to Crown in 1958. In 1960 the main building was struck by lightning and burned to the ground. In tearing down the cabins Park officials left the lovely old stone fireplaces, which are still standing to this day.

Musclow Lodge – Tea Lake

Details on the rise and fall of Musclow Lodge are found in *Gertrude Baskerville – The Lady of Algonquin Park.* However, a summary of its history is as follows:

> *"In 1936, Charles Musclow moved from Lindsay, Ontario, to a five-acre parcel or land near the Smoke Creek Bridge. The site was conveniently located at the intersection of Canoe, South Tea and Smoke Lakes with easy access to the newly built Highway 60. Musclow was a skilled craftsman and the main lodge that he built with its central living room with stone fireplace and a screened in porch overlooking Bonita Narrows was perfectly constructed. Most of the furniture was hand-made from beaver cuttings, He also built a boat that was later*

348. MacDonald leasehold correspondence. 1950, Algonquin Park Museum Archives.
349. Ibid.
350. Ibid.
351. Ibid.

used to ferry guests up to the Canoe Lake or Joe Lake train stations and around nearby lakes.

The lodge officially opened for business in 1937 and was called Camp Comac, though the name was soon changed to Musclow Lodge. During 1941 they had over 200 guests, but it wasn't enough business to support his growing family so Musclow built log cabins for other leaseholders during the off-season. From this work he gained a reputation as a superior builder in the district. In 1942 he decided to sell the lodge to Lou Handler, owner of Camp Tamakwa, and moved his family to British Columbia. The camp still owns the lease and all of the buildings are used as summer residents for longtime staff and associates of Camp Tamakwa."[352]

The Turtle Fishing Club

In 1933, J. R. Booth Jr., grandson of J. R. Booth of Ottawa, leased two acres at Lake Traverse on the south side of the Petawawa River where it enters the lake. In addition, under the watchful eye of the local Park Ranger, he got permission to cut 300 Jack pine logs at 3 cents per lineal foot from the local lumber camp called Lake Traverse Camp. Booth also asked permission to build an airport strip, which was denied. As recounted to Don Konrad in 1976:

"Bill Fiebig was one of eight men chosen to build the lodge. He was paid $40 a month including room and board, working 10 hours a day, six days a week. His job was to shape the logs with gougers and axes. The gigantic logs were laid together so tightly they didn't require chinking. The main dining room was 20 feet by 30 feet and each adjoined bedroom was 16 feet by 24 feet. Each bedroom had its own fireplace and walk-in closet. It was called the Turtle Lodge because when you looked at it from the air it looked like a turtle with the kitchen being the head and each bedroom the legs. J. R. Booth loved turtles and had used the symbol of a turtle as the bark mark on his saw logs to identify them during the spring log drives in rivers.[353] *At one point there were over a dozen workers including Swedes, Finns and Italians. The lodge was turned into a tourist resort for fishermen and vacationers, mostly American, who hired guides to take them into White Partridge Lake by horse-drawn wagon and canoe. They even brought in a Rolls Royce by rail. There was no road into Traverse in those days and the fancy car was used to transport guests from the station to the lodge on a road that was no more than a cow path. The car took a beating from the stumps."*[354]

Each spring, Booth would bring in friends and associates on fishing trips into the Park and would use his now-named "Turtle Club" as a base. As Park Superintendent Frank MacDougall noted in 1934:

"Mr. J. R. Booth is making a fishing trip during the later part of May and I believe he is interested in getting a price on the use of a [government] aircraft for either part or the whole time of his trip. We have taken a large order for propagation of fish with the Department of Game and Fisheries. They are setting aside a number of lakes into which we are putting parent Kamloops rainbow trout, and land-locked salmon."[355]

Though it was a magnificent building, by 1937 it seemed that Booth had all but abandoned the place, as

---

352. Excerpted from ***Gertrude Baskerville: The Lady of Algonquin Park,*** by Gaye. I. Clemson, 2001.
353. John Ross Trinnell, ***J. R. Booth: Life and Times of an Ottawa Lumber King,*** pg. 116.
354. Article in ***The Pembroke Observer*** by Don Konrad, dated October 31, 1976.
355. Turtle Club leasehold correspondence, 1934, Algonquin Park Museum Archives.

Park Rangers reported that the Turtle Club had been broken into. Fortunately, men from a local lumber camp who happened to be passing by saw the offenders, who fled and dropped the articles they had stolen, including a lantern and a few dishes. The Ontario Provincial Police were advised of the matter, but over the next few years, the Turtle Club was broken into several more times. As there wasn't any type of caretaker, the Park Superintendent suggested "that all contents be moved from this building and that the entrance be nailed up."[356]

In 1942, the lease was assigned to Clarency Wesley Camp and Wilhelm Moe and that year a travel permit was issued for a car to be used between Lake Traverse Station and the camp. In 1946, Camp and Moe gave the lease to the Ottawa Lions Club of Ottawa, which wanted to establish a boy's camp. Unfortunately, appropriate train connections meant leaving Ottawa late at night and arriving at Lake Traverse at 3 a.m. in the morning, so the group decided that its plans weren't feasible.[357]

Over the next few years, there were several requests to buy the lease in order to operate a commercial lodge or a children's camp. These requests were all refused by Park officials. In 1950, Osmond F. Howe asked about the lease with the idea of forming a non-profit fishing club. This also was refused. However, in 1952, a group of men led by Joseph Pigott Sr., Chairman of Pigott Construction of Hamilton, bought the building and formed a fishing club. After much correspondence with Park officials, their "Turtle Fishing Club" was granted a lease in 1956. The lease was set to expire in 1974, and the Ministry of Natural Resources began to discuss what to do with the structure. As the then-Park Superintendent wrote:

> *"As you know I have always been cool to the idea of the Department buying up the Turtle Club lease which expires in four years. However I have had a good look at the structure and talked with the staff about its possible uses. It is a magnificent building, well constructed and appears to be in reasonably good condition. I would recommend that we acquire it for use as a Junior Park Ranger Camp and occasional workshop centre. There is plenty of work that could be done in the area by Junior Rangers. Lake Traverse is accessible by public road and the building has some historical significance. Electricity is nearby at the Radio Observatory and could be brought in relatively cheaply."*[358]

Later, in spite of the fact that expansion of the Junior Ranger Program was not feasible, the MNR went ahead with the purchase and acquired the lease in 1973. Soon after, negotiations began with the Big Pine Committee for the Promotion of Tourism in Renfrew County, which wanted to move the lodge out of the Park and use it as a museum. Correspondence suggests that after negotiations were concluded in the summer of 1978, the building was dismantled and moved and the area cleared of debris by the committee. As Kanawa Canoe Museum Director David Brown wrote in 1977:

> *"We are very interested in obtaining the large log building located at The Traverse known as the 'Turtle Club.' Our interest lies in both preserving this interesting building for its historic value and in using it to house portions of our expanding collections. We would propose with your approval to dismantle this log building,*

---

356. Ibid.
357. Ibid.
358. Turtle Club leasehold correspondence, 1970, Algonquin Park Museum Archives.

move and re-erect it on the Heritage Trail."[359]

Unfortunately neither the lease records nor the Renfrew County web site indicate if this actually happened.

Poplar Point Camps

Another very popular business for a time was Poplar Point Camps, a fishing and guiding business established by Ralph Bice. In the 1940s, his base was in Kearney and he operated mostly during the spring and fall fishing seasons. Over the years, he used Park shelter huts and he later established a network of camps on Rain and Eagle Lakes. Bice was a prolific letter writer and stickler, it seems, for the rules. In 1950, he wrote to express his concern that he was encountering people, often guiding American tourists, who lacked proper licenses.[360] In 1954, the DLF decided to get serious about enforcing its policy that outfitters not leave any equipment, such as canoes, tents, or boats cached in the Park between trips. This change in policy was of great concern to Bice, who had always been careful to get the proper permissions but was affected by the policy nonetheless. After a few years he was mostly limited to operations from his base on Rain Lake.

Commercial Lodges and Outfitters in Operation Today

Today there are three outfitters, three lodges, and an art gallery/boutique that operate in the Park, though they are not operated by Algonquin Park leaseholders. All continue to be very successful year after year. Those commercial entities that have leaseholder roots include Killarney Lodge and Bartlett Lodge on Highway 60, Arowhon Pines Resort several miles inland on Baby Joe Lake, and the Portage Store on Canoe Lake.

Killarney Lodge

In 1933, Burt Weldon Moore, a traveling salesman from Toronto, was issued a lease to establish a tourist lodge on a low-lying peninsula on the north shore of Lake of Two Rivers with easy access to Highway 60. Moore had a lifelong passion for the outdoors and a dream to open a 'guest house'. Like so many others, he built a central lodge building and individual cabins, each with a view of the lake. Initially these cabins were a mix of both tent-platform cabins and log cabins. The logs to build all of the buildings came from the nearby McRae Lumber Company mill. Moore was a prolific letter writer and the archive records are full of his weekly, and sometimes daily, communiqués to Park officials from various Ontario motels. In 1948, while fishing just off Killarney Lodge Burt drowned and his son Elwood took over the management of the resort. In the 1970s, Elwood's health started to fail and he sold the lodge to Paul and Nancy Beggrow in 1972. The Beggrows, had been good friends of the Moores and had been regular guests for years. In the early 1980s, Paul, while still only in his fifties, began to have health problems and sold the lodge to Eric Miglin in 1984. Eric, and his wife Poppy Rowland continues to run Killarney Lodge to this day and winter in Toronto with their four children.

---

359. Turtle Club leasehold correspondence, 1978, Algonquin Park Museum Archives.
360. Bice leasehold correspondence, 1950, Algonquin Park Museum Archives.

Arowhon Pines

In the early 1930s, Lillian Kates came to Algonquin Park by train to visit her daughter who was attending Camp Wapomeo on Canoe Lake. With a free afternoon she hired a guide to take her on a short paddle around the area of Joe Lake Station. Tucked away on Teepee Lake, a short paddle north of the station, she stumbled upon the now defunct Camp of the Red Gods. Without a moment's hesitation she decided to acquire the lease and in 1934 started Camp Arowhon on the site. Several years later, as the quality and frequency of the train service declined, she became concerned that other than the Hotel Algonquin there was not nearby accommodation for visiting parents. To solve the problem she applied for a lease on Little Joe Lake for an area covering a little over four acres. It took two years to build Arowhon Pines Resort, which opened in 1941. Jack and Paul Lucasavitch, two local expert woodsmen cut, hewed and notched by hand all of the log walls and built the five-sided main lodge. The central fireplace chimney in the dining room came up by rail from Toronto in two pieces. It was towed up the lake on a barge and hoisted into place with a homemade "gin pole" and a small hand winch. In the early years access was by boat from Joe Lake Station or the Portage Store and in 1956 a public road was finally approved. In 1970, Lillian retired and management of the resort was taken over by her son Eugene who with his wife Helen continues to run it today. Recognized in the world famous Relais et Chateaux, travel guide, Arowhon Pines is well known for its fabulous cuisine, rustic yet luxurious accommodation and tranquil surroundings.

Bartlett Lodge

The site on which Bartlett Lodge sits was originally a summer home for Dr. William Bell that was built apparently around 1900. Dr. Bell an outdoor enthusiast, not only drew up the Park's first canoe route map of Algonquin Park canoe routes, but also was also interested in building a health spa for his recovering Ottawa patients. His plans never came to fruition for unknown reasons and he sold his lease in 1905 to Ed Colson who was a Park Ranger at the time and later took over management of the nearby Highland Inn. Later the site was acquired by Alf and Jim Bartlett, sons of a former Park Superintendent George Bartlett. They converted it into a tourist resort and named it Bartlett Lodge. The lease records indicate the Bartletts acquired their lease in 1923, but recent building repairs on the main lodge found markings that suggest that it may well have opened in 1917. The Bartletts ran the lodge until 1961 when it was transferred to Gordon Daw, the great grandson of another of George Bartlett's sons named Gordon. He added a small store where, where for a time, leaseholders could buy bread, candy and milkshakes Daw's parents Charles and Lorna Daw helped manage and run the lodge with him until 1980 when they sold it to Mark Freeman. In 1997 Kim and Marilyn Smith assumed ownership of the lodge and initiated extensive renovations including the recent addition of a solar cabin. The Smiths also own nearby Camp Tanamakoon. Today the lodge can accommodate 38 guests in 12 one, two or three bedroom cabins and also supports a gourmet restaurant that attracts visitors from miles around.

The Portage Store

A detailed history of the Portage Store can be found in *Algonquin Voices – Selected Stories of Canoe Lake Women*, but in summary:

> *"In 1935, in anticipation of Highway 60's completion, Molly Colson (former manager of the Highland Inn*

and co-owner with her husband of the Hotel Algonquin on Joe Lake), realized that cars were soon going to replace the railway as the primary access vehicle into the Park. She applied for and received approval to operate a canoe livery and store on a five-acre parcel of land at the south end of Canoe Lake in what was then called Portage Bay. On the site they built a small log cabin store, which they managed until 1939. In the spring of 1939, they sold the lease, the store, a sleeping cabin and an icehouse to Basil Hughes, which he operated for a couple of years. When called overseas in 1942, Hughes sublet the property back to Ed Colson who managed it on his behalf until 1950, when it was sold to a music teacher named Hilda Capp and her accountant brother-in-law Cardwell Walker. Capp enlarged the gift shop and asked for permission to both build cabins to accommodate overnight guests and install a gas pump. Both of these requests were denied. Unable to make a success of her efforts, she sold the lease to a group of women leaseholders from Canoe Lake composed of Janey Roberts, Isobel Cowie, Marg McColl and Fran Smith. For three summers, the 'Ladies Who Ran the Portage Store' rented out canoes, sold groceries, ice and massive amounts of ice cream, ran a gift shop, hand-pumped gas and served sandwiches to local cottagers, canoe trippers and day tourists.[361]

In 1957, unbeknownst to the 'Ladies,' Park officials had decided that the property needed to be acquired and replaced with a more modern business and managed on a concession basis. After extensive negotiations they acquiesced. The old store log cabin was pulled down and replaced with the current structure, which included a grocery store, gift shop and restaurant, canoe trip outfitting depot, canoe and boat rentals and gasoline sales. The new concessionaire was Ken Simpson, who ran the Portage Store operation and opened another at Lake of Two Rivers, which he ran until 1974 when he turned it over Alquon Ventures, which still runs both today and is owned by Eric and Sven Miglin from Huntsville."[362]

Other Entrepreneurial Ventures

In addition to outfitters, lodge owners, and fishing guides Algonquin Park attracted a few other entrepreneurs. One interesting one was Tea Lake resident Hunter Hamilton who in 1935 with his wife, Kathleen, asked to lease five acres of land nearby at Tea Lake Dam. This was the former site of what was called Camp 3 during the Highway 60 construction project. As he wrote that year:

"My purpose in doing this would be to earn a living by growing vegetables and maybe small fruits which I would sell to the summer cottagers and the two camps, Ahmek and Wapomeo. My plan is to have a boat and call at each cottage every day or so with fresh vegetables, the same as they do at Lake Temagami. I would plan on building a substantial house where my wife and I could live all the year round if necessary and might even build some small cabins to rent to tourists. The location of Camp 3 seems to me to be suitable for such a project because there is so much clear ground that can be utilized for this purpose and in addition the people on Canoe Lake and Smoke Lake should provide a market for my produce. If I were able to get this site I would buy the camp buildings and tear them down and clean up the spot so that it would be a credit to the Park."[363]

Unfortunately, at least for the local leaseholders, Park officials decided this scheme was unworkable and refused

361. Excerpted from ***Algonquin Voices: Selected Stories of Canoe Lake Women,*** 2002, pgs. 64-92.
362. For more details on the history of the Portage Store, see ***Algonquin Voices: Selected Stories of Canoe Lake Women***, pgs. 64-92.
363. Hunter leasehold correspondence, 1935, Algonquin Park Museum Archives.

to grant Hamilton a commercial lease. Another short-lived venture at Tea Lake dam was the establishment of an Indian craft centre by Doug Stringer. It was apparently quite successful, but lasted only a few years in the mid 1970s.

Another proposal, found buried and likely misfiled in the Ministry of Government Services Archives of Ontario, was a proposal to build a 200-foot panoramic tower a half mile south of Highway 60, west of the Rock Lake access road. This site was one of the Park's highest points, offering a view across much of Algonquin Park and hundreds of its lakes. This idea never saw the light of day, but according to the 1963 proposal:

> *"The tower would contain two high-speed elevators, which would carry passengers to the lower of the two observation levels. A curved stairway would allow visitors to the upper of the two levels. Visitors to the upper tower floors would hear a 10-minute automatic taped address describing the points of interest that could be seen from the tower, a history of the early days before the Park when some of our early explorers wintered in the Park area, the fascinating story of the early lumbering days in the Park and the beginning of the Algonquin Park story itself, i.e., how it was conceived, and by whom, and how and why it was maintained in its wilderness state. Another suggestion is that a VHF receiver and transmitter be located in the upper panorama room, which could be used to report fires. Uniformed information officers could be on hand to answer questions and, with the aid of a large detailed relief map in the upper tower, would be able to describe the vectoring of smoke between tower locations. They could also describe the problem of getting firefighting personnel and material to the fire area, the enormous cost of these procedures and a story about the extreme care with fires in forest areas. On both levels of the upper tower, telescopes on fixed bases would be available to the visitor without charge. This 'Algonquin Panoramic Tower' would attract an enormous number of visitors from all over the United States and Canada. A film counter and tearoom at ground level would complete the facility. The ridge itself is well suited to the erection of the tower. To begin with, it is solid rock for excellent anchorage the upper surface. It is almost completely level and would give excellent parking for about 100 cars. The short road in from Highway 60 could be built readily without blasting and has no more than a 7% grade."*[364]

Every lake had its multitalented lake caretakers, who often lived in the Park year-round and who provided life support for keeping cottages functional. In the 1940s, Sandy Haggart and later Brooks Transport and Armashaw Transport operated a daily service (except Sunday) from Whitney to Huntsville. With stops at various locations along Highway 60, including Gertrude Baskerville's cabin at the Smoke Creek Bridge, they would deliver the mail and pick up orders from various roadside boxes established by leaseholders along the highway.[365] As recalled by Rory MacKay:

> *"At the road was built a wooden box with a hinged lid, covered in asphalt shingles and a flag that could be raised or lowered on it. When the flag was up, a person who delivered groceries, milk or other supplies would pick up the order along with an amount of money. A day or two later the ordered supplies would be left in the box."*

---

364. Correspondence found in Ontario Archives, dated 1963.

365. For additional details on the life of Gertrude Baskerville's 35 years alone in Algonquin Park, see ***Gertrude Baskerville: The Lady of Algonquin Park,*** 2001.

On Canoe Lake there was Everett Farley, Frank Braucht, Len (Gibby) Gibson and Joe Cousineau.[366] On Bonita Lake was Jack Coons. On Cache lake there was Ken Unger, and on Rock Lake there was Billie Baulke.[367] On Smoke Lake there was Jack Hamilton who, with his sons Ken and Crawford, continued to be a local fixtures long after he'd left Nominigan and set up his own lease near the Smoke Lake Landing.[368] These men were true "Jacks of all Trades" and could handle just about any job a leaseholder needed done. These would include cutting wood for fireplaces and stoves, cutting ice in the winter and arranging storage for it in the various lake communal ice houses, shoveling snow off roofs in the winter, opening and closing cabins in the spring and fall, repairing water pumps and water systems, electrical work, making repairs to windows, doors, and docks, and any manner of carpentry task. Some even became representatives for major retailers. As was noted in the archival correspondence:

> *"Ken Unger was the Lake representative for Eaton's whose Huntsville store could supply you with everything from blankets to cooking oil. Ken would fill your order and get the supplies to your cabin. He also had a taxi service. If you gave one long blast of your car horn from the parking lot he would come over load your bags, get you to your cabin and unload all of your goods for $2.50."*[369]

On Canoe Lake, Farley arrived in 1931 from Oshawa to work for the Canoe Lake Lumber Company as a lumber foreman. In his early years, he lived in one of the houses left over from the logging and railway days up on Potter Creek. Later, after a short stint on Smoke Lake, he built a beautiful split-level cabin out of cut logs, with hardwood floors, a three-piece bath (which was unheard of at the time), and a beautiful big fireplace. Later he added a boathouse and a shed and a stable where he kept three horses and a cow. The horses were always being used to haul ice or timber or as transportation. Farley would cut ice in the winter months for camps and cottagers. Over the years, everyone on the lake grew to depend upon Farley. He would build cabins for new arrivals. He would open existing cottages in the spring, close them up in the fall, and make whatever repairs were wanted or needed. He also used to look after the level of the lakes at Tea Lake Dam for Ontario Hydro and would advise residents by telegram when the ice was out in the spring. He started a water taxi service with an inboard cedar strip motorboat he called "Jazzy," which chugged up the lake and could be heard for miles. Residents would call or write and he would pick up them up at either the train station or at the Portage Store. At the appointed hour, he would always be there waiting in his boat to take them across to their cabins. In what eventually became a local tradition, he would help unload their gear, sit awhile, make conversation, and join the new arrivals for a quick celebratory drink before chugging off down the lake.

Frank Braucht was born in Nebraska in 1878 and as an adult migrated north to Canada. He settled in Guelph and became a woodworking teacher. At an Older Boys' conference in Galt, he heard Taylor Statten speak, and in 1925, he joined the Camp Ahmek staff as the handyman. From then on he spent many summers at Taylor Statten Camps. Braucht was a master craftsman who loved to carve wood and make furniture and other

---

366. Additional details as to the lives of Farley and Braucht can be found in *Algonquin Voices: Selected Stories of Canoe Lake Women*, chapters 2 and 3.
367. Additional details on Baulke life of can be found in *Rock Lake Station,* 2005.
368. Today this legacy lives on with resident Rob Gamble providing the anchor at Cache Lake, Al Clare, doing the same on Canoe, and David Gatley supports the Rock Whitefish area.
369. Richard Eldridge and Orville Osborne, *Cache Lake Reflections.* 1995 pg. 88.

wooden objects. In 1932, he took out his own lease and built a log cabin with a huge fireplace. Mounted on the front face was a glorious thunderbird that he had carved. Though taciturn and sometimes quite gruff, Frank was a man apart. He lent his log cabin to people whom he considered the "right sort" for Algonquin Park. They included several that went on to become Canoe Lake residents, including Les and Marg Hogg, Marg McColl and Isobel Cowie, Janie Roberts and Harold McCleod. All his guests were expected to help with various chores around the place, including standing up to their waists in the water in the bay to haul out driftwood. He didn't want them to go soft. Among the most famous of his guests was Olive Diefenbaker, who came up every summer for 10 years. She was known as Olive Palmer then and taught with Frank in Guelph. For many years he also hosted various Boy Scout troops who would camp in a little clearing on a hill to the east of his cabin site. Frank loved to teach, and he taught many on the lake their skills for surviving in the bush. At one point he even organized a lake carving club that became known as "The Chiselers Club." In 1944, he built a lighthouse that stands to this day on a point now called Lighthouse Point, maintained by nearby resident Charles Gray.

In 1945, Joe Cousineau, who up until that time had rented a cabin on Brulé Lake, requested a lease along Potters Creek at the level spot just below where the Barry's Bay Lumber Company had its mill. He wanted to build a cabin and a woodworking shop, as he had just been hired by Taylor Statten to help repair and canvas the camps' canoes and sailboats. He also requested a lease for his son nearby. There is no official record that he was granted either of these leases. However, the 1950 Canoe Lake and District Leaseholder map did show a Cousineau site just south of the trestle bridge. According to Mary Colson Clare, Cousineau built a beautiful two-story log cabin complete with hardwood floors. He seems to have left the area in the 1950s, with his cabin apparently burned down by the DLF.

After WWII, Jack Coons had established Huntsville Electric and became well known in the Park doing electrical and other work for the various camps and lodges. In 1953, he decided to move permanently to the Park to work for Taylor Statten Camps and took out a lease on Bonita Lake. His original cabin was a previously built structure, which was disassembled and floated down the narrows from the Smoke Creek Bridge and reassembled on the site. Jack was a mechanical genius and while at Ahmek designed and built the camp's highly innovative sewage disposal system, a heating system for hot water, and an ingenious lathe used to make paddles, which was used for years. He was also a crack ham radio operator, and would use his radio all hours of the day and night.

Also important to mention was the Lucasavitch family from Whitney. In addition to his fame building finely handcrafted log cabins, the patriarch Felix Lucasavitch would help with opening and closing cabins and with wood burns. As Laird Saunderson from Source Lake recalls:

> *"Felix used to bring a horse in and cut the ice from the lake in the winter for the communal icehouse. Many of the cottages had drip fridges at that time, and I know we got ice blocks from him. We used to love to lie on the cool sawdust in our bathing suits on a hot day. Felix used to ride in on the railroad tracks on a self-pumped and propelled 'Sylvester 21' rail car, as I remember. It was some kind of see-saw pumping machine with which he could propel himself along the rail tracks and then pull it off when he wanted to stop."*[370]

---

[370] Recollections from Laird Saunderson, 2003.

Park Experiences

Kish Kaduk Lodge c1940s Clemson Collection

Killarney Dining Room Postcard c1940s

(left) Killarney Lodge Today Miglin Collection

The Portage Store 1936 Clemson Collection

Portage Store Today Miglin Collection

Mr. and Mrs. Edwin Thomas and Daughter Rose Outside of Canoe Lake Station 1920 APMA #73

Canoes, Motorboats, Tents, Camping Supplies, Guides and Complete Outfitting for Fishing and Canoe Trips

Kish Kaduk Lodge

GOVERNMENT PARK STATION, ONT.

Mail Address:
Government Park Station,
Via North Bay, Ont., Canada

Wire and Phone Address:
Via Brent, Ont., Canada

Ruth I. Paget
Manager

Highland Inn
ALGONQUIN PARK
CANADA

Killarney Lodge

Lake of Two Rivers

GOOD TROUT AND BASS FISHING
WE SERVE GOOD MEALS

ON NEW ALGONQUIN PARK HIGHWAY
18 miles east of Huntsville

Large Cabins, Well Furnished -- Coil Spring Mattresses -- Rock Drilled Spring Water -- Boats for Hire.
Modern Conveniences -- Running Water in Every Cabin -- Good Bathing Beach.

ALGONQUIN PARK P. O.

INDIAN CLEARING
ALGONQUIN PARK

POST OFFICE ADDRESS
ROCK LAKE STATION
WHITNEY, P. O.
ONTARIO,
CANADA

Samples of Commercial Lodge Letterhead

Winter at Minnesing Lodge 1954 APMA #618

Minnesing in Winter from Air APMA #962

Glen Donald Lodge on Source Lake 1958 APMA #1526

Park Airplane Landing on Ice in Front of Minnesing Lodge 1954 APMA #618

View of Algonquin Hotel (C), Colson Store (L), and Joe Lake Station (R) from the water c1915 APMA #183

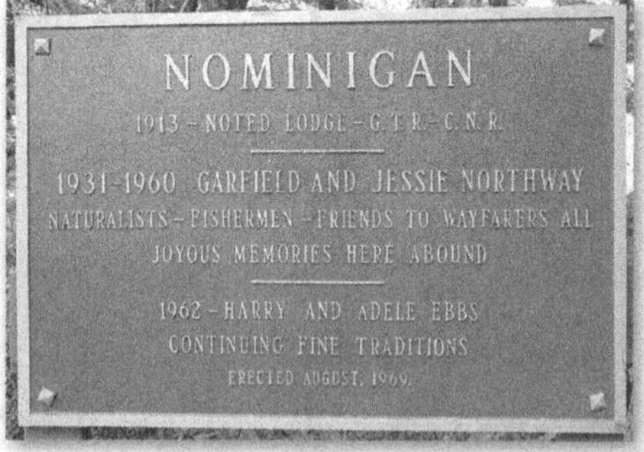

Nomnigan Plaque APMA #3830

Postcard of Whitefish Lodge c1950s Clemson Collection

Cache Lake's Ken Unger on a Delivery APMA #6021

Waubuno Lodge APMA #5983

George Brower (R) with Camp Waubuno Campers 1950s APMA #5966

Alf Bartlett, Original Proprietor with his Brother Jim of Bartlett Lodge 1923 APMA#182

Interpretive Program Tent 1946 APMA #3457

Rory MacKay Park Naturalist and Cottager 1978
APMA #4470

J. R. Dymond Leading a Hike 1936
APMA #1465

Nature Talk at the Cache Lake Rec Hall 1960/61 APMA #734

J. R. Dymond

(left)
Postcard of Killarney Lodge Point c1950s

Musclow Lodge c1940s Clemson Collection

My Summer Rendezvous

By Frank Braucht

Beside a northern lake,
On a quiet, wooded shore,
Where once the Indian roamed
In search of nature's store;
Where isles are set in azure blue,
Where cooling breezes blow;
Where northern-lights and myriad stars
Are matched by sunsets' glow;
Where flickering campfire light
Paints pictures in the dark,
And human spirits soar,
As upward flies each spark;
Where friendship, love and peace,
Unruly passions shame;
Where rich and poor alike,
Make happiness their aim;
There let me pitch my tent,
And find the needed rest
For body, soul and mind,
And learn God's ways are best.

Epilogue

It's a breathtaking afternoon, complete with blue sky, white puffy clouds and a soft breeze. As the yachting set would say, the sun is nearly reaching the yardarm. I squint my eyes, look to the west and watch the sunlight reflect off the water surface seemed like a thousand diamonds. From the ridge behind me, I can hear the infectious laughter of my children and their second cousins, who have retreated from the heat and sun of the afternoon to the coolness of the cottage above. It sounds like they are playing one of the many board games that our "arts and crafts" cupboard contains. My cousin Ken descends from above carrying a tray full of cheese and crackers and some gloriously cold beer. He pulls up a Muskoka chair, and I continue sharing with him the concerns that I and the rest of the Algonquin Park residents' community all have. In a little over a decade, all of our leases are going to expire. Unless Park policy changes, we all will be forced to remove our cabins and leave the Park. He stops me in mid-sentence and asks what I realize is a question that has been haunting me for some time now. "Why are you still here?" A long and deep silence fills the air.

A Portage Store canoe with visiting afternoon paddlers passes by only a few feet from our dock. For some unexplained reason, the much heavier father is sitting in the bow and his young son is attempting to steer the canoe from the stern. Because of the weight imbalance, the canoe won't glide in a straight line and the pair zig-zag their way up the lake. Both are also sitting with their knees way above the gunnels, making the craft very unstable. A wrong move or a gust of wind will soon have them both in the water. I note that luckily they are wearing their life jackets. I unconsciously check the direction of the wind and the angle of the sunlight. I note to myself that even at their slow pace, there is enough time before sun down for them to make it back to Portage Store Bay. I recall also that both Missy and David, who live on the point, and David and Carolyn by the shoal are all up this weekend. They will be able to make sure that the two make it across the lake safely. It's such a ritual for those of us who live on well-traveled lakes, this keeping an eye out for visitors, that I'm not really conscious of my thoughts.

I reflect on my cousin's question and wonder to myself, why I haven't left the Park long ago. Why did I not cut my losses and sell the lease back to the government, or to someone else along time ago? Why have I never considered, at least not seriously, about buying some land to cottage somewhere else outside of the Park? Why did I instead replace the deck, invest thousands in a new Envirolet composting toilet system and rebuild the fallen down sleeping bunkee? Is it because like so many of my lake neighbours, we are so head over heels in love with Algonquin that we can't imagine cottaging anywhere else? Is it because our collective family roots in this majestic place are too deep? In our family's case, its three generations going back over 50 years. With many other families, its five or six generations going back over 100 years. Is it because of our profound, deeply-felt connection with this community? Is it because we take very seriously the "guardianship" of our little corners of the Park?

During the first 50 years of our little community, we were welcomed with open arms and encouraged to set down roots. For the last 50 years, we have at times been seen as unwanted interlopers. Looking back with the eyes of 2006, it is almost laughable to read reports suggesting that our little community was the cause of the need to shoot over 100 marauding bears in the summer of 1953. I scratch my head, to read what look like authoritative suggestions that cottagers were the cause of lake pollution in the late 1960s. Especially surprising since in 2005, the bears and the pollution are generally gone, yet cottagers have remained, most low key but strongly supportive of the Park and its goals. From time to time I see media reports suggesting that we are a lucky, privileged few. Few and lucky, absolutely, privileged, I'm not sure, at least no more privileged than any other Ontarian who owns a family cottage. My father came to Algonquin in part because cottages in Muskoka were outside his economic reach. Thirty-five miles from the closest town, accessible only by water, most Algonquin Park cottages were and most still are today, only able to get light and heat with wood stoves, propane and kerosene lamps. Luckily for our family, Camp Wapomeo decided it needed electricity in the 1950s. The best route for the hydro line turned out to be right past our cottage backdoor. Our activities are heavily regulated, with occasional confusion as to appropriate governmental jurisdictions. But our little community is also an important part of the historic fabric of the Park.

As fellow leaseholder Brian Maltman so eloquently stated:

> *"The leaseholders are certainly not the only ones who love Algonquin Park and feel of it a sense of guardianship. Along side them are scores of scientists, writers, artists, naturalists, loggers, park users, and people who live and work in or around Algonquin, who also feel a deep commitment to this extraordinary place. This includes many who work for Ontario Parks in a myriad of ways such as clearing and maintaining back country portages and trails, leading nature walks, conducting naturalist research in the dead of winter, or enforcing regulations so that visitors and delicate ecosystems alike are kept safe.*
>
> *Many Park Superintendents of Algonquin, past and present, including the current incumbent, John Winters, go far beyond the requirements of the job, to become students of the park, and even part of its folklore. Commercial outfitting ventures and lodges have fostered the treasuring of Algonquin, by introducing it to visitors from all over the world. Without these, thousands of people would remain ignorant of the park's environment. The youth camps have introduced generations of children to the Algonquin world so effectively that many report fundamental changes in their lives and their*

sense of place in and responsibility for the natural world. Many leaseholders were first introduced to Algonquin this way.

Indeed as leaseholders we celebrate all of the others who also treasure Algonquin and work as much as we do to make it shine. For instance, we have the Natural Heritage Education Program, the outstanding interpretive initiative begun by Smoke Lake leaseholder J.R. Dymond, (who also founded The Federation of Ontario Naturalists, now called Ontario Nature) After the program's founding it was nurtured by researchers like Douglas Pimlott, brought to adulthood by Ron Tozer and Dan Strickland and is now in the capable hands of Rick Stronks. The Algonquin Forestry Authority, and the logging companies that operate under its guidance, studies and practices modern silviculture within the multiple-use model. The Wildlands League and Algonquin EcoWatch, among others, continue to help promote preservationist principles that have become woven into the very fabric of Algonquin's management."

I started down this road, naively believing that I could be unbiased in my recounting of the stories and experiences of our little community. But I realize now, after all this time, that such a thing is likely impossible. I turn to my cousin and share with him this fundamental truth. I can't leave Algonquin. This is my spiritual home and will always be so as long as I live. This is my community, with all of its crazy characters. This is where my roots are planted deep. Algonquin needs our leaseholding community. It needs us to know her and protect her in ways that casual visitors most likely have no time or inclination for.

As Dr. Charles Stevenson from Source Lake wrote:

"Mrs. Stevenson and I love this camp more than any home we have ever had. It means everything to us, and our children regard it in the same way. We have always done everything we can to preserve the natural wild beauty of Source Lake and have enjoyed the acceptance of our responsibility to keep the canoe tripper campsites here and on Bruce, Owl and Raven lakes as clean and as tidy as we can. All of the leaseholders on this lake are conscientious in the same way, which makes us a very happy and dedicated group."[371]

As Ralph Humber from Lake of Two Rivers wrote in 1967 and is just as true today:

"We came to the Park 40 years ago and love it intensely. It gives us health and a healthy look to life, as when man is closer to nature he understands it better. To us the Park is an inspiration and we protect it with all our might."[372]

And Ruth Welham-Umphrey from Whitefish Lake echoed in 2000:

"All of us love and cherish Algonquin and do all we can to take care of it. We pick up trash the tourists and casual campers leave, put out the fires they set, provide shelter when they are caught in a storm, ferry them back to their camp when their motor quits, and fish them out of the lake when they dump their canoe. Algonquin never leaves us. We carry it in out heart all year round. The thought of it sustains us through cold winters and when summer comes we return to our heart's home."

371. Stevenson leasehold correspondence 1973, Algonquin Park Museum Archives.
372. Humber leasehold correspondence files, 1967, Algonquin Park Museum Archives.

And Judy Bolt Willson from Smoke Lake in 2003:

> *"We love and respect the Park and the privilege of being there. As if it was our own, we are its loyal guardians."*[373]

And Helen Steinberg from Rock Lake:

> *"The longer we are here, the stronger our realization that we are centered here, and drawn toward what is important in our lives. The grace, the strength and the stability of our family has developed and grown each summer, as we are together here. It is a living thing that we savour and share. It is nurtured each year by the repeated rituals in our lives, by opening and closing and chess on the porch, by mouse traps and trillium and water lines, by early paddles and late night drinks shared with friends. We had no idea when we purchased this lease that it would change us so."*[374]

My cousin and I raise a toast to the four winds and laugh as the tears spill down my cheeks. We sit in silence and watch the sun set in the west.

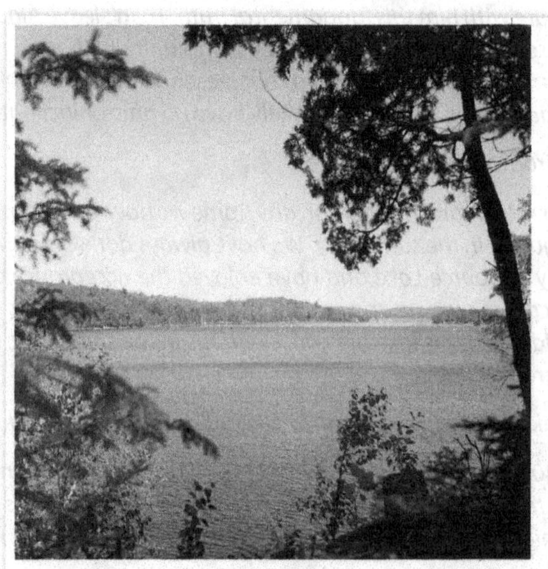

View from Clemson Deck 1950s, Now Totally Filled in With Trees Clemson Collection

373. Recollections from Bolt Willson Family, 2003.
374. Recollections from Helen Steinberg, 2003.

Bibliography

1. Addison, Ottelyn, ***Early Days of Algonquin Park***, McGraw Hill, Ryerson, Toronto, 1974.
2. Addison, Ottelyn with Elizabeth Harwood, ***Tom Thomson, The Early Years***, Ryerson Press, Toronto, 1969.
3. Bice, Ralph, ***Along the Trail in Algonquin Park***, The Friends of Algonquin Park reprinted 2001.
4. Bignell, Jan and Bob, ***Pringrove: The Later Years***, Muskoka Printing, Dwight, Ontario, 1998.
5. Bowman, Margaret and Eagles, Paul, ***Tourism Spending in Algonquin Provincial Park***, Master's Thesis, 2002.
6. Clemson, Gaye I., ***Gertrude Baskerville: The Lady of Canoe Lake***, self-published, Markham Ontario, 2001.
7. Clemson Gaye I., ***The Canoe Lake Chronicles***, self-published, Markham Ontario, 2001.
8. Clemson Gaye I., ***Algonquin Voices: Selected Stories of Canoe Lake Women***, Trafford Publishing, Victoria, British Columbia, 2002.
9. Clemson Gaye I., ***Rock Lake Station, Settlement Stories Since 1896***, Trafford Publishing, Victoria, British Columbia, 2005.
10. Eldridge, Richard and Osborne, Orville, ***Cache Lake Reflections: A Madawaska Voyage***, *An Anecdotal History of Cache Lake, Algonquin Park,* ***Ontario***, Trailside Productions, 1995.
11. Keyser Esther, and John Keyser, ***Paddling My Own Canoe***, Friends of Algonquin Park, 2004.
12. Garland, George. D., Editor, ***Glimpses of Algonquin***, Friends of Algonquin Park, 1989.
13. Killan Gerald, ***Protected Places: A History of Ontario's Provincial Park System***, Dundurn Press Ltd in association with the Ontario Ministry of Natural Resources, Toronto, 1993.
14. Killan Gerald and Warecki George, *J. R. Dymond and Frank A. MacDougall,* ***Science and Government Policy in Algonquin Provincial Park 1931-1954***, Scientia Canadensis, Volume 22-23 #51, 1998/99.
15. Lundell, Liz- Editor, Lloyd D - Concept, ***Fires of Friendship – Eighty Years of The Taylor Statten Camps***, Fires of Friendship Books, Toronto 2000.
16. MacKay, Niall, ***Over the Hill to Georgian Bay – A history of the Ottawa***, *Arnprior and Parry Sound Railway*, Boston Mills Press, 1983.
17. MacKay, Roderick and Reynolds, William, ***Algonquin***, Stoddart Publishing Co. Ltd, Toronto, 1993.
18. Mackey, Doug and Mackey, Paul, ***The Fossmill Story, Life in a Railway Lumbering Village on the Edge of Algonquin Park***, Past Forward Heritage Ltd., 2000.
19. Meehan B. Curator, Millard L. Text, ***Algonquin Memories – Tom Thomson in Algonquin Park***, Exhibition for the Algonquin Gallery in Algonquin Park, 1998.
20. Noble, William, ***Report on Ontario Archeology***, Ontario Archeological Society, Publication No. 11, 1968.

21. Northway, Dr. Mary, ***Nominigan – The Early Years,*** self published, 1970.

22. Northway, Dr. Mary, ***Nominigan - A Casual History***, self published, 1969.

23. Pigeon M. McCormick, ***Living at Brulé Lake Algonquin Park 1936-1950***, Friends of Algonquin Park, 1995.

24. Pigeon M. McCormick, ***Living at Cache Lake Algonquin Park***, Friends of Algonquin Park, 1995.

25. Robins, John D., ***The Incomplete Anglers Second Edition***, Friends of Algonquin Park, Whitney, Ontario, 1998.

26. Saunders, Audrey, ***The Algonquin Story***, Ontario Department of Lands and Forests, Toronto, 1946.

27. Shaw, S. Bernard, ***Canoe Lake Algonquin Park – Tom Thomson and Other Mysteries***, General Store Publishing House, Burnstown, 1996.

28. Shaw, S. Bernard, ***Opeongo***, General Store Publishing House, Burnstown, 1996.

29. Tozer Ron and Strickland Dan, ***A Pictorial History of Algonquin Park***, Ministry of Natural Resources, 1980.

30. Tozer, Ron, ***50 Years of Interpretation***, Interpscan 22(2): 7-8, 1994.

31. Trinnell, John Ross, ***J. R. Booth: Life and Times of an Ottawa Lumber King***, Tree House Publishing, Ottawa, 1998.

32. Wright, Helen E. Mooney, Joe Lake, ***Reminiscences of an Algonquin Park Ranger's Daughter***, HEW Enterprises, Eganville, 1999.

33. Wright, Helen E. Mooney, ***Trailblazers***, HEW Enterprises, Eganville, 2001.

34. Reports and briefs, including presentations to the Provincial Parks Council from Jean Beaupré (1985 & 1989), Michael Davies (1986), Algonquin Park Residents Association (1986 & 1989), Cache Lake Leaseholders Association (197 & 1986), George Garland (1971), and Algonquin Park Residents Association, ***A Park for People***, 1969.

35. Minutes from the Canoe Lake and District Leaseholders Association 1939– 2004.

36. Minutes from some of the Smoke Lake Leaseholders Association meetings 1960s and 1970s.

37. Minutes and various editions of the ***Cache Flash*** newsletter from the Cache Lake Leaseholders Association 1927 – 1985.

38. Lease correspondence and interview transcripts in the Algonquin Park Museum Archives, 1905-1991.

39. In-person or telephone interviews with Edith Alger, Frank and Valerie Argue, Lise Belanger, Michael Budman, Theresa Bertolone Burnett, Robert Burnett, Catherine Thompson Brackley, Jim Brackley, John Brooks, Michael Budman, Doug Campbell, John and Sandy Churchill, Marion Stringer Cherry, Mary Colson Clare, Isabel Clemson, Ed Commack, Elizabeth Hogg Cook, Mary and Si Cline, Peter Dalglish, Ines Wischnewski Davis, Greg and Sue Day, Nick Declano, Thom Dernoga, John Doering, Carolyn Roe Fink, Grace Fraser Hancock, Eric Fredeen, George Garland, Helen and Dan Gibson, Hugh Gibson, Brian Grant, Charles and Dorothy Gray, Nancy Gray, William Greer, Sue Ebbs Hayhurst, Sylvia Hayhurst Telford, Marg Hogg, Viiu Kanep, Eugene Kates, Graham Knightly, Don Lloyd, Harvey Lloyst, Jim Loney, Brian Maltman, Manning Family

William Matthews, Nancy Martin, Joy McCaskill, James McDonald, Islay McFarlane, John MacMurchy, Cathy Minor, Cliff and Tamar Nelson, David Ouchterlony, Mary and Keith Percival, Margo and Allan Powell, Hazel Peterson, Peter Purcell, Sue Rabick, Midge Rasey, Jennifer Richardson, Cathy Rotar, Joan Hewitt Sanderson, John Ridpath, Janie Roberts, Raymond and Marlene Sawchuck, Missy and David Sharpe, Bruce and Sherry Sandilands, Jane Sims, Kim Smith, John Standwick, Janie Statten, Brian and Helen Steinberg, Al Strike, Sara Stroup, Robert and Mary Taylor and Joan Ridpath Yule.

40. Written recollections from Algonquin Park residents including the Allan Family, Valerie Young Argue, Tom Bartlett, Helen Beaton, Sharon Beesley, Ernie Bilkey, Judy Bolt, Jane Dise Bowles, Jill Campbell, Rose Campbell, Anne Chisholm, John Colson, Betsy Hogg Cook, Isobel Cowie, Michael Davies, Mary Jane Kase Davis, Art Eady, Jo Anne Edwards, Dan Findlay, Jim Forrester, Carol Freeman, Robert Freeman, William Furse, Fountain Family, Lela Gamble, George Garland, Bernard Goldman, Katie and Rob Gordon, Judy and Robert Hagerman, Grace Hancock, Jim Hayhurst, Cathy Taylor Helyar, Robert Henderson, Jackie Henry, Terry Hutchins, Esther Keyser, Bea Lawford, Sandy Lewis, Bev Louden, Roderick MacKay, Norma McCord, Terry Taylor MacTaggart, Bill and Nancy Martin, Debbie Merritt, Barbara McKinnon, Walter McNeill, Eric Miglin and Poppy Rowland, Robert Miller, Mary Eleanor Riddell Morris, Leon Muszynski, Robert Nightingale, John Olsen, David Ouchterlony, Pretty Family, Richard Pultz, Elizabeth Reininga, Susan Roesch, Laird Sanderson, Allan Sargeant, Peggy Sharpe, Anne Sinclair, Robert Taylor, Charles Tator, Ron Tozer, Ruth Welham Umphrey, Richard Veenis, Gordon Willson, A. Ross Wilson, Mary Margaret Armstrong Withey and Eva Wischnewski.

41. Transcripts in the Algonquin Park Museum Archives of interviews with Jack Wilkinson and Rose Thomas, George and Willa May, Tom Murdock, Mary Pigeon, Lorne Pigeon, Mrs. Chilson, Ralph Bice, George and May Pearson, Lorne Pigeon, Gibby Gibson, Adam Pitts, Gerry Brown, Robin Hepburn, Allan Helmsley, Dr. George Garland and Dr. Edmund Kase.

Printed in the United States
By Bookmasters